Charles Henry Pearson

English history in the fourteenth century

Charles Henry Pearson

English history in the fourteenth century

ISBN/EAN: 9783337204068

Printed in Europe, USA, Canada, Australia, Japan

Cover: Foto ©ninafisch / pixelio.de

More available books at **www.hansebooks.com**

ENGLISH HISTORY

IN THE

FOURTEENTH CENTURY

BY

CHARLES H. PEARSON
LATE FELLOW OF ORIEL COLLEGE, OXFORD

RIVINGTONS
WATERLOO PLACE, LONDON
Oxford and Cambridge
1876

[A—83.]

PREFACE

I HAVE tried in this little book to give a brief outline
of the history of the fourteenth century in England.
More and more, as I have studied it, the sense of its
especial completeness has grown upon me. That
Dunbar and Falkirk led up to Crécy and Poitiers;
that the well-being of the English Commons under
the first Edward was the secret of that miraculous
strength which England put forth under Edward III.;
that disgrace abroad and disorder at home, followed
as " the day the night " on the demoralisation of
successful war; and that Richard II. suffered for
the sin of his fathers as certainly as Edward III.
inherited the results, the aims, and part at least of
the heroic nature of the first Edward;—these, and
other such lessons of history, seem to me to stand
out from our annals with marvellous distinctness.
Our records are often imperfect where we could most
wish them to be complete. Many men of the time,
even Edward III. himself, are little more than
splendid names to us. About many facts of the

time, as, for instance, about the rising of the serfs, we have only one-sided or imperfect narratives. But the broad outlines of the time seem generally certain and clear.

The reign of Edward II. is among the least attractive in history. Its constitutional value has been well brought out by Lingard; and its economical history, by Professor Rogers, is an original contribution of the highest value. I am inclined to believe that what more is to be known about it will be found in the personal history of the baronage. Writing briefly, and without notes, as my plan demanded, I have purposely abstained from conjectures, however probable I might think them. My conviction, for instance, is that the abduction of the Countess of Lancaster (p. 71), and the insults to Edward at Knaresborough (pp. 72, 82), were connected with scandal affecting the queen; that Edward promoted the Earl of Surrey's violence; that the nickname of King Arthur given to Edward at Knaresborough was in allusion to the story of Guenever; and that the quarrel in which the whole state was involved was thus envenomed between king and earl by the most intolerable of outrages and the bitterest of insults. But to have discussed this point adequately would have required a space disproportionate to the whole plan of my book.

For the reign of Edward III. the works of

Longman, Pauli, and Henri Martin are admirable guides. For two or three facts not mentioned by these authorities, or given in the common sources of history, I am indebted to the " Corpus Chronicorum Flandriæ " and Mr. Cooper's "Appendices to a Report on the Fædera." The case of Captain Marant (p. 221) is one of these ; and I regret that I did not insert it in the account of the surrender of Calais as a further explanation of Edward's conduct. For the history of the Black Prince's Spanish expedition, I have consulted Garavary and other such Spanish histories as were accessible in the Melbourne Public Library.

At the time when my last sheets were written, Mr. Gairdner's "House of Lancaster and York," and Mr. Maurice's "Tyler, Ball, and Oldcastle," had not reached Melbourne; and though I have since worked through them carefully, and I hope profitably, it has, of course, been impossible for me to make the use I should naturally have made of them.[1] I confess they have not shaken my belief that John of Gaunt's patronage of Wycliffe was unconnected with any sympathy for Lollard opinions ; nor in spite of Mr. Maurice's apology for Tyler can I place him in the same rank as Gryndecobbe and Lyster. For the view I have taken of Richard's character, I am especially

---

[1] For the same reason I have only been able to make the most cursory use of Mr. Green's " Short History of the English People."

indebted to Mr. Sanford's admirable " Estimates of the Kings of England."

I had purposed at one time to add a chapter on the literary movement of the fourteenth century. But my space was limited; the chapter on the results of foreign aggression grew to dimensions I had not anticipated ; and it seemed undesirable to slur over the important constitutional struggle of the reign of Richard II.

I am indebted to my publishers for kindly sending me the proofs of every sheet to correct ; and I hope the list of errata will not be a very heavy one. But the task of correcting from a great distance, after a long interval of time, is always a difficult one ; and I fear the mistakes that remain uncorrected may still be more serious than they should be. I have spared no labour to remove them.

CHARLES H. PEARSON.

9 BURLINGTON TERRACE, ALBERT STREET,
MELBOURNE, *Nov.* 30, 1875.

CONTENTS

CHAPTER VII.

SUBJUGATION OF FRANCE.

CHAPTER VIII.

THE LOSS OF THE FRENCH CONQUESTS.

CHAPTER XI.

RICHARD'S GOVERNMENT.

CHAPTER XII.

RICHARD'S TYRANNY AND FALL.

ERRATA.

Page 23, line 18, *for* then *read* had.

,, 24, ,, 16, delete Torksey.

,, 31, ,, 3, *for* 14th *read* 13th.

,, 32, ,, 5 and 7, *for* Achol *read* Athol.

,, 32, ,, 21, *for* is a poor *read* was a poor.

,, 107, ,, 21, *for* Ravenser *read* Ravenspur.

,, 118, ,, 1, *for* seen *read* seem.

,, 159, ,, 12, *for* Guines *read* Guienne.

,, 161, ,, 9, *should read* of Maupertuis.   In front they, &c.

,, 167, ,, 25, *for* 20,000 had *read* 20,000 peasants had.

,, 168, ,, 8, *for* knew also, &c., *read* and knew also that his own death was determined upon by the Regent in revenge, &c.

,, 169, line 24, *for* Charles the Bold *read* Charles the Bad.

INTRODUCTION.

State of England in the 14th Century.—Towards the end of the thirteenth century England was perhaps the best ordered and most prosperous state in Europe. Politically, indeed, its power was small, for our kings only retained a portion of their old dominions in France, and these, it might seem, merely by sufferance. Scotland was independent under a native dynasty; a great part of Ireland was in reality unconquered. Nevertheless, three quarters of a century passed in comparative peace had doubled the population, and more than doubled its wealth; respect for law had grown to an extent unknown elsewhere; and the serfs were rapidly being enfranchised. The annexation of North Wales had delivered the English marches from the dread of invasion. There were no towns in England except London that could vie with the wealth of Ghent or Bruges in Flanders, or of Venice and Florence in Italy; but the English towns were parts of a compact dominion, at peace with one another, and protected by the armies of a whole kingdom. Our kings could not bring into the field as many thousand soldiers as gathered under the banners of the French monarchs, nor were our gentlemen trained to war like the French

chivalry ; but, thanks to free institutions, we had a yeomanry such as no other country could boast, and a
seafaring population that was only restrained by stern
laws, rigorously enforced, from waging war on its own
account over every known sea.

Country and Climate.—In many respects the English
country and climate were different from what they now
are. As late as the time of Henry VIII. a Greek traveller in England described the country as abounding in
morasses or oak forests favourable for hunting. The
romance of Blonde of Oxford describes its hero eloping
with a lady, and hiding himself every day in the woods
that bordered the high road ; the Earl of Lancaster
actually carried an armed force across part of England
in this way ; while a statute of Edward I. directed that
the forests should be cleared away to the space of 70
yards on each side, that the traveller might be able to
guard against lurking highwaymen. Still industry was
reclaiming the desert everywhere. The great Andred-
Wood of Kent, Sussex, and Surrey, which had stretched
120 miles by 30, was being wasted away for the Sussex
iron-works ; and the eight Kentish estates which had
been formed in it by the time of the Conquest were now
multiplied by the lands in six new hundreds. Even
the royal forests were perpetually encroached upon by
squatters, who bribed the forester to pass by their shingle
huts, and fields fenced against the deer, without inquiry.
An Italian travelling among us in the reign of Henry
VII., spoke of England as diversified by pleasant, undula-
ting hills and beautiful valleys, nothing being to be seen
but agreeable woods or extensive meadows, or lands in
cultivation, and the greatest plenty of water springing
everywhere. Often the eye rested upon fair gardens, with
the laurel, the myrtle, and all Italian fruit-trees, except

the olive and the orange. But though nearly forty vineyards are recorded in Doomsday Book, and an early writer, William of Malmesbury, declares that the wine from the Vale of Gloucester was scarcely inferior to that of France, either the climate changed after his time, or his national predilections had biassed his taste; for his countrymen of a later time steadily imported their wine from Bordeaux, and incurred the reproach of drinking dregs by their fondness for ale and beer.

Earthquakes.—It is not impossible that the climate has actually changed since England was covered with bush and swamp. It seems certain that the rainfall is less, and probable that it is more evenly distributed; that there were greater floods and less fog in the twelfth and fourteenth centuries. A year in which the snow only lay for half a day during the winter months is recorded by one of our chroniclers as a miracle; and a frost like that of A.D. 1281, when men skated from Lambeth to Westminster, and the great masses of ice breaking up bore down five arches of London Bridge, has no parallel later than the reign of Charles II. Earthquakes were violent and frequent. In the ten years from A.D. 1275 to A.D. 1285 no fewer than five are recorded, two of which are said to have been great and horrible, while a third was so violent that it shook down several churches in Kent,

> " Chambers, chimneys, all to burst,
> Churches and castles foul 'gan fare,
> Pinnacles and steeples to ground it cast,
> And all was for warning to be ware."

Even volcanoes are recorded, though not in England itself. A great one broke out in Guernsey during the reign of Henry III., flames bursting up out of the sea, consuming large parts of the cliffs, and sending showers of ashes over the land.

Production of Cattle and Sheep—Game.—Resembling Canada in its seasons, with a soil not inferior in fertility, and with much land that had never been broken up, England ought to have carried a large population, and even to have been a granary for other countries. This, however, was far from being the case. In the two hundred years that succeeded the Norman conquest the population seems to have doubled, and probably numbered about three millions and a half in the reign of Edward I. It is doubtful if it ever rose above four millions, and it suffered great decrease at times from pestilence and war, as under Edward III. and Henry VI., recovering itself again under peace and in good years. It was often thought that the population of England was not in proportion to its fertility, and that if all the available land was brought under the plough England might export grain to the neighbouring countries. In fact, however, the imperfect agriculture of the times would not have allowed a population of more than four millions and a half, an acre in the fourteenth century producing only a fourth of the wheat that is now raised from it. Probably much land was wasted in forests ; but even forests had their use in times when no coal was burned, except in London and a few places along the coast ; and on the other hand, much land was ploughed in the Middle Ages which is now pasture or park. From an early time, however, the great price given for wool in Flanders made grazing especially profitable in England, and the woolsack was a very real symbol of the great material source of wealth. The stock generally were as poor as the farming. Oxen averaged about half their present weight ; sheep yielded only half the fleece that is now shorn from the small-framed merino ; and a law (A.D. 1535) intended to increase the size of horses, provided that brood mares of at least thirteen hands high should be kept in parks. But game, especially feathered game, was abundant. Till the reign of Henry VII. partridges and pheasants might be killed like rooks or crows, and partridges fetched about the same price as poultry in the London market. Hares were rare or unknown, and rabbits dear—being, we may suppose, kept down by foxes and stoats. Fish was plentiful, and many farms near the coast paid their rent in salmon or herrings; many inland holdings in eels.

London.—The rich counties of England during the Middle Ages were such as were best adapted to the commerce with Flanders. Norfolk was far beyond all others in importance; and Kent and Lincolnshire, Wiltshire, and Suffolk, came next, but far behind. The city of Norwich is said to have lost nearly 60,000 inhabitants during the Black Death,—a number very nearly as great as its whole population forty years ago. But London was unquestionably the first city in England. As early as the reign of Henry II. it was said to be one of the great cities of the world, possessing 140 churches, and adorned with palaces, and enriched by a trade with "every nation under heaven." In the time of Edward II. an English friar, who had been on pilgrimage, and had seen the grand cities of northern Italy, was still able to describe London as the most famous and richest of all cities under the sun. The great cathedral of St Paul's, with its tower 520 feet high, and its nave 720 feet long, was unsurpassed among English edifices; and Westminster Abbey, Westminster Hall, and the Tower, were other splendid witnesses to the genius of native architects. Our churches were then the richest of the world. The Italian describer of England gives the palm for magnificence to the tomb of Edward the Confessor, in

Westminster Abbey, over all that he had seen anywhere in the world, and declares that the jewels with which its gold shrine was studded literally lighted up the religious gloom of the abbey.   Nor was the wealth of the London citizens less remarkable.   "In one single street named the Strand, leading to St Paul's," says the same narrative, "there are fifty-two goldsmiths' shops, so rich and full of silver vessels great and small, that in all the shops of Milan, Rome, Venice, and Florence put together, I do not think there would be found so many of the magnificence that are to be seen in London." This wealth was no new spectacle.   The German nobles who accompanied Cœur de Lion on his return from Germany, declared that if the emperor had known the extent of the riches London could display, he would have exacted heavier sums of ransom.

Castles—Monasteries—Roads.—To ourselves the London of Richard's or even of Henry VIII's time would have seemed rather picturesque and curious than rich ; and the many wooden houses, sometimes only of a story high, might well have appeared unsubstantial and mean.   But even to modern notions the great buildings scattered through England in the shape of castles are very wonderful.   Cornwall had no marches to defend, and lay outside the civil wars that at times desolated England, but more than thirty castles could be traced by a traveller in Cornwall in the fifteenth century, and out of these about half were then standing.   In Lincolnshire alone there were fifty monasteries ; and in all England more than 1,700 pious foundations of the most various kind—convents, colleges, priories, and hospitals, mostly endowed within the space of two centuries— bore witness to the great wealth accumulated in the country.   As long as rents were paid in labour, it is

easy to understand why a great foundation might keep
works constantly going on in order not to waste any
of its dues. But labour-rents were generally commuted for payments in money by the end of the thirteenth century, and the activity of our architects did
not slacken. No doubt, in some respects private life
in the Middle Ages had fewer wants and extravagances
than now, and in the absence of other investments, it
was natural to put money into buildings or precious
stones. But against a rude and inexpensive style of
living we must set the cost of oppressive taxation and
of legal expenses, which no man could hope to escape,
and the waste of numerous retainers, who had once been
necessary for protection, and were afterwards maintained
for parade. Altogether, therefore, the great work done
in building during the Middle Ages is very marvellous;
and it seems strange that a practical and commercial
people, spending so freely where it was often possible
to spare, should have suffered the great highways of
commerce to remain comparatively neglected. Chaucer's
pilgrims took three days and a half for the journey of
less than sixty miles from London to Canterbury. It
is true that men travelling on business, with their be-
longings on sumpter horses, would often in summer make
long journeys at the rate of thirty, or even thirty-five
miles a day. But the great difference of the prices in
neighbouring districts for articles of bulk, such as wheat,
shows that the carriage of heavy goods was very costly
at all times. The difference between the prices of wheat
in Bedfordshire and Derbyshire, during the same season,
represents a cost for cartage of from £14 to £16 a ton
in money of the present day. The great fairs of Boston,
Stourbridge, and Abingdon, to which men from all the
neighbouring counties brought the year's produce for

sale, and where they laid in store for the winter's use, were all in places to which there was convenient water carriage. It was among the causes of decline in Winchester, that the merchants of that city had to buy their goods in Southampton Water.

Power of the Kings—Edward I. and the Earl of Surrey.—This prosperity of England had not been attained without good government. Ever since the Conquerer restored order in England the kingly power had been administered, with two or three brief and disastrous intervals, by wise and capable princes, or in their default by trained and patriotic ministers. Henry I. and Henry II. had been superior to most kings of their time, and Edward I. was the greatest statesman of his age. The fearful anarchy under Stephen, when "men said openly that Christ and his saints slept," had given Englishmen a wholesome distaste for class privileges; and nowhere was the power claimed by the baronage so jealously restricted as in England. Indeed, there seemed danger lest our lawyers should refine away native liberties, by transferring the servile precepts of Roman lawyers into our law-books. Extreme doctrines about treason, about the prescriptive rights of the Crown, and about the divine foundations of the king's authority, were only too common in the thirteenth century. The two worst of our early sovereigns, John and Edward II., were more than a match for the baronage single-handed; and the weakest, Henry III., triumphed finally over an insurrection which had enlisted the clergy, the commercial classes, and half the baronage, under the guidance of the ablest politician and soldier of his times. Yet even those victories had been dearly bought. The successes of John and Edward II. had invited foreign invasion; the succession to John's throne had been secured for his infant son by the surrender of all the king fought for; and Edward II.'s bloody revenge on his foes was followed closely by his deposition and death. Even Henry III. had been compelled to compromise. Practically, therefore, our king's exercise of power was always restrained, except in the most unwise, by a knowledge that their subjects would not brook innovation. It was often hazardous for the Crown to assert its undoubted rights. No inquiry could be more necessary than that which Edward I. instituted into the rights of jurisdiction and franchise which the lords of manors throughout England claimed. But when his commissioners called on the Earl of Surrey to produce his titles, the descendant of a royal bastard threw his sword upon the table, "Here, sirs, is my warrant. My ancestors came over with William the Bastard, and conquered their lands by the sword, and by the sword I will hold them against all who seek them." Yet, in fact, the strong will of the king triumphed, and the Earl of Surrey was amongst the first who submitted.

Taxation, and Revenue of the Crown.—Apart from the sanctions of law and the support of his people, the king's power rested chiefly on his revenue, and especially on the Crown lands. The old theory of the Constitution had been that the king was to live from these, and from certain feudal dues, the most important of which were those which an heir paid on succeeding to his estate. The early taxation, which took the form of a land tax, was only to be assessed when the realm was in danger. Practically, however, our kings never carried out this theory. They perpetually impoverished the exchequer by granting away Crown lands to reward distinguished service, or to gratify favourites, and they asked the Estates for extraordinary aid in war. The clergy and nobles were soon weary of complying with these irregular demands. Besides, it was difficult to adjust a land tax properly, as the Church claimed that its contributions were never to be increased. Nor did it seem fair that the growing wealth of the commercial classes should escape altogether untouched. Two changes were therefore introduced towards the end of the thirteenth century. A tax was levied on the wool, which was our great article of export; and this in a short time became the most important part of the royal revenue. It was always an unpopular one, often known as the "maltolt" or evil toll; and it was considered a divine judgment when Laurence de Ludlow, a famous merchant who persuaded the English traders to submit to the tax, was drowned at sea in a ship laden with wool. The second new tax, which to modern notions would be even more oppressive, was a tax on personalty. Collectors entered every house and appraised its contents, from the kitchen utensils to the fowls in the back-yard. A certain proportion of the valuation, variously fixed by Parliament at a sixth, a tenth, and a fifteenth, was thus levied to the king's use. Altogether, in times of peace, the ordinary Crown revenue amounted to about £60,000 a year under Edward I. Reduced roughly to modern values, this would show a taxation of about 5s. a head, or from an eighth to a ninth of what the population now pays in England. But much taxation was levied and spent in districts, and not a little took the form of personal service.

Three Estates of the Realm—Clergy.—Of the three estates of the realm, the clergy came first in rank, and were perhaps most important. Seventeen prelates, and about twenty-five abbots, holding by barony, and so entitled to a seat in the Upper House, were always a formidable power in Parliament, though their power was not as great in the fourteenth century, when they were still outnumbered by the lay baronage, as in the fifteenth, when the secular nobles had been reduced to thirty, or fewer, by the wars of the Roses. The clergy succeeded, however, during the fourteenth century in maintaining or establishing their claims to three important privileges— that they should only be taxed by themselves, that they should only be tried in spiritual courts, and that no laws affecting them should be passed without their consent. Being thus virtually independent of the state, they had all the influence of great landowners, whose estates were supplemented by every kind of forced or voluntary contribution. They probably owned a third of the land, and the income from tithes alone must have been enormous— the clergy, for instance, getting a tenth of the wool shorn in the country, while our kings found it difficult to levy a twentieth. Roger Mortimer, Earl of March, was considered a wealthy man, because his rental amounted to £1,150 a year, or less than £20,000 of our money. But the Bishop of Winchester had an income of £3,000, or from £40,000 to £50,000 in present value; and the Abbot of St Albans had a rental of more than £2,000 (£30,000). Among the barons who took up arms against John, only the Earl of Gloucester had been able to bring more than forty knights into the field; and even his train of two hundred knights was matched by the splendid retinue of twenty-six bannerets, and a hundred and forty knights, who followed a Bishop of Durham into Scotland. Nevertheless, the prelate in question was so far from being impoverished, that he died " with great store of goods, precious stones, silver vases, horses, and costly raiment." Add to all this the discipline administered by the clergy in the ecclesiastical courts, the influence they derived from their frequent employment as great officials, and the prestige which their exceptional learning and the control of the universities gave them in a half-civilised age, and it will be understood that the Church was a very real power in England, which no Government cared to provoke needlessly.

Earls.—Among the second estate, the lay lords, the earls, were pre-eminent by position, and generally by wealth.   Out of twelve English earls, who were living at the accession of Edward II., three were of the king's blood, and two were his brothers-in-law ; two others, who actually died without heirs male during the reign, had agreed that, in such an event, their lands and honours should revert to the Crown.   Of the other five earldoms two were united in one family during the reign of Edward IIL, and one was held by a foreigner, John de Dreux.

The new earls created during the century, if we except the unworthy favourites of Edward II. and Richard II., were either already members of the royal family, or intermarried with it in the course of a few years.   It is evident that the policy of our kings was to limit the number of earldoms, and attach the earls to the interests of the reigning family.   The policy answered well at times, and under capable kings ; but if there was general disaffection, the people instinctively turned for a leader to the nearest prince of the blood, and it constantly happened that his connection with royalty only made him more dangerous as a rebel.

Barons.—It is generally easy to say who was an earl, though the title was sometimes given by courtesy to an heir whose claims had not yet been recognised.   But it is not at all easy to determine who were barons in the thirteenth and fourteenth centuries.   Anciently a baron was a man who held a barony or " honour," and a barony was

an estate, so designated, held by military service of the
Crown, and with one principal manor, which was called
the head of the barony (*caput baroniæ*), and which could
not be alienated. This, of course, was very different from
the modern peerage. With us a nobleman inherits a title,
and is none the less a nobleman though he has not an acre
of land. Anciently the baron was baron in right of his
property, and was very apt to lose his right of summons
as a peer if he only inherited a small estate. There are
many cases of families who undoubtedly held baronies,
and who never received a summons to the parliaments of
Edward I., or only received it for a time, or now and then.
For the practice of settling the landed property on the
eldest son, which is now almost universal, was very rare
in England during the Middle Ages. Accordingly, as
there were not many properties that could endure constant
subdivision, the great noble of the Conqueror's time was
represented in a century by a number of small gentlemen,
one or two of whom, it might be, were legally barons.
Again, partly perhaps because women had better chances
of life in warlike times, a great number of inheritances
devolved upon female heirs. In these cases the estates
were often held conjointly, or, as it was called, "in pour-
party," the barony being in abeyance for the time, unless
an arrangement, ratified by the Crown, was made, so that
one of the heirs should succeed to the barony. Then,
again. if the baron was convicted of treason, or died child-
less, his barony reverted to the Crown. A great many of
these *escheats*, as they were called, were kept as part of
the royal estate ; and though it was usual to bestow a
portion on relatives, and to give away baronies from time
to time to royal princes or favourites, some of the most
important honours were never separated from the Crown.
There was, therefore, great fluctuation in the number of

barons.   Particular monarchs, as Henry I. and John, might create a number of fresh baronies; but far more disappeared by forfeiture to the Crown or by division among female heirs, or by one man uniting several properties.   The Earl of Cornwall, Henry III.'s brother, possessed no fewer than eighteen baronies; and the great family of Braose enjoyed more than twenty at various times.   On the other hand, there is a case on record where a man held by the three hundredth part of a barony.   In this case it is pretty certain that the heirs could never have united to exercise their baronial rights together.

Baronies by Tenure and Baronies by Writ.—By the time of Edward I. the inconveniencies of baronies by tenure began to be sensibly felt.   The number of qualified barons was rapidly dwindling; and a legal House of Peers would have been composed of rather more than a hundred gentlemen, some of them with scarcely any stake in the country, while some of the largest landowners would have been excluded.   Public feeling was against this anomaly.   A law-book of the time declares that any man holding land to the value of a barony of two hundred and sixty-six pounds rental ought to be summoned as the peer of a baron.   On the other hand, Henry III. had already laid down the rule that no one should attend unless summoned by writ.   This was probably intended to prevent the gathering of discontented men in arms; but it acted powerfully on practice.   Accordingly, from the time of Edward I. baronies by tenure cease, and are replaced by baronies by writ.   These differ from the present peerages, which are constituted by patent, inasmuch as the writ was only to a particular parliament, while the patent ennobles the possessor for life, and his heirs male to all time.   The difference was in favour of the Crown during the fourteenth century.   So long as it did not omit the most important names, it could pack the Upper House freely with officials and men of small importance, who were under its influence.

Baronial Rights.—The power of the English baronage and gentry was more sensible on their own manors than in the conduct of general politics. Every estate was held on certain conditions, and enjoyed certain franchises, so that the powers of neighbouring land-owners might differ very widely. But the rights actually exercised by John de Warenne in his barony of Lewes will serve as a fair instance of the almost royal rights which the Crown sometimes gave away. All felons taken red-hand, that is, with the evidences of guilt upon them, were carried to the earl's prison, and hanged on the earl's gallows, or fastened in his pillory. If the case was one of suspicion only, they were still kept three days in his jail before they were handed over to the royal bailiff. If the charge was merely one of detaining property unlawfully, the earl's court tried it. He it was who held the view of frank-pledge, where the police of the district was regulated, and the men capable of bearing arms mustered. His officer regulated the manufacture and sale of beer and bread. Any ship cast on the shore, if there was not a living soul on board, went to the earl. And by perhaps the most valued privilege of all, the earl had full forest rights throughout the estates of the barony, except that he could not imprison poachers. These were the special franchises of the barony. The right of determining civil suits among the tenants belonged to every lord of a manor, and was too unimportant to be inquired into by Edward's commissioners. It of course enhanced the lord's influence over all who held of him. Considering that the free tenants on his estate were often connected with him by blood, and always by the oath of homage and fealty, which made them in some sort his subjects,—that his friendship might be very profitable, and his enmity very dangerous,—it is scarcely wonderful if they followed his lead often against king and law, and sometimes even against the Church.

Private War and Duels.—In one respect the English barons were less powerful than is sometimes supposed. The right of making private war upon one another was never allowed them in England, and the fact goes far to explain the great comparative prosperity of the country. It cannot, of course, be said that the law on this subject was always respected. But the exceptions belong almost invariably to times of general disturbance, when neighbours who had a grudge against one another, or an unsettled claim to land, fought out their quarrel under colour of the general interest ; or to exceptional districts like the Welsh marches, where the gentry had a dangerous habit of discussing their differences in armed conferences. Edward I. once threw the two greatest subjects in England, the Earls of Gloucester and Hereford, into prison, and declared all their lands forfeit for life, because they had driven off one another's cattle from some land which each claimed as his own. The extreme sentence was, in fact, remitted, and the offenders let off with fines, but the example was not lost upon Edward's subjects. In the same spirit tournaments were forbidden, except under royal licence. Even duels were forbidden, except as part of a judicial process, or after inquiry before the king in council. In 1305 Nicholas Segrave was accused of treason by a Sir John de Cromwell, and desired to purge himself by the duel. The king refused permission, on the ground that the army was then in the field ; and Segrave in his anger left the camp, and crossed the sea in order to force a fight in France by an appeal to the French king's jurisdiction. In this case Edward's just anger was heightened by several considerations. Segrave had quitted the camp without leave, and had prosecuted an appeal in the French court—a practice of which our kings were justly jealous. The sentence was death and confiscation of goods, accompanied by the judges with a recommendation to mercy, which the king at first rejected contemptuously. But the interest of the offender's friends and relatives was strong, and he was at length pardoned.

Occasional Acts of Lawlessness.—While the law was thus explicit, there is no question that it was not always enforced as rigidly as by Edward I. But the most common breaches of the peace during the fourteenth century were of a kind which it is very difficult to repress in half-civilised countries. Every district had its lawless men, trained in the use of arms, who preferred any occupation to honest labour; who picked quarrels that they might exact hush-money, or sold their services to the neighbouring lords and gentlemen, and made forcible entries on the land, or fired the homes of their employers' enemies. In this case only the subordinate agents appeared; though even gentlemen of birth suffered death at times as felons for robbing a fair or breaking into a monastery. But the carrying off of heiresses was a greater temptation than common plunder, or even than revenge on an enemy. The lady once taken from her friends and married to her captor by some hedge-priest, it was very difficult for her friends not to hush up the matter. The Countess of Lancaster, wife of a prince of the blood, was carried off in this way, and married again, under colour of pre-contract, in the reign of Edward II. A statute of Richard II.'s reign at last provided that in such cases the lady's lands should pass to her next of kin. Sometimes the law was openly defied for a long period. Hugh de Spenser, Edward II.'s unworthy favourite, kept a lady of family, Elizabeth Comyn, in prison for a whole year, till she purchased her deliverance by a heavy sacrifice of property. This, however, was an exceptional act of violence. The laws and ordinary practice of English life in the Middle Ages cannot be estimated from it, any more than English institutions of the eighteenth century by the powers extending to life or death which certain Highland chiefs practically exercised. The real importance of such a case is, that it shows what sort of order would have prevailed if the nobles had ever succeeded in wresting power from our kings.

A Nobleman's Household.—The great number of a nobleman's household—that is, of the persons who looked to him for sustenance and reward—was one element of his importance. "A baron," says a treatise of the sixteenth century, "may have a steward and clerk of his kitchen, a yeoman of his horse, a gentleman usher (but covered, and not bareheaded, when he goeth abroad), and a yeoman usher, a groom of his chamber, a yeoman usher of his hall, and his groom (but no marshal), a server armed, a carver (but unmarried), a foreman." Besides this retinue, such a lord could probably have in his house several sons of the small gentry, who served as pages, and were taught the courtesies of life. In the romance of Blonde of Oxford, such a page, who happens to be French by birth, is admitted to familiar intercourse with the ladies of the family, teaches them French, and plays at chess and dice with them. In the romance of Fulk Fitz-Warin, the young Fulk is sent at seven years old to be brought up in the household of one of his father's old friends, and at eighteen is fortunate enough to save his guardian's life in a fight. Gradually the fashion of clothing retainers in liveries came in, and great nobles got to vie with one another as to the numbers they could produce on public occasions.

Where there was any enmity between the masters, the
followers were apt to come to blows, and the practice became so fruitful of disorder, that by a statute of Henry
IV. it was enacted that even the king's servants should
not wear his livery except when they were in attendance
at court. It was long, however, before the practice died
out; and Sir John Butler, of Warrington, is said to have
been murdered for a refusal to wear Lord Stanley's cloth
on the occasion of a royal visit to Latham.

Knights.—The highest gentry of the fourteenth century must, in many respects, have been a grand race.
Chaucer has left us a charming picture of one—

> " Of his port as meek as any maid
> He never yet no villainy ere said
> In all his life unto no manner wight ;
> He was a very perfect gentle knight."

And the reproach of a song of Edward III.'s time—

> " All so well can a knight chide as any scold of a town "—

points in its very satire to the same ideal of courteous and
quiet manner. The French prisoners at Poictiers " found
their enemies very courteous," says Froissart. The scattered notices we glean here and there seem to attest hearty
friendship and good fellowship between the gentry and
the meaner men in their company. Lord Audley gave
away the splendid estate bestowed on him by the Prince
of Wales to the few squires to whom he said he owed
everything; and Sir John Chandos lost his life in a fight
against overwhelming odds, trying to rescue a squire.
Mere bravery is not uncommon; but the English won
the palm for bravery over the best soldiers of France and
Spain. " You will find in their army," said a Spanish
nobleman to his sovereign, " the flower of all the chivalry
in the world—men who will rather die on the field of

battle than retreat one foot." When the Count of Eu, who had been some time prisoner in England, at last came back into France, he spoke so enthusiastically of the honour, courtesy, and gentleness he had found among the English, that he was suspected of treason, and put to death. The political satires of this time in general deal very tenderly with knights and gentlemen. Their devotion to the country excused and redeemed their faults.

Merchants.—The position of merchants was higher than might have been expected from the warlike and feudal character of the age. They took place at the squire's table with doctors of laws, " parsons and vicars of dignity," heralds of arms,

> " Worshipful merchants, and rich artificers,
>   Gentlemen well nurtured and of good manners,
>   With gentlewomen, and namely (*specially*) lords' nurses ;
>   All these may sit at a table of good squires."

And another rhyme couples merchants with franklins or small gentry. The Mayor of London, as a dignitary of peculiar rank, took place with barons, mitred abbots, and the three Chief Justices. Four kings dined with Picard, who was mayor in 1363. Magna Charta provided for the unhindered passage of merchants about the country, and that no undue tolls should be taken of them. As a separate class, they were tried by juries of merchants only. Most remarkable of all, perhaps, is the great encouragement given from an early time to foreigners. The Hanse merchants were especially favoured, having a guildhall of their own, in which they were governed by their own aldermen. They enjoyed the privilege of storing their corn in bonded warehouses, from which they might take it out and sell it as was most convenient; and they imported so freely from the rich grain districts of the Baltic that in the reign of Edward IV. they provoked a protective ordinance, which forbade the trade when prices were low in England. Next in importance were the Lombards, who had succeeded the Jews as the great money-lenders of the country. They had an exchange in Cornhill; and the only national debt that the country has never paid is for a sum borrowed from the Bardi of Florence by Edward III. when he was prosecuting his French wars. Mainly, of course, the London merchants were a class by themselves, united in guilds or companies, which finally monopolised the city freedom; so that no one could be a citizen if he was not a member of one of these associations. But knights and gentlemen sometimes put out their younger sons as apprentices to mercers and drapers. A noble would join a merchant in a speculation; the smaller families of gentry intermarried freely with the wealthier citizens; and the successful London merchant constantly bought land that was held by military service, and founded a knightly family. Then, as now, the mayors and sheriffs were occasionally knighted for distinguished service. As soldiers, the Londoners were not of great reputation; but their ships did good service, and on one occasion a single citizen equipped a small squadron to clear the sea of pirates, and captured sixteen vessels.

A Mediæval Manor.—If we pass from towns to the country, we shall find that England was divided into manors, each of which was held of the king or of some great lord. Under him were free tenants, who were personally free, and could do what they liked with their land, so long as the lord's rent was paid; and beneath or beside these there were various classes of serfs. Taking a single manor from the Domesday of Cambridgeshire under Edward I. we find it thus described:—" Lord William de Say has a messuage (or building) in Great Linton containing one acre, a hundred and sixty acres of plough land, seven and a half acres of meadow land, twenty acres of pasture and forty acres of wood in demesne, which he holds by one knight's fee of the Earl of Brittany, and the said Earl holds them in chief of the king." In other words, William de Say farmed nearly 230 acres in Great Linton; but he owned more than 500 acres besides, which were let to various tenants. For all this he had to provide one heavy-armed soldier, who was to serve for forty days, or, in place of him, to pay the commutation assessed by Parliament. Under William de Say were twenty-three free tenants of the class of small squires, franklins, or farmers. " Robert de Linton holds 43 acres of land of the Lord William de Say, and pays £1, 7s. 8d. a year." There were also 49 free burgage tenants, who rented shops in the burg or town. " Thomas de Maleton holds a shop of the said Lord William de Say, and pays 10d. a year." Several of these were free tenants of the Abbot of St Jacle, who was another landowner in the manor, owning, however, only 21½ acres. Below these came a body of tenants called " *customars,*" as they paid for their lands by certain customary dues and services. They belonged to the class of villans. " John Kendrick holds of the aforesaid Lord William de Say sixteen acres of land, with a house, in villenage, and pays 3s. 7d. a year, and gives two hens (value 2d.), and twenty eggs (value ½d.), and owes ten days' work, each the value of ½d., from the nativity of St John Baptist (June 24) to August 1, and from August 1 to Michaelmas; thirty-two days' work, to the value of 13d., and is to plough 11 acres a year at 3d. an acre, and to give suit to the court and pay rentage." These last phrases mean that John Kendrick was to attend the court of the manor whenever it was held, and to pay a tax to his lord whenever his lord paid a war-tax to the king. Like the customars were the cotters. "Gilbert Crispin holds an acre of land, with a messuage, in villenage of the same lord, and must render thirty-two days' work, each the value of $\frac{1}{2}$d., from Michaelmas to August 1, and is to own $7\frac{1}{2}$ acres of corn in the autumn, to the value of 3d." On this property of Great Linton there were no serfs proper. The distinction between the villan and the customary tenant was that the villan's labour was valued by the lord at his own price, and in some cases he could be turned off the land without compensation.

Gradual Enfranchisement of the Labouring Classes.—Taking now Linton Magna, a part of Linton parish, in Cambridgeshire, and comparing its state in 1278 with its state 200 years before, when the Domesday survey was made, we find that the land accounted for—in other words, the land brought under cultivation—then increased from 600 to 760 acres. The adult male population in the Conqueror's time consisted of 24 serfs under one non-resident lord, and ten burgesses in Cambridge belonged to the manor; that is, ten serfs had been allowed to leave the manor and work or trade in a neighbouring town. In Edward I.'s time the chief landowner seems still to have been an absentee, but was probably represented by a steward. The population is now composed of 101, of whom 29 are free tenants and 49 free burgage tenants having shops. Twenty are customars and two cotters. In other words, the freemen on the estate are now nearly four to one compared with the serfs: and the population has more than trebled. It did not attain anything like this rate of increase during the next five centuries and a half. Now, results like these, or only a little less remarkable, meet us throughout the four counties for which we have a second Domesday or census of Edward I.'s time; though Cambridgeshire seems to have been most fortunate in the great proportion enfranchised. To take an instance on a large scale : the population in the hundred of Bampton in Oxfordshire increased from about 401 to about 1156, and the free tenants from 4 to 363. If we could assume that the same rule held good throughout England, we should infer that the class of freemen had risen from between a fifth or a sixth to between a third and a half of the population, and that many who remained serfs had been improved in position by acquiring customary rights. Had the population increased generally in numbers as in those counties, it would have amounted to nearly five millions. But the gains had been much greater in the purely rural districts than in the towns, except in special cases, such as that of Norwich. In several cases of county towns, such as Lincoln, ~~Torksey~~, Colchester, Sandwich, and Hythe, the number of burgesses taxed under Edward III. is slightly below the numbers given as belonging to the respective towns in the census of William the Conqueror. On the other hand, many places that were mere villages two hundred years before had come to be small towns in the fourteenth century.

Position of the Serfs.—Generally, then, we may say that the English population had increased greatly since the Norman Conquest, was just becoming enfranchised, and was bringing forest and waste land under the plough very rapidly. It is more difficult to say what the condition of the mass of the people was. Legally there is no question that the serf was in some respects very badly off. He could not acquire property, and he could not plead in a civil action against his master. His labour was due to his lord, and was given without wages. In practice, however, it is certain that the condition of the agricultural classes was much better than was implied in their legal rights. The lord made most profit in the long run if he let his serf acquire property which he could tax in certain proportions from time to time. Instead of clothing and feeding him, he found it convenient to give him a house, a bit of land, and something like three days in the week on which he might labour for himself. There can be no doubt, I think, that the master had the power of inflicting a reasonable chastisement in strokes when the serf refused to work; but it is pretty certain, also, that the laws were jealous of the master's power, and that it was not safe to abuse it. A lawyer of Edward I.'s time, who wrote a treatise on law, and laid down rules for the management of an estate, says that the most lawful and ingenious manner of chastising servants is by fines and scoldings. At the great rising of the villans in Richard II.'s time, they did not complain of ill-usage by their lords. They complained that their rights had been encroached upon, commons enclosed, and mills built at which they were bound to grind; and they demanded that land should be set aside for them on which they might catch game and fish. They were in fact suffering only from the extension of agriculture and from trade monopolies.

General Wellbeing of the People.—A ballad which seems to belong originally to the time of Edward I., represents that king as losing his way in the chase, and taking shelter in the house of one John the Reeve, who is a royal bondsman. John is at first very unwilling to entertain guests whom he sees to be gentlemen, though he does not know their rank. He fears if he lets them see his wealth that his dues to the Crown will be increased; but at last his shyness wears off, and he begins to boast of his prosperity:—

> " I go girt in a russet gown,
>   My hood is of home-made brown,
>   I wear neither burnet nor green
>   And yet, I trow, I have in store
>   A thousand pounds and some deal more,
>   For all ye are prouder and fine.
>   Therefore, I say, as mote I thee, (*as might I thrive*)
>   A bondsman it is good to be
>   And come of churl's kin."

The entertainment he gives them bears out his boast :—

> " By then came in red wine and ale,
>   The boar's head into the hall,
>   Then shield (brawn) with sauces seere (*several*),
>   Capons both baked and roast,
>   Woodcocks, venison, without boast,
>   And dish meat dight full dear.
>   Swans they had piping hot,
>   Coneys, curlews, well I wot,
>   The crane, the heron, in fere (*together*),
>   Pigeons, partridges, with spicery,
>   Yolks, flomes (*cheese-cakes*), with fruitery :
>   John bade them make good cheer."

In this description, as in that of Chaucer's Franklin, the object no doubt is to paint the substantial comfort of a prosperous yeoman ; and the picture is perhaps a little over-coloured.   But the author of " Piers Plowman," who belongs to the latter half of the fourteenth century, draws almost as cheerful a portrait of the condition of hired labourers :—

> " Labourers that have no land
>   To live on but their hands,
>   Deigned not to dine a day—
>   Night-old worts (*stale cabbages*),
>   May no penny ale them pay (*satisfy them*),
>   Nor no piece of bacon,
>   But if it be fresh flesh or fish.'

It is true this is given as a contrast to the condition of the ploughman, who lives on his own land, and who is reduced to feed on bread made of bran and beans, eked out with leeks and baked apples, till the new harvest comes in. Similarly, in another poem of the same period, the ploughman is represented in abject poverty, his hood full of holes, his dress insufficient to keep out the cold and wet, and his wife "barefoot on the bare ice," helping to drive his lean steers, while their little children lie at the end of the furrow. But even this man talks of beans and bacon and common corn bread as his ordinary fare.

Take again a popular description of England, translated roughly from Latin verse, of the twelfth century, and enlarging the vague descriptions of the classical writer :—

> " England is a good land, fruitful of wool ;
> England full of play, freemen full worthy to play ;
> Free men, free tongues, heart free, free be all the people.
> Here hand is more free, more better than their tongue.
> Strange men that needeth, their land well oft relieveth ;
> When hunger grieveth, their hoard all such men feedeth.
> Their land is good enow, wonder much fruit beareth, and corn.
> Land, honey, milk, cheese—this island shall bear the prize."

In its English form, we have this description from a writer of the reign of Richard II. We cannot now say whether he wrote it, or at what time such expressions as " free be all the people" were interpolated. But we may surely assume that to some of that time England appeared a land flowing with milk and honey, full of mirth, and inhabited by a free and free-handed race.

Effects of the Prosperity of the People on the French Wars.—The importance of this feature in English life, the rude wellbeing of the commons, was very apparent in our wars. The dependence of our armies on their commissariat was subject of early remark. " When you behold our barons and knights going upon a military expedition," says Peter of Blois in the twelfth century, " you see their baggage horses laden, not with iron but wine, not with lances but cheeses, not with swords but bottles, not with spears but spits." "I have it on the best information," says the Italian tourist before quoted, "that when the war is at its greatest fury, they (the English) will seek for good eating and all their other comforts, without thinking of what harm might befall them." But as a consequence the English yeomanry were the strongest men of their day in Europe. Rather undersized by modern standards, as the coats of mail preserved in the Tower show, they were able to send their deadly hail of arrows from a distance of more than 200 yards; so that it was even forbidden to practise at less than eleven score yards. They had also, as Fortescue pointed out in Henry VI.'s time, the money to equip themselves at their own cost, and the leisure to train for war; while the French commoner came into the field without defensive armour and with no better weapons than long knives. The current French vaunt that the English made their belly their god, was met with the fierce rejoinder that it was like fighting with women to fight the French. On one occasion the English women stood with slings by the side of their husbands, and inflicted a bloody defeat on a French invading force. The wisest captains of France were slow to meet their enemy on anything like equal terms in the open field. The English soldier who lost a battle or a fortress was almost certain to be taxed with treachery by his countrymen.

Law Courts and Officials.—The great evils of which popular songs during the fourteenth century complain are the oppressions of royal officials and of the various law courts, and the insolence of great men's retainers. It takes centuries to produce a high tone of honour among officials, and in times like the Middle Ages, in England,

it was easy for the venal sheriff or bailiff to amass money
and escape inquiry. Sometimes it was the lands of a
minor that were seized unlawfully in the king's name;
sometimes the imposition of a tax gave the opportunity
of uneven assessments; constantly hush-money was demanded because some trifling law had been violated or
some royal right encroached upon. The ecclesiastical
courts were equally corrupt, and had greater opportunities
of oppression. Heresy, blasphemy, incontinent life, neglect
to keep the Church holidays or to pay the Church dues,
were all offences for which men might be summoned and
punished, according to the guilt proved, with fine, imprisonment, or death.

> " Give money to the dean where thou thinkest to dwell,
>   And have leave long enough to serve the fiend of hell,"

says a people's ballad. But have a false charge brought
against you, says another poem, and wish to make purga-
tion, the officers will assign you from town to town, and
you must needs pay ransom though you be clear as crystal.
It is little wonder if the people accordingly sympathised
with the outlaws of society, and disliked the stern legality
which, with all its oppressions, was yet better than anarchy; little wonder if lawyers' lives were in danger in
every popular rising. Nor can it be doubted that the
insolence of great lords' retainers pressed heavily upon the
poor.

> " When God was on earth and wandered wide,
>   What was the reason that he would not ride ? "

asks an old song; and the answer is—

> " He would not have a groom to go by his side,
>   Nor grudging of any gadling to jaw or to chide."

But allowing for these evils, and not extenuating them,
the fact remains that the English commons were protected as well as fleeced by law, and had a feeling of

brotherhood for nobles and gentry.   In the risings of the
peasantry in France, the French villan tried to exterminate the upper classes, and insulted the last agonies of
his victims ; the English villans contented themselves
with the deaths of a few unpopular great men and lawyers ; and if the leaders entertained more far-reaching
plans, they at least never tried to carry them into effect.
The country, therefore, had great elements of strength,
for it was well-served and firmly knit together with a rich
and brave people.   One peculiar feature of the times
added, no doubt, to the Englishman's capacity for war.
Like modern backwoodsmen or bushmen, he was forced
to be shifty and skilful with his hands, from the mere
fact that skilled artisans were confined to the towns.   For
nearly eighty years England had kept out of great wars.
The time came when Edward I. suffered himself to be
drawn into a new policy ; and the first invasion of Scotland may be regarded as the first in a long series of events
which gradually transformed England into the chief military power of the day.

CHAPTER II.

STATE OF SCOTLAND IN THE THIRTEENTH CENTURY.

Its People, Military Power, and Natural Resources.—Scotland, like England, enjoyed almost unbroken peace during the 13th century, and its tranquillity was the more beneficial as its sovereigns were fairly capable and judicious rulers. The people were always fiercer than their southern neighbours; the blood-feud was more distinctly recognised as an institution beyond Tweed ; and down to a late period it required all the influence of a great general to restrain the Scotch soldiery from wanton licence and barbarity in an enemy's country. On the other hand, the English common law had been adopted ; the oppressive forest laws of England were unknown ; and a few wealthy towns carried on an important foreign commerce, which enriched the nation and brought merchants and artisans into the country. Except that the nobles had a little more power and the peasantry rather more freedom than in England, it was difficult to distinguish the English-speaking population of the two countries. The kings, Keltic or Highland chieftains by descent, had intermarried so freely with the royal and noble families of England and France, that they were spoken of as Frenchmen "in manners, language, and civilisation," as early as William the Lion's reign (1212 A.D.)   The nobles were partly of Norman extraction, holding estates in England, and owing a divided allegiance to the English crown.   The Comyns, Bruces, and Balliols are of this class.   Or they were of old Scottish descent, like the Strabolgies of Athol, or the Macduffs of Fife, then allied with the great families of England, and perhaps, like the Earl of Athol, claiming kinship with English royalty.   The people of the eastern part of the Lowlands, from Tweed to Forth, the most numerous part of the population, and its sinews, were as English as the Northumbrians, from among whom they had emigrated in the first instance.   The rest of the kingdom was less homogeneous.   Galloway had a population of Keltic extraction, and governed by its own customary law ; and the Highlands of Scotland were like a separate principality, the people having no common feeling or interest with their English-speaking neighbours of the Lowlands, and the chiefs rendering little more than a nominal allegiance to the Scotch crown.

Friendly Relations with England.—A great part of Scotland is a poor country, unfitted for tillage ; but, compared with the border counties of England—Northumberland, Cumberland, and Westmoreland—the Lothians could support a large population ; and rude as the Scotch husbandry was, it was rewarded with large crops of the hardier grains—rye, barley, and oats.   The rivers were full of fish, game was abundant ; and then, as now, there were large sheep pastures, wool being the great article of export.   Altogether, therefore, it seems probable that the population of the whole country may have numbered from half-a-million to a million.   The proportion of rich men among these was much smaller than in England.   The iron-clad soldiers, in a full muster of the English army, numbered about one in ten ; in a Scotch force they

perhaps did not exceed one in sixty.   The common soldiers
of an English force were mostly archers, recruited from
the yeoman class, who could afford to buy good weapons,
and had the leisure for careful training.   The Scotch
archers were few comparatively, and the national Scotch
weapon was the spear, which was chiefly wood, and its
use easily learned.   In one respect only did a Scotch
army have the advantage of its southern enemy : it could
easily be mounted from the hardy ponies which roamed
in droves over the open country ; but horses that would
bear a mounted knight had to be imported from Spain.
There were still large forests in Scotland, and wood was
accordingly the common material of the better houses,
while the huts of the poor would be built only of wattles.
The castles, mere strongholds of the gentry, and not intended for defence against trained soldiers, were often
enclosed only by earthen ramparts with palisades at the
top.   War with England, therefore, was not an enterprise
to be lightly undertaken.   When the Scotch were still barbarous, and had nothing to lose, a Malcolm or William
might pour down over the borders, inflict heavy loss,
carry off a large booty, and retire unpunished if he
avoided battle in the open field.   But by the time of
Edward I. Scotland had towns, and villages, and farms, on
which the havoc of war could be retaliated.   Its nobles,
trained in the soldiership of the times, could not hope for
success in a protracted struggle with England, and had
every reason to keep the peace, as they valued their
Scotch homes or their southern fiefs.

Disputed Succession—Edward I. asked to Arbi-
trate.—There was, however, an unsettled question between the neighbouring countries.   The richest part of
Scotland, the Lothians, had belonged to England under
the Saxon kings, and had only been lost in Canute's

reign. It was a question whether the Scotch kings did not owe homage to the English crown for this portion, at least, of their territory, if not for the whole country. Henry II. had once settled the question by forcing William the Lion, when he took him prisoner, to bind himself to the desired submission; and Richard I. had annulled the settlement by suffering William to buy his independence. Lawyers on either side might dispute whether a king could grant away the rights of his crown; whether William could make Scotland vassal, or Richard dispose of the English suzerainty. Practically, the English claim was often advanced during the 13th century, and never really conceded. The Scotch kings did homage for their English possessions, and the English lawyers registered their claim to a further homage for Scotland, or worded the oath vaguely, so that either party might interpret it in his own fashion. Both countries were, in fact, anxious to be at peace. If there were Scotch nobles holding fiefs in England, there were also many Englishmen owning Scotch estates; and it was convenient for great nobles on either side that a country should be close at hand in which they could take refuge from a king's displeasure, or from the law. Moreover, the recollections of war during Henry III.'s reign were either of defeat in France, or of civil bloodshed in England. The feudal baron had ceased for a time to be a soldier by trade, and dreaded the expense of military service. Add to this, that Alexander III. of Scotland was well known and very popular in the English court, and that Edward contemplated joining the two countries by a marriage of his son to Alexander's grand-daughter and heir, and it will be understood that the peace of the two countries was unbroken, almost unruffled, and seemed likely to be eternal. Never were Scotchmen and Englishmen more nearly one.

Recognition of English Superiority.—These prospects were not to endure. The death of Alexander III., in 1286, was followed, only four years later, by the death of the fair maid of Norway, the grand-daughter who was to have brought Scotland, as a dower, into the royal family of England. From that moment Edward's policy was changed. Till then he had been careful to keep his claims in the background, not wishing to irritate national pride, when it seemed probable that his objects would be achieved peaceably. Now Scotland was to pass to another dynasty ; and he owed it to England that the critical interval, when the succession was still disputed, and the kingdom less than ever able to cope with foreign invasion, should not be allowed to pass over without a formal settlement of the points in dispute. But he was too conscious of his own strength to act precipitately. There were thirteen rival competitors, some, it is true, of little account, but among them embracing almost every interest in Scotland, and if civil war was to be avoided, it was necessary that a strong power should intervene. Men naturally turned their eyes toward the great king with a European fame for justice and piety, whose indirect influence over the rival nobles was so great that he might almost dispense with the employment of an armed force. Who it was invited Edward to act as umpire is not exactly known ; but whether it was the regency or the whole baronage, it is certain that the invitation was formally made, and was acquiesced in by all classes.

Claims of the Competitors.—Edward was well disposed to undertake the task of arbitration. He appointed a conference at Norham on the borders, and ordered the barons north of the Humber to attend with their feudal retainers, so that a small army, raised in the least costly manner, might be present to back his decision. Meanwhile, he desired the Scotch Estates to consider whether they admitted his claims to be feudal superior of Scotland, which he laid before them in the shape of a legal case, supported by all the evidence that could be procured. The Estates took three weeks to deliberate. During that time they might easily have prepared to meet Edward in the field. But there was no union in their councils, the rival claimants being jealous one of another, and many who were already English feudatories not caring to endanger the estates they held immediately of Edward. It is probable that a few of them were bribed. The nobles and bishops agreed unanimously to allow the justice of the English claim; the towns seem to have impugned it, but were so powerless by themselves that their remonstrance was contemptuously put aside. Edward now carried out his claim to its practical consequences. He put English garrisons into the Scotch fortresses, and associated one Englishman with the regency and another with the chancellor. Then he received the oath of fealty from all who held by barony of the crown. His position, however, was still only that of a trustee administering an estate till the rightful heir should be found. To decide which of the thirteen claimants was entitled, a court was appointed at Berwick-on-Tweed two months later. Berwick-on Tweed was at that time the great commercial port of Scotland; and by choosing a place within the borders Edward appeared to recognise the principle that his justice as overlord or suzerain was to be done in Scotland itself.

Decision in favour of John Balliol.—Though there were thirteen claimants, it could not be said that there were thirteen claims. Most of the rival suitors had no possible standing-ground in law, and probably only came into court with the idea of proving their pedigrees,

and establishing their connection with the royal family of
Scotland. One real claimant, the Count of Holland,
could only prove if his three chief rivals—Bruce, Balliol,
and Hastings—were disqualified by their ancestor's attaint
for treason, or because he had sold his succession for an
estate. But these arguments were so little convincing
that the Count at last withdrew from the suit. Then the
question was narrowed to one of two issues. Was the
kingdom of Scotland to follow the laws of an ordinary
estate, or to be divided among all descendants of the three
daughters of David, Earl of Huntingdon, the last prince
of the blood who had left children. It was the interest
of Bruce and Hastings to urge this; for although Bruce
claimed kingdom and crown, his cause was manifestly
the weaker, and he was prepared from the first to compound for a share of the inheritance. It was Edward's
interest to take this view, for Scotland divided among
three earls was much more likely to remain a province of
England, than Scotland united and held by a royal vassal.
There were plausible grounds in Scotch law for taking
this view, as the principality of Galloway had been
declared divisible by the Scotch kings, who had even
enforced the principle by a civil war. But there was
another law case more to the point, in which a Scotch
earldom· had been declared indivisible; and Edward's
court accordingly held that the dignity of king was indivisible also. This decision removed Hastings from the
suit. Next the court had to decide whether Balliol, the
great-grandson of the eldest daughter of Earl David, or
Bruce, the grandson of the second daughter, had the better
title to the crown. In modern times there could be no
doubt on the point, but the custom of the Keltic clans (and
Scotch royalty, it must be remembered, was Keltic) favoured
the descendant who was a generation nearer in point of time

to the common ancestor.   Scotland as a kingdom, however, was governed by laws like those of England, and Edward's court pronounced accordingly, and gave the kingdom to Balliol.   He was quickly put in possession of his inheritance, and the English garrisons withdrawn from the fortresses.   In return, he made formal homage to King Edward, kneeling before him, as was the custom, and placing his hands between his lord's hands, while he swore to become his man of life, and limb, and earthly honour, and to do him the services due from the realm of Scotland.   Should Balliol be false to this oath, he was to pay the forfeit with his kingdom ; should he venture so far as to attempt his lord's life by war, he might be drawn and quartered.

Irritation caused by the English Sovereignty in Scotland.—In a very short time the king and nobles of Scotland discovered that their position as vassals of the English crown was intolerable.   Appeals from King John to King Edward were lodged by every litigant against whom judgment had been given in the Scotch courts ; and while this added indefinitely to the cost of legal proceedings, and was thus an injury to the whole country, it was also a great disparagement of the royal dignity.   Indeed, when King John neglected to appoint proctors at Westminster, he received a summons to appear and plead in person.   Presently Edward was involved in a French war.   He now called on the Scotch nobles to serve like his English vassals for the defence of the kingdom, and though this did not oblige them to service in France proper or in Flanders, it implied service in Gascony, or a commutation in money.   The time seemed well chosen for resistance, for a French fleet was ravaging the English coasts, and the last formidable rebellion in Wales had broken out.   The Scotch nobles formally refused

the service claimed of them, and Balliol procured a Papal
absolution from his oath of homage. So great was the
danger that even Edward hesitated to confront it. He
proposed that the Scotch king should surrender the three
fortresses of Berwick, Jedburgh, and Roxburgh, and
that these should be restored to him at the end of the
war with France, if the Scotch during that time gave
no assistance to the enemy, and did not admit either
Frenchman or Flemings into their ports. Although the
claim of personal service was evaded by this arrangement,
it was in no sense given up, and the demand that the
Scotch should sacrifice almost their whole national commerce in the interests of English policy, was felt keenly
by the people as an insult. King John himself seems
to have been a mere puppet in the hands of his council.
But these, a committee of the great nobles, bishops, earls,
and barons, acted resolutely. The English residents in
Scotland were treated as public enemies, their lands confiscated, and themselves driven out of the country. In
particular, the lands of Annandale were taken from Robert
Bruce V., son of King John's late rival, and given to
John Comyn of Buchan. This example of violence was
unfortunately exceeded at Berwick, where the English
merchants then lying in the harbour were attacked in
a sudden outburst of popular fury, from which few escaped
with their lives. The news filled up the measure of
Edward's wrath. Careful to the last in observing the
forms of law, he summoned Balliol to answer for these
excesses ; and not till the Scotch king neglected to appear
were his lands in England confiscated, and war against
him declared.

Massacre of Berwick and Battle of Dunbar.—
The war was not of long duration. A bloody storm at
Berwick, where Edward allowed a general massacre in

revenge for the ravages and insolence of the inhabitants, was retaliated by the Scotch in England, where Balliol burned two hundred boys alive in a school at Corbridge. But the Scotch were soon recalled from the borders by news that Dunbar was invested; and in the attempt to relieve it, they sustained so decisive a rout from the Earl of Surrey, that all thought of resistance was at an end for a time. Hundreds of well-born prisoners from the Scotch baronage and gentry passed through England, some two by two on the same horse, others, with their feet fettered, in carts. Balliol himself was admitted to an abject submission, and kept in an easy captivity. Edward made a triumphal march through Scotland, keeping sharp discipline among his men, and paying liberally for all the provisions brought in. It is said Robert Bruce asked for the forfeited kingdom, which by custom should have been granted to him, though in strict law he had no claim to it. Edward replied by asking sharply, whether he thought the king had nothing better to do than to conquer kingdoms for him The long-coveted prize was at last within Edward's grasp, and he was not disposed to let it escape him. The Scotch earls, barons, and knights were forced to do formal homage to the English king. In return there was a general amnesty, though a few who might be formidable from their power were required to live in England for a time. An English regent, justiciary, chancellor, and treasurer were appointed for the conquered kingdom. English garrisons were put in the chief fortresses, and Berwick was made the seat of government. Edward's intention, no doubt, was to make the change as easy as possible.

English Rule in Scotland ; William Wallace.— But nothing could make the transition from independence to vassalage tolerable. An escheater went through the

country, taking formal possession of the estates for which
their owners had not done homage, and which were
accordingly declared forfeit by the English justiciary.
The gentry and farmers found that they were obliged
to cart their wool to Berwick or Ayr, the only parts
from which it might be exported, and on which a tax
was first levied upon it. The nobles and knights found
that the obligation to serve Edward in war would be
rigidly enforced, as the king was now concentrating his
whole strength against France. The clergy were exasperated at an influx of English friars and other ecclesiastics. Worst of all was the license of the English
soldiery in their garrison towns. They were filled with
an overweening confidence in themselves from their easy
victory, and being quartered in what was still a hostile
country, and where a guerilla war was very often maintained, they indulged in every kind of outrage, from
insolence and plunder to the ill-use of women and murder.
No redress was to be obtained from the highest English
officials. The regent, the Earl of Surrey, whose connection with Scotch royalty might have made him favourable to the nation, was habitually absent from the country,
being unable to bear its inclement climate. Ormesby,
the justiciary, was a hard, stern man ; and Cressingham,
the treasurer, a rapacious and dishonest minister, only
anxious to enrich himself, and not very scrupulous as to
the means. With such causes for discontent, a revolt
could not be long delayed, and only wanted a leader.
One was found in an obscure gentleman of Renfrewshire,
William Wallace, whose wife is said to have been killed
with some circumstances of peculiar horror, for assisting
Wallace to escape from the English soldiery, one of whom
he had killed in a broil. Wallace was ill-qualified by
position to command a Scotch army. He was not even

a knight when he first took up arms, and to the last his authority was barely endured by the proud Scotch nobles. But at this time most of the baronage were serving in Edward's army, or afraid to risk the forfeiture of their lands, and Wallace did incalculable service by provoking a war, in which the Scotch learned that their enemies were not invincible. He generally had the prudence to avoid pitched battles, in which the heavy armed English soldiers, outnumbering him by twenty to one, must have gained an easy victory. His tactics were those which Robert Bruce developed and improved afterwards, —to harass the enemy by invasions, to hang upon their flanks, ravaging the country, and cutting off stragglers if they entered Scotland ; and if he was himself forced to fight, to take up a position on strong ground, and await the enemy's attack, so that his own raw levies might not be disordered by complicated movements.

Battle of Stirling.—Wallace's first successes were followed by a general rising, and it became necessary for the English viceroy to march with as large an army as he could collect into Scotland. It must be said, to the praise of the Earl of Surrey, that he was sincerely anxious to avoid war. He obtained large powers to treat from the king, and seemed to have made peace with the nobles, when he learned that the troops they disbanded were joining another army under Wallace. Surrey now marched upon the new enemy, and again tried the effect of negotiations. Wallace rejected the very idea of terms, and both sides prepared for the battle. To the English it seemed as if the victory was certain, for their iron-clad cavalry far outnumbered any force that the Scotch could bring into the field. The Earl of Surrey seems, accordingly, to have neglected the commonest precautions. Instead of taking his army across by a ford of which he was told, where sixty could cross at once, he led them, after much time had been wasted, across a narrow bridge, which only allowed the passage of two horsemen at a time. What he had been warned of ensued. When a small portion of the army had crossed, the Scotch descended from the hills on which they were encamped, surrounded the English troops, and hurled them back in a disorderly mass upon the Forth. A hundred knights and five thousand light-armed soldiers are said to have perished in the rout. There were still men enough to retrieve the day, but the aged Earl of Surrey was unmanned by the danger he had run, and fled precipitately. England lay open to the invader, and Wallace's troops spread over the north, burning, plundering, and slaying in every direction.

Battle of Falkirk.—But within a year Wallace had been crushed. Edward ordered his generals to keep on the defensive till he could take the field in person, and when he was at last able to enter Scotland, did it at the head of such an army as had never yet been mustered. So thoroughly was Edward exasperated, that having to send a detachment into the country against some forts which held out, he chose for his general John Marmaduke, whom he had often censured for cruelty, and told him that he might now strike and spare not. The Scotch policy was to avoid an engagement, and it seemed for a moment as if they would starve Edward out of the country. But Wallace could not resist hanging upon the English flanks with a large army, in the hope of surprising the king by a night attack ; and Edward, learning that he was in the neighbourhood, with the Earls of Angus and March, moved suddenly upon him, and forced him to accept battle at Falkirk. Without sufficient cavalry, and without archers, Wallace could do nothing but draw up his spearmen in a strong position behind a bog, and trust that the English would charge in the headstrong, chivalrous manner which knights gloried in. Edward was too trained a soldier to allow such a mistake. His archers poured in their deadly shafts on the helpless masses of the Scotch; and when these were disordered, the cavalry, whom Robert Bruce had conducted round the marsh, poured in, and completed the rout. There was a fearful massacre, and though Wallace escaped with life, he was henceforth without credit and without power.

Subjugation of Scotland. — The conduct of the Scotch war for independence now fell into the hands of the Scotch nobles; and as long as England was involved in a costly and perilous war with France, the Scotch rather gained than lost ground. But in 1303 Edward was able to turn the undivided strength of his kingdom against the north; and all hope of intervention from France, or of successful mediation by the Pope, seemed absolutely at an end. The last Scotch fortress was surrendered; the last army disbanded; and the Scotch nobles sued for peace, and were allowed to compound for their forfeited estates by fines. One noble, John de Soulis, refused to make any peace with his country's enemy, and died an exile in France. One gentleman, the famous Wallace, was so far excluded from the treaty, that he was summoned to surrender at discretion, with the understanding that his life should be spared, but without hope of retaining his estates. He unhappily rejected these terms, was captured by the treachery of Sir John Menteith, and being taken prisoner to London, suffered the horrible death reserved for traitors, with the addition that he was disembowelled alive. Otherwise Edward's policy in Scotland was large and generous. He was resolved to govern it as a province and part of England; but he maintained Scotch laws under English judges, and the Scotch Parliament under an English viceroy, and he employed Scotchmen freely to command the fortresses.

Rebellion of Robert Bruce. — But the Scotch crown had too many rightful heirs for Edward's claim to be even yet established. If the Balliols were out of the question, their right passed, in the first place, to Robert Bruce, the sixth Earl of Carrick. Robert Bruce's father, a young man of singular beauty, had been riding through Carrick in Ayrshire one day, when he crossed a hunting cavalcade in attendance on a lady of rank. Bruce and the lady exchanged salutations and kisses, after the fashion of courtiers in those days, and Bruce was about to pass on, when the lady placed her hand on his bridle, and carried him off, no very reluctant captive, to Turnbury Castle. In a fortnight they were married, the lady bringing as her dower the earldom of Carrick, and an alliance with the old Scotch nobility, which perhaps explains why her son Robert renounced the English politics of his father and grandfather. Nevertheless, the young Earl of Carrick was rather precipitated into rebellion than a deliberate rebel. Before the last conquest of Scotland he had made a compact with John Comyn the Red, Lord of Badenoch, whose claims to the crown were only second to his own, that they should support one another in all future emergencies. After the peace, Comyn seems to have acquiesced in the new settlement, and either to prove his loyalty, or because Bruce was soliciting him with plans of insurrection, had the baseness to send his copy of the compact to Edward. The king naturally summoned Bruce to answer for his conduct, and Bruce, having gained a short delay by denying the authenticity of the document, thought it wisest to fly for Scotland that same night. Once over the border, he summoned a meeting of his kinsmen, and laid the case before them. It was agreed that Bruce's young brothers Thomas and Neil Bruce, should wait upon Comyn, who was then at Dalswinton, near Dumfries, invite him to a conference with Bruce in the church of the Grey Friars, and kill him while they were on the road. Comyn must have known that he was in danger; but he was at a distance from his own property and people, and probably did not dare to refuse compliance. He treated the young Bruces with such courtesy and confidence that they had not the heart to carry out their plan of assassination. And thus, fatally for Robert Bruce's reputation, Comyn came alive to the appointed meeting-place. An angry discussion ensued, and as Comyn, who doubtless thought himself protected by privilege of sanctuary, positively refused to support Bruce in the rising which was now unavoidable, Bruce at last stabbed him where he stood; and Bruce's followers, when they learned what was done, closed in to despatch the wounded man, and slew with him his uncle, Robert Comyn, who had aimed an ineffectual blow at Bruce.

English Cruelties in Scotland.—In Scotland this crime caused little horror, though it alienated the powerful Comyn connection from Bruce's interests. But generally, the feeling was one of enthusiastic joy that war with England was to be renewed under a powerful noble and soldier of promise, who could never now draw back from his followers. Five earls and four bishops assisted in the coronation of King Robert; and the Countess of Buchan, a Macduff married to a Comyn, publicly renounced the cause espoused by her family, and rode off to place the crown, which her brother kept, upon the new king's head. In England, where the nation had by this time identified itself with the king's policy,

the murder in a church was regarded as an inexpiable
crime, and Robert Bruce as traitor and felon alike.
Aymer de Valence was sent north at once, and Edward
prepared to follow with the whole forces of the kingdom.
But they were not required. A short battle before
Methuen, in which the Scotch were treacherously
surprised, ended in a complete rout of Robert Bruce's
forces. He himself was nearly taken, and his best
friends and nearest relatives were brought in prisoners
day by day, as the conquerors followed up the pursuit,
or stormed some new stronghold of the insurrection.
Hitherto Edward had treated his vanquished enemies
as prisoners of war; but his character, as he grew
old, seemed to harden, and the soldier and statesman
were alike lost in the judge. Among his victims
were Nigel, Alexander, and Thomas Bruce, the king
of Scotland's brothers; Sir Christopher Seton, his
brother-in-law, and who had saved his life; Sir Simon
Fraser, whose beauty excited the compassion of the London populace; Sir Herbert de Moreham, the tallest and
handsomest man in Scotland; and the Earl of Athol, of
the English blood-royal; as also Bruce's marshal, standard-
bearer, and chaplain. The Countess of Buchan was confined in a cage, fashioned like a crown, on Berwick
ramparts, "so that all might look at her for a wonder."
Mary Bruce, the sister, was condemned to a similar cage,
but was afterwards put into a convent with her sister
Christian and Bruce's daughter Marjory. The queen,
Mary Bruce, as daughter of the loyal and powerful Earl
of Ulster, was only kept in honourable captivity. In the
Lowlands there was a reign of terror, the work of young
Prince Edward, and disapproved by his father, who
wished only the rich to be sufferers. Men were hanged,
burned, or dragged at horses' tails, without distinction for

knightly rank or for the separate clerical office. The wives
of rebels were outlawed. Many Englishmen sympathised
with the Scotch cause, or admired the gallantry of the
Scotch leader. Robert Ros, Baron of Wark, had openly
joined the Scotch in their first revolt; an English noble
had warned Bruce to escape from Edward's court; and a
Conyers and Seton of English family had been among his
first followers. Henceforth it became dangerous to find
any excuses for Bruce or admire his gallantry. The
founder of the house of Hamilton, said to have been an
English courtier, and who spoke in defence of the royal
rebel, was challenged, and fought a duel to prove his
loyalty, but found England too hot to hold him afterwards.

Robert Bruce.—And now comes the romantic part
of Scotch history, when the singular courage and energy
of a few men, outlawed, fugitives, and without money
or followers, sustained the unequal contest against the
whole power of England. Robert Bruce was distinguished by singular personal advantages; tall, broad-
shouldered, open-chested, and sinewy, with a bright,
frank face and a ready tongue, he seems to have
attracted the love of women wherever he went, and was
often aided by their devotion in his worst perils. The
third best knight in Europe, by the judgment of Englishmen, he sustained the spirit of his followers by deeds of
personal daring and cheerful endurance of privation, till
it is said there was not a soldier in his host who did not
love the king better than a brother. One charming
story tells how he sat on a bank and read romances of
Charlemagne and the twelve peers to his men, while
their little force was crossing Loch Lomond in a boat
that would only hold three at a time. At another time,
when he was stricken down by disease, the news that
the enemy were at hand roused him from his sick-bed,

and he declared himself cured.   More martial traditions
told how he struggled with and despatched three High-
landers who had almost dragged him from his horse,
how he defended a pass single-handed against a whole
troop of the enemy, and how he forded the moat at
Perth in water up to his neck.   But a higher praise
than of mere daring belongs to him.   He seems from
temperament and policy to have been genuinely humane.
Tried as he had been by the judicial murders of his own
relatives, he never retaliated on his captives, and as a
rule strictly forbade massacre when he stormed a town.
He treated the captives of Bannockburn with singular
courtesy.   The same praise cannot be given to his great
follower, Douglas, who appears never to have forgiven his
father's death in an English dungeon, and the spoliation
of his own inheritance.   When he first recovered his
castle he butchered the captive English garrison, mingling
their blood with wine and stores of food, the Douglas
larder, as it was called in savage jest.   In the early part
of the war, at least, it seems to have been his rule to make
no prisoners, and if we cannot pass harsh judgment on a
man who fought with a halter round his own neck, we are
the more bound to recognise the magnanimity of his leader.

**Characters of Edward Bruce, Douglas, and Ran-
dolph.**—But altogether Bruce's captains were well worthy
of himself.   His brother Edward, in the early days of the
war, deliberately charged with fifty men on a body of
1,500, counting at first on the cover of a mist; and
then, as the mist rolled off, hoping, rightly as the event
proved, that the English would think they were the van
of a larger body.   Douglas, victor in fifty-seven out of
seventy engagements, was unrivalled as a partisan leader.
He made it so unsafe to garrison his castle, that it got
the name of Castle Dangerous.   He took Roxburgh by

a sort of Indian stratagem, making his company approach on all-fours, like the small oxen or ponies of the country. In the last invasion of England he retreated in presence of a superior force, which was never able to touch him, though he wasted the country before it, and had almost carried off the young king a prisoner. It is curious to read of this stern soldier as a man with a bright sweet face, and a lisp like a modern dandy; very courteous and *debonnaire* among friends. As Douglas was the soldier of Scotch independence after Bruce, Thomas Randolph was the statesman. As the Scotch king's nephew he had fought with him at Methuen, and owed his life after the battle to the intercession of his captor, Thomas Gordon. For some years Randolph was steadily faithful to the English cause—partly, it would seem, because he despised the guerilla war which his uncle waged. A second captivity and Bruce's arguments converted him, and from that time he never wavered in his more natural allegiance. But though he began his service with an important exploit, the capture of Edinburgh Castle (A.D. 1314), Randolph never reached the military fame of his brother-in-arms, Douglas, and seems to have won Bruce's confidence by his wisdom in council, as he conciliated the affection of friends and enemies by the singular charm of a frank and equable disposition.

Death of Edward I., and Revival of Scotch Independence.—Probably even this brilliant company of heroes would have failed to free Scotland, if a few years longer life had been granted to Edward I. But the great king died about a year after the battle of Methuen (July 7, 1307), while the host intended to complete the subjugation of Scotland was still gathering at Carlisle. His dying orders that his body should be carried along with the army till the subjugation of Scotland was achieved, were probably intended to force his successor into energetic action. Edward II. did not scruple to disregard them. He had been savage, out of mere wantonness, in the repression of rebellion; but he was only half-hearted in the desire to reduce Scotland, and was already weary of war, which he was not competent to conduct, and anxious to enjoy the sweets of royalty in the company of his favourites. With his departure from the north, the army intended to subjugate Scotland scattered again to their homes. Edward II. seems at first to have hoped that the Scotch would accept terms of peace. When it appeared that they had no thought of submission, and as his two viceroys, the Earls of Pembroke and Richmond, resigned office, or were thought incapable, he left the further conduct of the war in the hands of the northern nobles. In less than two years Bruce had triumphed so emphatically over this divided command, that Scotland was resuming her place among nations, negotiating with France and Rome, and making truces with England on equal terms. Roxburgh, Edinburgh, and Stirling were still, it is true, held by English garrisons; and districts, such as Dunbar county, retained a nominal allegiance to the English crown; and a few Scotchmen fought in the English ranks. But the liberation of the rest of the country was only a question of time and money; and after Edward had made an unsuccessful campaign (A.D. 1310–1311), and returned with discredit and impaired authority to England, Robert Bruce was even able to draw tribute from the border counties of the north. Before seven years had elapsed Stirling was the only English fortress still unreduced.

CHAPTER III

MISGOVERNMENT OF EDWARD II.

Death of Edward I.—The death of Edward I. showed how incalculably precious the life of a single man might be to the State. During his long reign of thirty-six years Edward had ₊raised England from almost the lowest place among nations to be at least the third great power in Europe. The nation's military fame had been retrieved; its territory consolidated; its commerce increased and regulated by wise laws. The worst abuse of royal rule, the great size of the forests, had been partially remedied. Above all, Parliament had been remodelled and almost created. In place of the obsolete baronage, which held by the tenure of estates, a new peerage had grown up, which rested its claims to power on the possession of property; and the towns had been formally admitted to a share in the counsels of the nation. But the evil as well as the good of Edward's actions was destined to live after him. He had tried to buy up the English earldoms, or attach the earls by intermarriage to the fortunes of his own house; and the change which transformed our highest nobles into princes of the blood was dangerous under all but a capable king. He had steadily refused to let Parliament interfere with the appointment of ministers; and the absolute power of nomination, which was scarcely safe even in his own hands, might easily be perverted to the gain of favourites. Above all, Edward had revived the warlike spirit in his people. Even those who at first shrank from the heavy burdens which his enterprises entailed, were dazzled by the results of the brilliant policy which annexed Scotland and Wales, and held the whole power of France in check. England swarmed with captains and soldiers, demoralised by the hope of plunder and the licence of camps.

Character of Edward II.—Edward II., perhaps the most unfortunate of our kings, was a man of singular endowments marred by fatal defects. " God had given him greater advantages of birth and nature than any other king," says an ancient chronicler. " He was a man," says another, "of fine person, of great bodily strength, but of no settled character. For, despising the society of his peers, he attached himself to buffoons, singers, tragic actors, coachmen, diggers, and rowers— being fond of managing a ship and other mechanical arts; indulging in drink, easily letting out his secret thoughts, quarreling with standers-by for slight causes, following others' counsel more than his own, lavish in gifts, sumptuous in entertainments, quick of speech, many-handed, unlucky against his enemies, embittered against those of his own household, ardently loving some one friend whom he would fondle, enrich, promote, and honour." It was his misfortune to inherit the legacy of a war; and his disgrace that, with every chance in his favour, he not only lost the conquests his father had made, but endangered English rule in Ireland, and saw hostile armies ravaging the north. It was his misfortune that his reign was marked by unexampled famines and murrains; but he aggravated the misery of his people by a stringent taxation, which only enriched his favourites. He had received from his father a carefully-sifted and capable staff of officials, and he gradually filled up the highest places in Church and State with unworthy and venal officers. Incapable as a soldier, though perhaps personally brave, he was merciless to his conquered enemies; and alienated the English people by his cruelties after Boroughbridge, as he had before alienated the Scotch by his savage reprisals after Methuen. His immorality was accounted scandalous by men whose standard of morals was not rigid; and all his tastes had the same unkingly stamp. "He too much loved the vile company of mariners," says Sir John Gray of him. "If he had spent as much trouble on warfare as he spent on farming," says another writer, "very prosperous would England have been, and its name very glorious on earth." Accordingly, some writers have supposed that Edward was really fond of industrial progress, of agriculture, and the mechanical arts, and was unfortunate and unpopular because his tastes were misplaced in a warlike age. The excuse will not bear investigation. The English nobles of Edward's time were essentially country gentlemen, whose farms were ordered with minute precision, and who freely indulged their various tastes for agriculture or art. Robert Bruce, for instance, amused his declining years with architecture and ship-building. What Englishmen condemned in Edward II. was the carelessness that found pleasure in yachting or farming while the English border was in flames; what they recoiled from was the bad taste that preferred vulgar associates to the company of statesmen and scholars. It is characteristic of popular feeling that an imposter appeared during the reign, professing himself to be the real king, for whom,

Edward, a peasant's son, had been substituted at birth.
The king's ignoble tastes made the story almost credible.

His Favourites.—Nor was Edward's fondness for
his favourites nothing more than a disgraceful infatua-
tion. If it was not the guiding principle of his policy,
it at least determined the fortunes of his reign. It was
said he abandoned the expedition into Scotland that he
might enjoy the society of Pierce Gaveston, his Gascon
schoolmate, whom he had promised his father never to
recall. It is more certain that he made further prosecution of the war impossible by bestowing the whole
accumulated treasure with which Scotland was to be
conquered on the unworthy favourite, who at once sent
it out of the kingdom. The Bishop of Lichfield and
Coventry, one of Edward I.'s best ministers, was imprisoned on charges that could not be sustained by the
new king, because he had opposed, or perhaps only
because he had not supported, Gaveston. The favourite
was treated from the first as a prince of the blood. The
earldom of Cornwall, the island of Man, the Honours of
Wallingford and Knaresborough, all of them royal appan-
ages, were bestowed upon him; he was married to the
king's own niece; and at the coronation was appointed to
bear the crown of Edward the Confessor. Gaveston's head
was turned, not unnaturally, by those signal instances of
the king's favour. Finding himself despised by the old
nobility, he surrounded himself with a train of insolent
retainers. He arranged a tournament at Wallingford, in
which the barons whom he disliked were encountered
and overthrown by picked antagonists. He indulged in
coarse sarcasms on men of the highest rank even in Parliament; calling the king's cousin, the Earl of Lancaster,
"The Player" and "Old Hog," nicknaming Aymer de
Valence, "Joseph the Jew," and speaking of the Earl of

Warwick as the "Black Dog of Arden." "Does he call
me dog?" said Guy de Beauchamp; "let him beware lest
I bite him." Worse offences than these were charged
against Gaveston. It was said that he kept notorious
robbers and homicides in his train; that he substituted
creatures of his own for the king's old ministers; and
that he issued blank charters with the royal seal. Within
a year (May 1308) Edward was compelled to promise
that Gaveston should quit the kingdom. The barons undoubtedly meant that he should return to Gascony, where
Edward's prodigality dowered him with ample estates.
But instead of this, the obnoxious favourite was made
viceroy in Ireland, and his banishment converted into a
new dignity.

Gaveston.—Gaveston's conduct as viceroy seems to
show that he might have done good service to a better
master. He defeated the natives in several engagements,
and slew one of their most formidable chiefs, O'Diuma-
saigh. The one official act recorded of him, that he cancelled a royal brief which infringed the rights of the
corporation of Dublin, seems indicative of a temperate
and conciliatory rule. But his habits, expense, and his
personal insolence clung to him. He wasted the revenues
of the country in holding court with royal state; and
quarrelled with the Earl of Ulster, the most powerful
subject in Ireland, his own brother-in-law, and to whose
care he had been specially recommended. At the
expiration of a year Ireland was scarcely safer for him
than England; and he ventured to return by connivance
of the king, who met him at Chester.

Conduct of the Nobles.—The English nobles took
different ways of expressing their discontent. Gaveston's
estates in the Isle of Wight, and probably in other parts,
were harried. Tournaments were arranged as an excuse

for bringing assemblages of armed men together. The
king put the law in force against these offences. But he
could not rule without Parliament, for his prodigality
left him constantly impoverished; and in March 1310
the nobles mustered in arms to attend Parliament, and
summoned Edward to dismiss Gaveston from his councils:
Gaveston withdrew, and the barons met in Westminster.
The king's partisans, such as they were, seem not to
have attended; and a sweeping measure was carried by
which a council of seven prelates, eight earls, and six
barons was appointed, with the name of "ordainers," to
take the entire management of the king's household, and
the administration of the realm for a year (March 16,
1310). Extreme as this measure may appear, and it was
in fact only short of deposition, it was justified by the
state of the royal finances. The customs were pledged
to two Lombard merchants,—the Frescobaldi; and the
queen, a princess of France, complained that she had not
the money necessary for the support of her household.
The ordainers took speedy measures for the relief of the
most pressing grievances. The taxes were handed over
to native receivers, the abuses of purveyance were
checked, and Magna Charta was published again. At
the same time, by a self-denying article, the ordainers
agreed that they would not themselves receive any grant
out of the royal lands. Having satisfied public impatience by these first measures, they proceeded to occupy
the year of office with a plan for necessary reforms.

Submission of the King to Parliament.—Edward
would have been more or less than man if he had not felt
this attack on the kingly power keenly. Not unnaturally
he resolved to leave the kingdom for the time. His presence was required in France and Scotland,—in France to
do homage for his southern fiefs, and in Scotland to check

the progress of Robert Bruce. It was said the king preferred the Scotch expedition only that he might be present to protect Gaveston from his enemies. The campaign was a costly failure. Out of the old nobility only the Earls of Gloucester and Surrey attended the king on his first march, the other earls excusing themselves on the ground of public business as ordainers, or because the Earl of Cornwall was still with the king. As it happened, the one achievement of the expedition fell to the favourite's share. At the head of a small division he foiled Robert Bruce in an attempt upon Galloway, and received the submission of all the west of Scotland as far as the Highlands. The success did not propitiate his enemies. The Earl of Lancaster, when he came up north to receive investiture of the earldom of Lincoln, which had just accrued to him by the death of his father-in-law, refused even to salute Gaveston. When the king at last met the ordainers in Parliament (August 1311) to discuss their scheme of reformation, it appeared that the expulsion of Gaveston was one of the main articles. Edward protested passionately against this demand. He was willing to yield every other point demanded, however prejudicial it might be to his kingly prerogative, if they would only desist from persecuting " his brother" Peter. It was impossible for the barons to comply. Gaveston was notoriously the cause of the king's mismanagement, the appointer of evil ministers, the inciter to hatred of the nobility, the issuer of blank charters, the man for whom illegal taxes were levied and insolent guards maintained at court. Under threat that his refusal should cost him the kingdom, Edward reluctantly gave way. Gaveston was banished, not only from England, but from all the king's dominions, under pain of death if he returned. Two other foreign favourites of the king were banished the court, and Edward was to disband his guard of archers. Henceforth his ministers and great officers of State were to be persons approved by Parliament ; or if it was necessary to remove one of them, his successor was to be approved by the king's council, and to hold his post on sufferance till the next meeting of Parliament. Compared with this great principle, that the servants of the Crown are responsible to the nation for their good conduct, the enactments of the ordainers against illegal taxation, purveyance, and abuses in the royal forests, are comparatively unimportant. An article, that Parliament was to meet once a year at least, gave an additional guarantee for the new system. The enactment that the king was not in future to leave the country or to make war without consent of the Estates, was a condemnation of the late campaign in Scotland. The credit and power of England had been compromised, and the Crown reduced to borrow from dead men's estates, because Edward had failed to secure the support of the great lords on whom all depended.

Fall of Gaveston.—The peace of England depended on the king's loyal acceptance of the ordinances, and especially on the renouncement of Gaveston. At first Edward bowed to the storm, and contented himself with giving the outlawed friend recommendatory letters from himself and as many great nobles as would sign. But it was not easy for Gaveston to adapt himself to his changed fortunes. Through his conduct to the queen he had made France and Flanders, which was then a French fief, unsafe to him. For the brilliant adventurer who had governed a king and presided over his court to sink into the position of a refugee, compelled to court obscurity, and without alliances among men of rank on the Continent, seemed an intolerable privation. He had left

England on All Saint's day (November 1); he was back before Christmas. A foolish message from Edward had recalled him. The king was furious at the further changes which the ordainers desired to make in his household, and resolved sullenly that he would defy them. When the outlaw's return was first rumoured, so great was the indignation excited that Edward himself issued warrants for his arrest (November 30, 1311). Seven weeks later (January 18, 1312), the king with his own hand, finding, it would appear, no minister who would act for him, sealed letters to the different sheriffs, declaring Gaveston to be a good and faithful subject, in the king's peace. With inexplicable madness, he followed up these briefs by declaring the favourite's forfeited lands restored to him, and loading him with fresh favours. In January he professed to abide by the ordinances. In March he appointed a commission, which comprised only one bishop and not a single great noble, to treat with the ordainers for the reformation of the ordinances. He was now in York, in parts where the royal power was somewhat firmer than in the south. He took advantage of his position to negotiate with Robert Bruce, proposing to acknowledge Scotch independence, and Bruce himself as king, if he would give Gaveston an asylum in Scotland till the danger to him in England should have passed by. Bruce replied by asking contemptuously how he could trust a sovereign who had broken a solemn oath to his own liege subjects? The Scotch monarch was too wary a statesman not to understand the worthlessness of such a compact. Nothing was more likely to draw the host of England across the border than the presence in Scotland of a public enemy such as the Earl of Cornwall.

Civil War.—Meanwhile the ordainers and their partisans acted vigorously. The Primate cursed Gaveston

solemnly ; and the earls prepared to collect their forces
and apprehend him,—even his brother-in-law, the Earl of
Gloucester, promising to acquiesce in whatever the others
resolved. Wishing to avoid an open war, they proclaimed
tournaments in different cities south of York as a means
of collecting their followers. The Earl of Lancaster,
whose great estates lay chiefly in the south, marched by
night and by forest tracks at the head of his retainers, and
surprised Gaveston's treasure and provisions of war at
Newcastle. The king and the Earl of Cornwall were
compelled to fly by sea to Scarborough, where the king
left Gaveston, perhaps that he might draw Lancaster's
army upon himself, and took refuge in Knaresborough.
The tactics proved fatal to the favourite. The earls contented themselves with blockading the king, while they
pushed the siege of Scarborough vigorously. If it were
reduced—and a mere castle could not hope to hold out
long against an army—Gaveston knew that no mercy would
be shown him. He proposed, it is said by the king's
advice, to surrender (May 19) on condition that his life
should be spared till the first of August. In the interval
terms of accommodation should be discussed ; if it appeared
impossible to arrange them, the *status quo* on both sides
should be restored. The Earl of Pembroke, who commanded the barons' army, agreed to this capitulation. It
was obviously in the Earl of Cornwall's favour. The
king, it was said, intended to procure the mediation of
the Pope and the King of France by the surrender of
Gascony. Should that resource fail, Gaveston would
still be better off than before, as the earls would find it
difficult to raise a second army.

Death of Gaveston.—Not unnaturally, the barons
were furious at the prospect of seeing their enemy escape.
They resolved in council to seize the prisoner on his way

to the south; and the Earl of Warwick accordingly surprised him at Duddington, in Northamptonshire, and carried him off, amid the hue and cry of the populace, to Warwick. Pembroke, whose lands had been pledged for the captive's safety, remonstrated warmly with the Earl of Gloucester, and was advised to act more cautiously in future. Presently the other earls arrived at Warwick. There was little doubt among them that Gaveston ought to be put to death, and no need to wait for a judicial sentence, as he was an outlaw. But there was some little hesitation about beheading one whom the king loved so well. The Earl of Lancaster, as the king's cousin and the greatest noble in the realm, took the danger upon himself, and presided over the execution, which took place on an estate of his own, Blacklow (June 19, 1312). The headless corpse was denied Christian burial for two years, as the sentence of excommunication had not been taken off. Then the king gave it honourable interment at Langley. Later events showed that he never forgave the executioners; but at the time the joy at the Earl of Cornwall's death was so universal, that only a minority in the king's council advised him to take up arms; and when, in spite of this, he attempted to raise an army, he found himself confronted by superior forces. The Earl of Gloucester mediated; and in the midst of angry conferences, the birth of a son and heir came to soften the king's grief and divert his thoughts. He gave up the thought of a civil war, and found an excuse for visiting the French court. At last, after two years of uncertainty and suspended government, Edward was formally reconciled to his baronage (October 1313). The stores taken from him in Tynemouth, and the Gaveston jewels, had been carefully inventoried and restored (February 1313). The schedule of the plate and jewels, which comprised several hundred pieces, shows that many had belonged to the royal treasure.

War with Scotland.—Edward's thoughts now turned to a renewal of the Scotch war. If he were successful in the north, his reputation would be retrieved and his power perhaps consolidated afresh. There was no time to lose, for in March 1314 Sir Philip Mowbray, governor of Stirling—almost the last English fortress—came in person to announce that he had agreed with Edward Bruce to surrender the fortress if it was not relieved within a week of the festival of John the Baptist. Edward could scarcely restrain his tears, and prepared to call out the military force of the kingdom. But, against the advice of his council, he adjourned the Parliament, which had been summoned for April 21, on the plea that the danger to the realm was too urgent. The reforming party naturally suspected that the king meant to set aside the ordinances when he found himself at the head of an armed force. The four Earls of Lancaster, Surrey, Warwick, and Arundel accordingly refused to attend, and their absence deprived the English army of at least half its military strength, for the Earl of Lancaster alone could bring a thousand heavy armed men into the field. Still, Edward's army was amply sufficient for the purpose. The Earl of Gloucester brought 500 knights with him, and more than 1,500 others mustered from different parts of England. The fourteen northernmost counties contributed a levy of 14,500 men ; 7,040 were summoned as light infantry from the Welsh marches, and 4,000 from Ireland. However writers of a later period may have blamed Edward for marching with insufficient forces, such was assuredly not the feeling of the time ; and it is said that many volunteers, anticipating the conquest of Scotland and a division of its lands, marched in the train of the army, with their wives and children and household gear. On this occasion, too, it would seem that good care was taken of the commissariat. More than 90 ships and 244 waggons carried the stores of the invading force.

Bannockburn.—As far as mere numbers went, the army under Robert Bruce—put by Scotch writers at 30,000, by English at 40,000—was probably not inferior to the English host; but in the equipment of its soldiers it was markedly deficient. The Scotch cavalry was a mere handful of men; the Scotch archers hardly more considerable. Had the English been as well trained and handled as they were equipped, the massacre of Falkirk would have been repeated. But the English were mostly a mere militia, under an incompetent and headstrong commander, who insulted all who offered him advice, and who let his troops pass the night before the battle in drunken revelry; the Scotch were by this time veterans, with two or three consummate generals at their head. They had the advantage of position, crowning the slopes of a hill, and they had secured the ground on their flanks by pitfalls, in which the English cavalry floundered, and by caltrops, which lamed them as they advanced. Those who struggled through were met by the shock of the Scotch spearmen, and overwhelmed, it would seem by sheer weight, after a gallant hand-to-hand struggle. The archers placed in the English flanks had been disordered and cut down by a charge of the Scotch cavalry. As the English van pressed forward, it became inextricably confused with the routed knights, and before long all was a hopeless mêlée, in which none thought any more except of struggling out into the open country, where flight would be possible. The Earl of Gloucester, the king's nephew, and second by birth and rank to no English noble, was slain on the field, not a single follower daring to strike in or rescue him. King Edward, with a spark of knightly feeling, spurred his horse, resolving to die with his subjects; but the Earl of Pembroke caught his rein, and led him away. So great was the panic spread by the fugitives, that the king himself could not find shelter till he drew rein at Dunbar. It was fortunate for him that he did not seek shelter at Bothwell, where the castellan, changing sides, made prisoners of many noble Englishmen.

Its Consequences.—The English loss at Bannockburn, though considerable, was not enormous. Altogether rather more than 500 men of social position were missing from the English muster-roll; and of these 154 were earls, barons, baronets, or knights distinguished in their counties by wealth and birth. At first many of these were considered as dead. As more authentic tidings reached England, it appeared that the men of rank actually slain did not much exceed forty in number. The others were treated courteously, and allowed to ransom themselves; or, like the king's brother-in-law, the Earl of Hereford, exchanged for Scotch prisoners in England. Among the common soldiers of the English army there were probably more in proportion slain and fewer captives; and as the pursuit lasted fifty miles, and many fugitives were slain by the country people, the loss altogether must have been severe. Nevertheless the larger part of the army reached Berwick in safety, and under a capable commander might perhaps have been so handled as to save the English frontier from insult. But Edward, when he learned that the Scotch were upon his traces, withdrew to York, and presently found that he was not safe even there. However, he mustered the county militia, applied to the Bishop of Coutances for the aid of

sixty mounted cross-bow archers, and took now the only
effectual means of securing England by summoning a Parliament.   He met with cold comfort from his peers.   They
ascribed the defeat at Bannockburn to the king's neglect
of the ordinances, which had deprived him of the services
of many loyal subjects, and declined to take any measures
for the prosecution of the war while so many barons were
in captivity.   The king was compelled to treat for a
souffrance, or truce, terminable at the pleasure of either
party, with the great enemy, whom he would only style
Sieur Robert de Bruce.   But if the barons were dis-
inclined to make war, they were not indifferent to political reforms.   They took advantage of the king's need of
money, and insisted on an entire change in the chief
officers of state, and on the removal from court of the new
favourite, Hugo le Despenser.

Ireland.—For a few months England was well administered.   Berwick was secured; the coasts of Scotland
blockaded till there was famine throughout the country;
the English frontier protected by a body of 500 hardy
armed men; and Robert Bruce compelled to break off
from the siege of Carlisle.   But the restless energy of the
Scotch generals found a new field of enterprise.   The
native race of Ireland had heard the news of the English
disaster at Bannockburn; and the chiefs of Ulster now
invited the Scotch to assist them in driving out the
common foe.   For several reasons the plan suited Scotch
policy.   It transferred the war from the desolated
English border to an untouched country; it might be
made part of a general scheme of revolt against the English crown, which should include the principality of
Wales; and it provided occupation for Edward Bruce,
who had lately demanded a share of the kingdom, and
had actually been declared his brother's heir, to the exclu-

sion of the king's daughter. That prince was accordingly despatched with an army of 6,000 men into Ireland (May 1315), and was soon joined by a number of the native chiefs. For a time he obtained considerable successes, owing chiefly to the disunion of the English commanders—one of whom, the Earl of Ulster, refused to let the royal justiciary appear in the province even to defend it. Yet the earl by himself was no match for the invader; and his fidelity was at least so doubtful, that the Dublin commonalty imprisoned him on suspicion. But Edward Bruce threw away the fruits of his victories and tarnished the title of King of Ireland, which the native chiefs conceded, by an indiscriminate cruelty, which ended in arming every man of English descent against him. In a great battle at Achenry (Aug. 1316), Richard de Birmingham defeated the king of Connaught and almost exterminated his tribe, the O'Connors. A winter campaign, in which Robert Bruce himself took part, and which carried the Scotch to Dublin and Limerick, was as disastrous to them as a defeat, from the hardships they underwent (Dec. 1316 to April 1317). A year and a half later Edward Bruce fell (Oct. 1318) in a battle at Dundalk against John de Birmingham. "And no achievement," says the Four Masters, Irish annalists, "had been performed in Ireland for a long time before, from which greater benefit had accrued to the country than from this; for during the three and a half years that this Edward spent in it, a universal famine prevailed to such a degree that men were wont to devour one another."

Wales.—An insurrection in Wales did actually break out in the year A.D. 1315, but it does not seem to have been connected with any intrigues of Robert Bruce. It was an outbreak of no unusual kind against English mis-

government. The royal officials for years past had mis-
used the processes of English law among the Welsh in
such a way as to excite great discontent, though the king,
as a native-born prince, seems to have been personally
popular. In most parts of Wales the natives were contented to petition for a redress of grievances; and, thanks
to Bannockburn, they received conciliatory promises.
But in Glamorganshire, the estates of the late Earl of
Gloucester, who died without heirs male, were entrusted
by Edward to Pagan de Turberville, who perhaps exceeded
the usual licence of officials, and whose very appointment
was a grievance to his predecessor in office, Llewelyn Braer,
a rich and influential native of the district. Llewelyn
was imprudent enough to make public threats of vengeance against De Turberville, was denounced to the
king, and summoned to attend the next Parliament at
Lincoln for judgment. He thought it safer to take up
arms, and was presently at the head of several thousand
Welsh. But the great English nobles could not look
tamely on at a revolt which threatened their own estates.
The Earl of Hereford, as chief landowner in the district,
was entrusted with the command of an army, and the
Mortimers and other lords of the marches co-operated.
Llewelyn was compelled to surrender at discretion, but
received an informal understanding that his life should
be spared. He was sent to London, and delivered to the
royal officers. Unfortunately for himself, he appeared
dangerous, or his estates appeared desirable to the younger
De Spenser, who had married one of the Earl of Gloucester's sisters; and by his instrumentality Llewelyn was
taken back to Wales, put through some form of trial, and
beheaded. His adherents were presently admitted to a
general amnesty.

Famine in England.—The general prostration of

England was increased by the greatest famine known in
our annals. The incessant rains of 1315, which lasted
from May to September, kept the corn from ripening; and
when it was at last reaped it had to be dried in ovens,
and even so was bad for food. The quarter of corn,
which generally averaged about 5s., rose in the south to
15s., and in the north to £1 10s. There had been bad
seasons in the two preceding years, and Parliament,
hoping to mitigate the evil by legislation, had drawn up a
tariff of the prices at which provisions were to be sold
(Feb. 2, 1315). As the rates fixed were below market
values, producers naturally declined to sell at all; and in
February 1316, the Estates were compelled to retrace their
steps, and leave trade free. Prices now rose to 40s. in
the north, or eight times the usual rate, though in the
south the pressure was not greater than in the preceding
year. Men of substance were compelled to reduce their
expenses by diminishing their households, and numbers
of unemployed poor were thus thrown upon the country.
Horses and dogs were greedily eaten; and it was said that
in some of the prisons the famished occupants seized and
devoured the new comers who were put in among them,
and even mothers were believed to have eaten their children. Disease came in the train of famine, the bad food
causing dysentery and typhus. Everywhere the dead and
dying might be seen lying about the streets. More resolute men banded themselves together and lived by robbery. This was especially the case in the north, where
the distress was greatest, and where the danger from the
Scotch was an excuse for carrying arms and going about
in companies. One moss-trooper, Gilbert de Middleton,
had the audacity to stop and rob two cardinals who had
come north to consecrate a Bishop of Durham, while he
held the Bishop Elect to heavy ransom. In this case the

outrage was so flagrant that the offender was pursued, captured, and hanged like an ordinary thief in London. But the chances of impunity were great enough to keep disorder alive. One Adam de Banaster, whose life was forfeit for a murder, took up arms against the Earl of Lancaster, under whose jurisdiction he fell, and had the audacity to display the royal banner. His first enter-prises were successful, and he collected a small army of 800 men. But a band of robbers, however formidable in the country, was no match for the forces of the greatest English nobleman. Banaster was attacked and killed, and his troop dispersed.

The Earl of Lancaster.—It is probable that Banaster was without authority from the king to display his flag. But the Earl of Lancaster and the people of England might be pardoned if they believed that Edward would shrink from no means of weakening or destroying his over-powerful kinsman. In A.D. 1316 (Feb. 17) Edward had been compelled to request his cousin to take the Presidency of the Council, and the Earl had agreed on condition that nothing should be done without the con-sent of himself and the other ministers; that ministers should be accountable to Parliament for their conduct; and that if these conditions were violated he should be allowed to resign. Within a year the earl was again in opposition, and refused to attend Parliament at Clarendon (Feb. 1317), or that which met a little later at West-minister (April 15, 1317). It was now the fashion in the king's household to speak openly of his cousin as an enemy to king and realm. But Edward was not satisfied with mere words. Thomas of Lancaster, though a patriot by ambition and interest, and religious after the fashion of his day, giving large alms and honouring the mendicant friars, was a violent and bad man, who kept outlaws and

assassins in his train, and whose adulteries were flagrant.
He seems to have had a quarrel with the Earl of Surrey, and
his misconduct had alienated his wife. The countess was
residing at Canford in Dorsetshire, when a body of men,
headed by one of the Earl of Surrey's dependants, carried
her off (May 11) to the earl's residence at Reigate. The
excuse for this violence was that the countess was bound
by pre-contract to an obscure gentleman, Richard de St
Martin; and the lady, now six years the acknowledged
wife of Earl Thomas, did not scruple to declare that the
claim was valid. Parliament decided differently when
the matter came before it. Meanwhile, the gross insult to
the Earl of Lancaster naturally provoked him to declare
war against the Earl of Surrey. And knowing or suspecting that the outrage had been instigated by the king, he
excused himself from attending Parliament summoned to
meet in July at Nottingham.

The King's Distress.—It was easy to foresee what
the consequences to the kingdom would be if the king
and his cousin were at open war. The nobles interposed,
and a "love day" was arranged, on which Edward and
the earl met near Lancaster, and exchanged embraces and
protestations of affection. But the earl received private
information that the king had resolved none the less to
seize him if he came to Parliament, and imprison or behead
him. Accordingly, when Edward went up north to York
to collect an army against the Scotch, the earl from his
castle at Pontefract guarded the high roads, and disarmed
all who came flocking to the royal standard. Edward
could do nothing with the small force that had followed
him, and was compelled to return south when the summer
broke up. As he marched through Pontefract the earl's
followers poured in and loaded him with insult. The
king ordered his men to prepare for battle, and peace was

only maintained by the mediation of the Earl of Pembroke.
As soon as Edward had left the north, his cousin resumed
the war against the Earl of Surrey, and occupied the royal
castle of Knaresborough and that of Alton, which was
then in the king's hands (October 1317). It had been
proposed to hold a Parliament in Lincoln in January, but
the danger of civil war was so imminent that the king was
obliged to adjourn it first to May and then to June, when
it was revoked altogether. Meanwhile the Papal legates
and some of the nobles negotiated at Leicester with the
Earl of Lancaster. The only terms he would listen to
were the faithful observance of the ordinances guaranteed
by royal charter, and leave for himself to prosecute his
feud with the Earl of Surrey.

The Earl Triumphs.—So great was the king's
extremity that he was compelled to promise even this, for
the Scotch, disregarding a Papal truce which the cardinals
had proclaimed, took Berwick early in the spring (April,
1318), by the treachery of an English officer, and then
descended upon the northern counties, ravaging as far
south as Knaresborough, and carrying off rich plunder and
many prisoners. Part of their army remained to invest
Norham, and it was known in England that it could not
hold out beyond Michaelmas. The queen and nobles
insisted on a firm peace being made; and Edward, who
seems to have meditated a second treachery, allowed Hugh
Despenser to leave the court, was again formally reconciled
to his cousin, and presided over a general peace-making.
The Earl of Surrey atoned for his outrage by the sacrifice
of some estates, which to save appearances was called an
exchange. A fresh Council was appointed according to the
ordinances, and commissioners were sent into every county
to redress the injustices of the royal officials. The Scotch
seem to have abandoned the siege of Norham, so that no

campaign was necessary for this year; and indeed, as the terms of reconciliation were not ratified till the autumn, an expedition on a large scale was impossible. But for a time there was content and the expectation of better things in England. The policy of the Earl of Lancaster had again achieved a complete and this time an almost bloodless triumph. Robert Bruce was under Papal ban; Edward Bruce had fallen at Dundalk; and a plentiful harvest reduced the price of wheat lower than it had been for seven years.

CHAPTER IV

DEATH OF EDWARD II.

Preparations for War.—Now that there was peace in England, the one thought of king and Council was to prosecute the unhappy war with Scotland, and retrieve the loss of Berwick. As a prelude to warlike operations, letters were sent to the Count of Flanders, the Duke of Brabant, and six principal cities in the Low Countries, to request that they would desist from trade with the Scotch rebels. The matter was of the last importance to England, for the Scotch were not only drawing military stores and recruiting engineers from Flanders, but were at this moment dependent for food on the Flemish trade. All the more were the merchants of Bruges unwilling to resign the lucrative commerce; and supported by their court, they returned a decisive negative to the English demand, and gave the title of King of Scotland to Robert Bruce. The Duke of Brabant and the town of Malines were more compliant; and the corporation of Ypres returned an evasive answer. But practically the English Government was compelled to rely on its fleet and on privateers for establishing a partial blockade by sea. Adventurers from the eastern countries were encouraged to make prizes by the permission to keep whatever they could capture. At the same time great efforts were made to bring a large force into the field. Fifteen thousand men were to be levied from the counties north of Humber and nearly 3,000 in Wales. If we add to these the men-at-arms of all descriptions who followed the earls and barons into the field, there can be little doubt that the English army must have numbered 30,000 at least in this campaign, though the militia south of Humber was not called out. Miners were forwarded from the Forest of Dean to assist in the siege operations, and carpenters were impressed from London, and wood-cutters from Essex. Nothing seemed wanting to the preparations, and Edward anticipated the fruits of victory by bestowing a number of vacant Scotch benefices on various English clergymen. By the middle of August his army was entirely encamped around Berwick.

Siege of Berwick.—But a doom seemed to attend the king's enterprises. An attempt to throw men into the town by a drawbridge fastened to a ship's mast and attached to the city wall, miscarried through the gallant defence of her garrison, and the ship stranded at the ebb of tide and was burned. The great sow or covered tower which the English had pushed up to the walls, and under cover of which they worked, was shattered by a huge stone which a Flemish engineer, Crab, discharged on it. Nevertheless, the reducing of a fortress is only matter of time, and the little garrison of Berwick was beginning to be hard pressed by the repeated assaults made on the walls, when news came that the Yorkshire militia had been defeated at Milton, near Borough Bridge, by the main Scotch army under Randolph and Douglas. Hastily gathered together and recruited in great measure from priests and monks, so that the affair is known as " the chapter of Milton," the English friars had fled before they even crossed spears with the Scotch veterans. England lay, accordingly, in the way of the invader, and as the army blockading Berwick was too small to be divided, it became a question in the English Council, whether Berwick or the north country should be sacrificed. The Earl of Lancaster, whose estates lay in the north, threw his whole weight on the side of giving up the siege. Finding himself worsted he revived his old quarrel with the king, complaining that Edward had declared his intention of making Hugh de Spenser seneschal of the castle, and Roger D'Amori governor of the town. Under colour of this grievance he withdrew his whole force from the besieging army and marched south. The general indignation was great. Men now remembered that Berwick had never been really attacked from the side where the earl's division was encamped. It was said that his forces and the Scotch intermingled like friends on the borders ; and it was soon believed that Thomas of Lancaster had received £40,000 from Bruce to favour the late Scotch inroad, which had nearly ended in the capture of the English Queen. Down to this time the charges of secret dealing with the public enemy, which king and earl by turn brought against one another, had always been interpreted to Edward's disadvantage. Now every soldier carried home one story, that Berwick would have been taken if the Earl of Lancaster had not been a traitor. The earl felt the disgrace keenly, and tried to confront public opinion by an offer to refer his conduct to arbitration, or to undergo the ordeal of hot iron or of the duel. No one answered the challenge, and he was formally declared innocent. But his power as a popular leader was gone.

Truce with Scotland.—It was hopeless for the time to think of renewing the war with Scotland. But the old policy of inaction could not be continued, for the Scotch had returned as the English army broke up, and were burning and plundering far and wide in Cumberland and Westmoreland. In Yorkshire more than seventy towns were so ruined that it was necessary to exempt them from taxation. Edward consented to treat, and a truce for two years was arranged. There were some murmurs at this in England, because Parliament had not been consulted. But in the north, where the population had suffered as much from the English defence as from the Scotch attack, the promise of quiet was universally welcome. Edward had another reason for concluding the truce. He was bound to render homage for his French fiefs, and was anxious to do it in person. The summer was consumed in preparations for the journey and in making it, though the king was only five weeks absent from England.

Domestic Troubles.—Troubles began again soon after his return. The princely inheritance of the Earl of Gloucester, who fell at Bannockburn, had passed after his death to his three sisters, who were now married to the younger Hugh de Spenser, to Roger D'Amori, and Hugh Audley. There had been a division of the estates among the husbands of the co-heiresses by a sort of family compact ratified by the king, and De Spenser had obtained almost all Glamorgan to his share. But it was his ambition to build up a little principality in the Welsh marches. He seized and held Newport in Shropshire from his brother-in-law, Hugh Audley, having entered it by stratagem. He perpetually importuned the king to resume the castles which had been committed to the care of Roger de Mortimer; and proposed his intention of revenging the death of his ancestor slain at Evesham on the two chiefs of the Mortimer family. At last by an act of insolent self-seeking he contrived to arm half the English baronage against him. William de Braose, heir to one of the greatest names and greatest properties in England, but a man of reckless extravagance, had settled the reversion of the estate of Gower on his daughter Aliva, when she married John de Mowbray. Nevertheless, being hard pressed for money, he made proposals to sell it in several quarters at once, to the Earl of Hereford and to the Mortimers. John de Mowbray hearing of these negotiations, established his right to Gower in the courts, and for greater security took possession of the estate. By the common law of England he was not justified in doing this till he had obtained the king's licence. The custom of the marches, however, was said to warrant the act, and, anyhow, so slight an offence deserved no heavier penalty than a small fine. Hugh De Spenser, however, persuaded the king to declare the estate forfeited, and denounced the barons who pleaded the march customs as guilty of treason. Not unnaturally they confederated against him, and were joined by the Earl of Lancaster, in whom the disgrace of Berwick still rankled ; and by Roger Clifford, whose mother, Maud de Clare, had been plundered by De Spenser of her fair share in the division of the Clare property. The confederates first demanded that the common enemy should be removed from the king's Council and kept in safe custody till their charges against him had received hearing. When Edward indignantly refused compliance, and declared the lands of Hugh Audley and Roger D'Amori forfeit, they levied open war upon the king and his favourite, captured the Welsh castles easily, as De Spenser was detested in the principality, and ruined or plundered his and his father's property in Wales, and in fourteen English counties, to the amount, as was afterwards said, of more than £50,000. The tenants came in crowds and renewed their homage. In the king's council a few were found who raised their voices for war, and Edward himself inclined to their policy, but the larger number maintained that Parliament should be summoned.

Rebellious Nobles.—When Parliament met (July 10, 1321), the Confederate Lords brought up their retainers to London in yellow and green uniforms with white scarves, and the mayor was compelled to maintain order by a police of 1,000 men. The younger De Spenser had tried to recruit partisans, and had actually concluded a league offensive and defensive with John de Birmingham, Earl of Louth, the victor of Edward Bruce. But the faction was powerless against public feeling and the barons' army. After a fortnight of angry conferences the king was obliged to give way, and the De Spensers were formally exiled. The father, now an old man, left England, accordingly, moaning and cursing his son who had caused him to be banished from the flower of all Christian lands. But the young De Spenser, whom the king had made warden of the Cinque Ports, fitted out privateers and hovered around the English coast, plundering merchant vessels, or, perhaps, rather seizing them to the king's use. The spoils of two alone are said to have been worth £40,000; and the money came opportunely at a moment when the independence of Edward's enemies had inclined popular feeling in his favour. The queen was passing across country on her way to Canterbury, and wished to spend the night in Leeds castle, which the king had given to Bartholomew de Badlesmere. That baron, the rich Lord Badlesmere, as he was called, had just marched at the head of his retainers to Oxford, where the barons in opposition were holding an armed conference. When the queen's marshals appeared at the gates to demand quarters and prepare a lodging, the Lady Badlesmere, fearing probably lest the castle should be treacherously seized, refused entry; the queen's retainers tried to enter by force, and were driven back with the loss of several lives. There was general indignation when this gross insult was known—the more so as Queen Isabella had often interposed her good offices to make peace between king and lords; and when Bartholomew de Badlesmere wrote approving his wife's conduct, the king suddenly found himself restored to his old authority. He at once called out the whole armed power of the country; and through the singular folly of the Earl of Lancaster, who declined to help De Badlesmere, with whom he had an old feud, the baron's army was not able to do more than make an armed demonstration at Kingston. Leeds was, of course, easily reduced, its garrison put to death or imprisoned, and the family of the insurgent baron sent to the Tower. Castle after castle now surrendered to the royal forces, and earls and barons began to find excuses for deserting the constitutional cause. But, in fact, success was hopeless under such a leader as Lancaster. Even now, when the south and east were in the king's hands, he alienated Earl Aymer of Pembroke by denouncing him as a traitor. Next, when the barons were thrown back upon the line of the Severn, he neglected to appear in time at the appointed rendezvous. The result was that the Mortimers, who had just inflicted a sharp defeat on the king's troops at Bridgenorth, laid down their arms suddenly, and threw themselves on the king's mercy. As Maurice de Berkeley followed their example, the west was soon pacified, and the two De Spensers thought it safe to return and demand a fresh trial. (Jan. 1322.)

Civil War.—It is probable that the insurgent lords, with the single exception of Bartholomew de Badlesmere, whom the king steadily singled out for punishment, might yet have obtained peace if they would have offered submission; but they imagined themselves too deeply implicated to recede, or felt too profound a distrust of Edward's good faith. Accordingly, at the very time when the Scotch were pouring over the northern border, the barons laid siege to the royal castle of Tickhill. The result was that Edward carried with him the whole military force of southern England, estimated at 300,000 men, when he went up north. Still much of this was an unwarlike rabble, not fit to enter the field against the picked men of the Earls of Lancaster and Hereford; and these actually defended the passage of the Trent for three days, expecting reinforcements which did not arrive, when they learned that Sir Thomas Holland, whom Lancaster had intrusted to bring up supports, had taken them over to the king, and that Edward had crossed by a higher ford, and was threatening to outflank them. Then a general rout set in. The Earls of Lancaster and Hereford turned their course northwards, hoping to reach Scotland; but a body of English borderers, under Andrew de Harcla, was collected in Borough Bridge to intercept them. The Earl of Hereford was slain in the attempt to force a passage. The Earl of Lancaster was seized treacherously in the night, in violation of a truce, and carried captive to York. Above a hundred barons and gentlemen of the first rank were among the prisoners.

Punishment of Rebels.—It was not in the character of Edward or of his worthless counsellors to show mercy to the vanquished; and if the secret treaty they published between the earls and Robert Bruce was not a forgery, it must be granted that Thomas of Lancaster had well deserved to die. Yet it shows Edward's character, that every one believed that the heavier crimes of treason and civil war would have been condoned if the earl had not been guilty of Gaveston's death, and that the king could not refrain from insulting and torturing his victim.

Sentenced to death without leave to reply, the earl was taken to the scaffold on a common plough horse, was greeted with shouts of "King Arthur," the nickname his followers had given Edward in Pontefract, and was forced to look on while several of his most trusted retainers were put to death. Altogether eighteen or twenty men of position suffered on the scaffold, five were sent into exile, and the remainder were kept close prisoners. The estates confiscated must have covered nearly half of England, and the king's adherents were largely rewarded. Andrew de Harcla, whose services had been of such special merit, was made Earl of Carlisle.

War and Peace with Scotland.—Edward was now for the first time since the first few months of his reign undisputed master of England, and nothing was more urgent than to bring the war with Scotland to a speedy conclusion. He was at once sanguine of success, and careful to make his preparations sufficient. Not till August could his full forces be gathered together, and when they entered Scotland it was in such numbers that Robert Bruce thought it safer not to meet them in the field. But the country they traversed had been cleared of every living thing, and when, after three days stay at Edinburgh, the English fleet was still kept back by contrary winds from sailing up the Forth, the famine in the camp was so great that Edward was compelled to order a hasty retreat. The Scotch now hung upon their march, so that it was not safe to forage; and by the time England was gained, the army was in such state that 14,000 men died of indulgence in food. Edward thought the campaign over, and allowed his men to scatter to their homes, while he himself took up his quarters in Newcastle. He was soon roused by the news that the Scotch army had crossed the border, and that the Earl of Carlisle, who had been appointed to guard it, was negotiating with Robert Bruce, and plundering on his own account. Urgent orders were at once sent out that the Crown vassals should repair to the royal standard, first at Newcastle, and, when Edward was obliged to fly from that town, at Blackmore, near Biland Abbey. A few thousand were accordingly gathered together, when the Scotch army appeared in force. After a short fight the English flank was turned by the Irishry of Argyle and the Isles, who climbed the hill sides while Douglas and Randolph were fighting at the ford. It was a great rout, if not an important battle: the Earl of Richmond was taken prisoner, and Edward himself was forced to fly hastily. The Scotch returned to their country laden with prey (Oct. 1322), and reduced Norham by the way. Edward's solitary satisfaction was to take vengeance on the Earl of Carlisle, whom he arrested and judged summarily. There seems little doubt that Andrew de Harcla was legally a traitor; but the part he had taken against the Earl of Lancaster, from whom he had received knighthood, made him so unpopular in England that the charges against him must be received with suspicion. It is highly probable, as is said, that he hated De Spenser. After the unhappy issue of the August campaign he might well think that peace with Scotland was desirable; and his real plan was perhaps nothing more than to force Edward to conclude a pacification, the terms of which should be arranged by six commissioners on each side. Perhaps a feeling that he represented public opinion in the north had something to do with the treaty which Edward actually concluded soon afterwards (May–June, 1323). By this there was to be peace for thirteen years between the two countries, but no trade or other communication except by special licence, under the pretext that the Scotch were excommunicated The title of king was still denied to the " Sieur Robert de Brus."

Quarrel with France.—But the Scotch difficulties were scarcely ended before Edward was involved in a serious quarrel with France. In 1322 Charles le Bel, brother of Queen Isabella, had succeeded to the French throne, and sent envoys to England, demanding that Edward should perform homage in person for Aquitaine. It was not De Spenser's interest that the king should leave England, and he first tried to persuade the envoys not to deliver the invitation, and then persuaded Edward that there was no need to comply with it. At last a special embassy was sent over to apologise for the king's remissness (A.D. 1323). It then appeared that there were other causes of complaint. The English seneschal of Aquitaine, Ralph Basset, had lately stormed and demolished the French town of Saint Serdos, slaughtering the garrison and all the population, on the pretext that the castle had been built within English territory. It is probable that there were other causes of quarrel between the two Crowns, and that De Spenser's piracies had been partly at the expense of French commerce. The occasion of confiscating so large a fief as Aquitaine was too favourable to be lost. A French army was marched into it; and although reinforcements were sent from England, the Earl of Kent, who commanded, could effect nothing; and only three towns were still in his hands when he concluded a truce till the next Easter. Negotiations were now carried on, but without any effect, and at last Edward resolved to send his queen into France. It was an hazardous measure, for during the late bitter feeling against France, everything had been done to insult and offend Queen Isabella; her lands sequestered, her household sent out of the kingdom, and she herself made to feel sensibly that De Spenser stood higher in the king's affections than his wife. Nevertheless, she was so far successful as to obtain a prolongation of the truce till the ensuing August. Then, as the French demands were outrageous, calling for the cession of the whole county of Ponthieu, Edward made preparations for a descent upon France. But when the forces assembled it appeared that no provision had been made for paying them; and, when Parliament met, De Spenser said openly that it would now be apparent who was the king's enemy by his counselling that the king should go in person. Nevertheless, so urgent was it that Edward should either lead an army or conduct conferences in person, that he was at last on the point of embarking when envoys from France arrived, bringing a new and acceptable proposition,—Let the king transfer his rights in Gascony to his young son Edward, and the whole difficulty might be arranged, and the prince's homage accepted. To the two De Spensers nothing was so important as to keep the king in England. They dared not follow him into France, apparently thinking themselves unsafe in an army; but they dared much less remain behind him in England, where the king's departure would have been the signal for a general civil war directed against themselves.

The De Spensers.—Yet, as it happened, the plan adopted by the De Spensers was directly ruinous to them. Ever since the defeat of the constitutional party efforts had been made throughout England to free the captives. Once it had been proposed to seize the elder De Spenser, now Earl of Winchester,—once Wallingford Castle had been surprised, in order to rescue Maurice de Berkeley. In both these cases the attempts had miscarried. But in A.D. 1324 the younger Roger de Mortimer effected his escape from the Tower, and took up his residence at the French court, where other English exiles presently joined him. So visible was their ascendency over the queen, that the Bishop of Exeter, who had come over to assist in the negotiations, found himself excluded from all trust, and at last stole back secretly to England, partly, it is said, from apprehensions for his personal safety. Meantime the queen, who had at first protracted her stay under the pretext of affection to her brother, now that her son had joined her, wrote to say that she would not return while a third person divided her from the king's affections, but would consecrate her days to grief and widowhood. She was strongly supported by public feeling in France, where Edward's debaucheries were no secret. The King of England professed unbounded astonishment when his queen's letter reached him, and declared, in a letter of remonstrance, that he had believed De Spenser to stand high in her favour. The bishops were persuaded to write and request her to return. When their letter also proved ineffectual, the king, by his favourite's advice, caused his wife and son to be publicly proclaimed outlaws and traitors.

Edward Defeated.—Ten months of feverish expectation now went by, during which Edward was vainly negotiating with the court of France, and summoning his wife and son to return to him, while the queen and Mortimer were collecting troops in France, Brabant, and Hainault. Edmund Earl of Kent, the king's brother, had joined them. Italian merchants were found to advance money, and the feeling of sympathy with their cause was so strong throughout England that the jails were crowded with prisoners. In one sense Edward had a very strong case. There was no question that his wife and son had been false to English interests, and that the young Edward had practically surrendered a part of Aquitaine; Mortimer's relations with the queen were matter of notoriety;

and the exiles were bringing a foreign army into England.
But the government of the De Spensers had been so outrageous, that the queen's march from Orwell and Harwich,
where her fleet landed (Sept. 14), resembled a triumphal
procession.   Edward tried to call out the London militia;
they excused themselves on the ground that they owed
no service outside the walls; but when the king had fled
in despair, they rose tumultuously to welcome Isabella,
and killed Walter de Stapleton, Bishop of Exeter, a late
treasurer, who had been collecting troops for the royal
cause. Meanwhile the queen marched on westwards
in hot pursuit of Edward.   At Bristol, which quickly
surrendered to her, the Earl of Arundel and the elder De
Spenser were taken prisoners, and hanged on the common
gallows.   The king and the younger De Spenser being
unable, through contrary winds, to make the Isle of
Lundy, took refuge in the Abbey of Neath, in Glamorganshire.   Meanwhile daily proclamations were made in
the queen's army, calling upon the king to return and
resume the reins of government in conformity with the
ordinances.   When it was found that Edward did not put
in an appearance, his son, the young Edward, was declared
guardian of the realm of England, and a chancellor and
treasurer assigned him (Oct. 26).   But three weeks later
(Nov. 16), Edward and the younger De Spenser were
betrayed by the Welsh into the hands of a party sent to
capture them.   From the moment the king entered
England again, the powers of the guardian were held to
cease *ipso facto*, and a deputation waited on the captive
monarch, to request that he would suffer the great seal to
be used.   Edward had, of course, no alternative but to
comply, and it was placed in the hands of the Bishop of
Norwich, who transacted all necessary business with it.

Execution of De Spenser.—The first thought of

the conquerors was to execute stern justice on the younger
De Spenser. He was arraigned before the peers at Hereford, and sentence pronounced in a speech of passionate
declamation. He was charged with illegal return from
banishment, with piracies on the high sea, with procuring
the judicial execution of the Earl of Lancaster and various
other nobles, and with causing others of the party to be
assassinated in prison, in order that he might seize their
lands, with treachery in the Scotch campaign, with encroachments on the franchises of the church, with
attempts to ruin the queen and the heir-apparent, and
with taking the king out of the realm. Among these
graver charges comes out one of individual wrong, but
marked by exceptional barbarity,—"and you caused
Dame Baretter to be beaten by your ribalds, and her arms
and legs to be broken, too despitefully, against the order
of chivalry, and against law and reason; wherefore the
good lady is for ever deprived of reason and of ruined
estate." There is no reason to suppose that any one of
these charges against De Spenser was false, except the
accusation of treachery in the Scotch war. But the last
words of the sentence, "withdraw, traitor, renegade traitor;
go and receive judgment, malicious and attainted traitor,"
are of unseemly violence; and the sentence was carried
out with circumstances of great brutality. The condemned nobleman was drawn on a hurdle, with a crown
of nettles upon his head, through a yelling multitude;
was mutilated before death as a heretic, and was then
disembowelled, the beating heart being drawn from the
body and cast into the flames (Nov. 24).

Edward Deposed.—Rather more than six weeks
afterwards Parliament met at Westminster. The peers
took an oath to defend the bodies of Queen Isabella and
of her son Edward, and to maintain their quarrel in life

and death against Sir Hugh de Spenser, and against Robert de Waldock, the late chancellor. There had been at first an idea that the king might be restored, and the Bishops of Winchester and Hereford were sent to Kenilworth to request that he would meet Parliament. They returned (Jan. 12), and reported that Edward declined to trust himself in the hands of his enemies and traitors, an answer which seems to show that the king was allowed royal state and a semblance of liberty. Probably the words of the reply lost nothing in the report. During two days, while Parliament was still deliberating, the two bishops who had been sent as mediators preached violently to large audiences against the king, on the texts, "A foolish king will destroy his people," and "My whole heart is sick." On the third day the primate appeared in Westminster Hall, took for his text, "Vox populi, vox Dei," and announced that Edward was deposed by the unanimous consent of the three Estates, and that his son was to succeed him in the kingdom. There was a general feeling of satisfaction ; but the queen professed to be inconsolable at the decision, and acting probably under her influence, the young Edward refused to accept the crown except with his father's consent. A deputation of the Estates was accordingly sent to Kenilworth, and the justiciary, William Trussell, who had presided over De Spenser's execution, renounced the homage due from the king's lieges to him in the following words—" I, William Trussell, proctor for the prelates, earls, and barons, and others named in my credentials, having full and sufficient power thereto, renounce and give back the homage and fealty due to you Edward, king of England, as king heretofore, by these persons aforesaid ; and I deliver and give the aforesaid powers in the best manner that law and custom give. And I protest in their name that they will not in future be in your fealty nor in your allegiance, and that they do not claim to hold anything of you as king. Also, they hold you henceforth as a private person, without any kind of royal dignity." Edward, who had put on a black dress for the interview, burst into tears and groans when he found his deposition thus formally consummated. But the decision was irreversible; and he had been promised, in a private conference with the Bishops of Lincoln and Winchester, that he should receive a handsome allowance, and be allowed to live in royal state, if he would smooth matters by resigning. He accordingly apologised for the errors of his rule, and expressed his satisfaction and gratitude that his son was chosen to succeed him.

And Murdered.—This interview was the last public pageant of Edward's life. During the next three months he remained in honourable custody under the Earl of Lancaster's care. He is said to have endured his fate with resignation; and some verses, which he composed on his misfortunes, show that his thoughts turned to religion. Unhappily for himself, in this extremity of his fortunes he expressed an ardent desire to be reunited to his wife; and the Earl of Lancaster consulted her on the subject, and urged compliance. Isabella had already received unwelcome advice to the same effect from the Pope. Her causes of complaint against her husband had been very real and serious during years when, as it seems, she had been a good wife to him; and she was now infatuated by a guilty passion for Mortimer. She arranged with the Bishop of Hereford that Edward should be removed from Kenilworth, and assigned to the care of Thomas de Berkeley and John de Maltravers, by whom, after some wanderings, apparently intended to prevent knowledge of his prison, Edward was taken to Berkeley Castle in Gloucestershire. For a short time he was

treated decently, through the good feeling of Thomas de
Berkeley, and received presents of costly clothes from the
queen, accompanied by letters of regret that the Estates
would not permit her to visit him. But, before long,
Thomas de Berkeley withdrew in disgust from the castle,
finding that his authority was overruled under colour of
secret orders from the court; and Maltravers, who had
already practised on Edward's life during the journey,
and had offered him the grossest indignities, was left free
to try the effects of foul air and poison upon his prisoner.
When it appeared that Edward's vigorous constitution
was proof against these arts, Maltravers and an associate,
Thomas de Gurney, murdered him barbarously by passing
a red-hot iron into his bowels (Sept. 22, 1327). In spite
of the precautions they had taken to heap mattresses over
his head, his piercing shrieks rang through the castle, and
furnished evidence against his murderers. They remained
in England, however, as long as the queen and Mortimer
were at the head of affairs. On the change of government
they fled. De Gurney was apprehended three years later
in France, and died on the journey to England, with suspicion of being murdered, those in power, it was thought,
fearing that he might make some indiscreet revelations.

His Character.—It is said that Edward's fate was
partly due to the dread entertained that his partisans
would take up arms. The statement is not improbable,
and is no evidence in the king's favour. Public opinion
had been swayed round once before as completely and
decisively in his favour by the injudicious conduct of
Lady Badlesmere. Such revulsions of feeling are common among half-civilised communities. Those who took
up arms against the government of De Spenser and his
colleagues expected, no doubt, that the taxes would be
diminished, justice better administered, and the country

restored to its old prestige abroad ; but, in fact, the taxes had to be increased to defray the expenses of the revolution, the course of government went on in the old track, the regency failed, as the king had failed, against the Scotch, and the only change might seem to be that an impure queen, governed by Mortimer, had replaced an impure king governed by De Spenser.   None the less was the deposition of Edward II. a necessary act in itself, and fraught with the highest results to constitutional liberty.   His better qualities,—an affectionate disposition, personal courage, and some taste for mechanics,—do little to redeem his many and flagrant vices.   Even before his accession he perpetually tried to interfere with the course of justice and of church preferment ; as king he gave everything by favour, and his special favourites were the arrogant and unwise Gaveston, the brutal De Spenser, and the primate Walter Raynald, who betrayed him. Broken laws, broken faith, a dishonoured public policy sanguinary executions at home, national indebtedness, and a licentious and wasteful court, were the great counts in the indictment against one who came to the throne under the best auspices.   The moderation and constitutional procedure of the Parliament in its dealings with him are beyond all praise.   Throughout the series of acts that preceded his deposition all care was taken to preserve the royal dignity unimpaired; and it seems, as if to the last, the Estates honestly wished to restore the king. Fortunately their intention was defeated, whether by Edward's unguarded violence or by the treachery of the mediators, and Edward, discrowned and a prisoner, retrieved by his resignation under affliction a portion of the esteem he had forfeited during years of despotic rule, and perhaps served his country by his death better than he could have done by his life.

CHAPTER V

FIRST YEARS OF EDWARD III.

The King's Minority.—Edward III.'s coronation (Feb. 1, 1327) was followed by a new settlement of public affairs by Parliament. All the proceedings against the late Earl of Lancaster and his adherents were finally reversed ; and the government of the country was intrusted to a council of four bishops, four earls, and six barons, under the presidency of Henry of Lancaster. Before the Commons broke up they addressed a petition of forty-one articles to the Council, requesting redress of various grievances, and in some cases a reform of official practices. To petitions of the first class, such as that the forest charters should be kept, the Council readily assented ; to petitions trenching on the king's power, such as that the Crown should keep wardships and marriages in its own hands, instead of selling or giving them away, a discreet answer was returned that the business must wait till the king was of age.

War with Scotland.—There was little doubt that the Council was honestly anxious to maintain peace with foreign nations. Unfortunately, if Edward's deposition had removed the danger of a French war, it furnished the Scotch with a motive and an excuse for renewing hostilities. By the international law of the times, a truce between two sovereigns, being made as it were for themselves, not for the people, expired of itself if one of the contracting parties died or ceased to reign. It is true the Council of Regency lost no time in directing the wardens of the marches to abstain from hostilities (Feb. 15). But the very document in which this order was given spoke of Robert Bruce, in the old offensive style, as a private person; and the unfriendly feeling of the dominant party in England could not be doubted, as Edward's loss of Scotland had been enumerated among the offences for which he had forfeited his crown. It is scarcely wonderful if the Scotch, who had already tried to surprise the Castle of Norham, now resolved upon open war, and were not propitiated by an English offer, couched in the same insulting language as before, to negotiate the terms of a final peace. While Edward's Council were despatching ambassadors, the Scotch were assembling an army; and before the end of April there was such alarm in England that the whole military force of the country north of Humber was called out, and a general right of plunder from the public enemy was proclaimed. Measures were taken to bring over troops from Hainault, and the southern soldiers were ordered to rendezvous at Newcastle-on-Tyne by Ascension day. Meanwhile a small force was sent northward to protect the frontier; but the Earls of Lancaster and Kent, who commanded it, were afraid to take the field against Douglas, who ravaged the borders in their very presence with the vanguard of the Scotch army. Robert Bruce himself was now a leper, and could not take the field; but Randolph and the Earl of Mar soon brought up two other divisions, by which the Scotch forces in England were raised to the number of 4,000 men-at-arms mounted on good horses, and 20,000 light-armed men, riding the small ponies of their country,

which they let loose to feed in the fields and woods.
Every man carried a sack of oatmeal and a griddle. He
could support life on this diet, and trusted for other food
to the invaded country. An army thus accoutred, and
unencumbered by artillery or commissariat, without even
a single waggon in its train, could make twenty-four miles
a day without undue fatigue.

Undecisive Campaign.—The force that gathered
round the young King of England at York ought to have
been sufficient for the conquest of Scotland. It numbered
8,000 men-at-arms mounted on large horses, 15,000 soldiers
on light horse, 15,000 spearmen from the towns, and
24,000 archers. Besides these were 500 men-at-arms
under Sir John of Hainault, whose presence, however,
proved a source of embarrassment; for either, as one
account states, because the Hainaulters insulted women,
or, as some supposed, from the intrigues of King Edward's
friends, a quarrel soon broke out between the English
archers and the grooms and pages of the strangers. Outnumbered and sorely pressed, the Hainaulters at last
fought their way out to a place of safety, but throughout
the remainder of the campaign they were obliged to use
more precautions against the English whom they had
come to serve, than against the Scotch whom they came
to fight. Nor did the Council dare to take strong measures against the offenders, as it was known that the
Scotch court cherished an idea of raising up allies among
the late king's adherents. All that could be done was to
keep Sir John and his men near the king's person, and
lead the army without more delay into action. But when
the English host came into the country between Durham
and Carlisle, which the Scotch were ravaging, they soon
found that it was more easy to follow the fires that
lighted up the Scotch line of march than to bring the

enemy to action.   At last, after seven days of wandering among morasses and forests, in which horses and men suffered the greatest straits for want of food, the king offered knighthood and a hundred a year to any one who would bring him in sight of the enemy.   In four days it was claimed by Thomas de Rokesby, a prisoner whom the Scotch released, and sent with a message that they were waiting for the English.   But the joy of the army on coming in sight of the foe at Stanhope was soon damped by the discovery that the Scotch were so posted on the hill-side as to be practically unassailable.   A proposal, in the true style of chivalry, that the Scotch should come down into the plain and form their line of battle without hindrance, was met by Douglas with a peremptory refusal,—he and his followers should stay there at their pleasure, and it was for the King of England to dislodge them if he disliked the ravage they had wrought.   For nearly three weeks longer the same tactics were pursued. The Scotch shifted their quarters indeed, but the new positions they took up were as little inviting to assail as the old ; and the two hosts never once crossed arms, except in a night attack when Douglas with 200 picked men burst suddenly into the English camp, crying, " Douglas ! Douglas ! you shall all die, thieves of England !" and rode up even to the king's tent.   At last the English had intelligence that the Scotch chiefs were meditating a great enterprise.   Imagining that a new night attack had been arranged, the English generals kept their force under arms till morning, and then found that the enemy had decamped, and were well on their way to Scotland.   Pursuit, with half-starved horses, was impossible, and would perhaps have proved disastrous, as Scotch reinforcements were coming up, so the English host withdrew sullenly to York, murmuring that the king had been betrayed, and that Mortimer, whose ascendency was already observed and disliked, had taken money from the enemy to secure them an unmolested retreat. It is more probable that French influence was actively used to procure a peace between these two countries. But, in fact, after this last failure, it must have been almost impossible to raise money in England for another campaign.

Terms of Peace.—Accordingly a peace between the two countries was arranged. It was agreed that the young David Bruce, heir to the Scotch crown, should marry Joan, the sister of the King of England. England was not to assist Scotch rebels in the Isle of Man or in the Western Isles, nor Scotland the enemies of England in Ireland; but in case of war between France and England, Scotland might aid its old ally at its own risk. By a subsequent article it was added that, in case of bad faith, England, and, we may assume, Scotland, should pay a fine of £2,000 to the Pope. The promises of submission extorted by Edward I. from Scotland were to be surrendered, and by a private article the Black Rood or part of the true cross, and the coronation-stone at Scone, were to be given back. Moreover, the King of England was to aid the Scotch with his good offices at the Papal court to procure the remission of the sentence of excommunication. On the other hand, the Scotch were to pay a sum of £20,000, in compensation, apparently, of the havoc they had wrought on the marches. By this treaty the independence of Scotland was definitely acknowledged. At the cost of infinite bloodshed and misery, our northern neighbour had been transferred from an almost certain ally into a watchful enemy.

The Earl of Lancaster.—It is noticeable that the young king was not present at the betrothal of his sister to David Bruce (July 19, 1328), and it is possible that he

and his counsellors disliked that he should attend a ceremony in which Isabella and Mortimer presided.   The
arrogance of the favourite was daily becoming more intolerable, and the barons were not disposed to submit patiently.
It was ordered that no one should attend the Parliament
convoked at Salisbury in the autumn of this year (Oct.
1328) with an armed escort.   In spite of the prohibition,
the two rival chiefs, Mortimer and Lancaster, appeared each
at the head of a small army, and only the mediation of some
great nobles prevented a battle.   The Earl of Lancaster
withdrew to Winchester, while the prelates and barons of
his party held counsel together in Salisbury on the best
measures to adopt.   Their deliberations were broken up
by a body of Mortimer's troops, who occupied the house
in which they were sitting, and threatened the lives of
all present if they proceeded with the matter in hand.
The Bishop of Winchester seems to have left the Parliament in consequence, and others either went with him or
declined to enter the town.   But Mortimer was prepared
for a civil war.   He caused himself to be declared Earl of
March, and conciliated the king's uncle, John of Eltham,
and Edmund Butler, by making them Earls of Kent and
Ormond respectively.   Then the Parliament was adjourned,
with provision for payment of the knights and burgesses,
and Mortimer marched, with the young king in his company, against the Earl of Lancaster, the proper regent of
the realm.   Earl Henry and his party were compelled to
fall back before a superior force, and the royal army stayed
for a week in Leicestershire, pillaging churches and houses,
as if it were in a foreign country.   Then the two parties
met in Bedford, and a great battle was expected.   But at
the last moment two of the king's uncles, Edmund Earl
of Kent and Thomas Earl of Norfolk, deserted the popular
cause, and passed over to Mortimer's army.   This gross

act of treachery paralysed the Earl of Lancaster, and he was glad to accept the terms negotiated by the Archbishop of Canterbury, that he was himself to be pardoned on making public submission to the king, but that a few of his chief adherents were to be excepted. A vague promise was added, that all wrongs complained of should be redressed in the next session of Parliament. Bad as these terms were, Mortimer, it is said, would not have granted them if he had not feared that a prolongation of the war would provoke a general rebellion. The Earl of Lancaster seems to have incurred some personal discredit by contriving the murder of Robert de Holland, who had betrayed the late earl in his worst need.

Foreign Policy.—The distracted state of the country during the king's minority had a great effect on the foreign policy of the Government. In the beginning of the year (Jan. 31, 1328), Charles le Bel, King of France, a brother of Queen Isabella of England, had died, leaving no heirs male, though his queen was expecting her confinement. The agents of the English Government put forward a claim that Edward, as next in order of succession, should be guardian of the kingdom till a child was born, and king in case the child born was a girl. It was argued that though Isabella herself was excluded by the Salic law, which forbade women to reign, her rights were transmitted unimpaired to her son. Many doctors of canon and civil law were retained to support this opinion; but it could scarcely be maintained seriously, for if women could transmit a title to the crown, Philip, son of the Duke of Burgundy, by Jane, daughter of Philip le Long, had a prior claim to Philip, and the children of Jane, Comtesse d'Evreux, a daughter of Louis X., stood first of all in order of succession. In fact, Navarre, as a separate kingdom, not held under Salic law, was actually adjudged later on to Philip Count d'Evreux, in right of his wife. It was impossible to hold that a principle which had been twice set aside within the last thirteen years in the case of French princes, could now be upheld for the benefit of a foreign prince, and the subtle distinction afterwards drawn by Edward's supporters, that he had been born during the lifetime of the king from whom he claimed, was invented for the purpose of this especial claim. Above all, the French people, high and low, had no wish to be governed by a foreign prince. The nobility, accordingly, decided that Philip de Valois, cousin of the late king, should be regent provisionally; and when the queen-dowager was confined of a daughter (April 1, 1318), Philip succeeded to the kingdom as his inheritance, and was crowned at Rheims (May 29, 1328). But the English Government had not been inattentive or indifferent to this setting aside of the king's claims. In March the French subjects and allies of England were warned that the king intended to assert his rights. In May the Bishops of Worcester and Chester were appointed commissioners, to take possession of all that had lately devolved on the king as rightful heir of the realm of France. But this resolute tone was soon dropped; within three months of his coronation Philip had won a great battle at Cassel over the revolted Flemings, and Flanders, under its count, a French vassal, was thus virtually reannexed to France. Considering that France was then unquestionably the first power in Europe, and that the English experience of war had for twenty years been eminently discouraging, even a strong government might well have shrunk from continuing to assert Edward's claim. For an unpopular ruler like the Earl of March peace was an absolute necessity. The state treasure was exhausted; Parliament could not be trusted to grant funds, and no army could be assembled that was not likely to turn its arms against the queen and her favourite.

Edward in France.—But if Edward's claims were not to be prosecuted, it was necessary to renounce them; for Philip gave frequent and sharp notices that he should proceed to summary confiscation of the contumacious vassal's fiefs, if homage for them were not rendered. Accordingly, on a second formal summons, Edward answered in person, and the two kings met at Amiens (June 6, 1327), each at the head of a brilliant cavalcade. The standard-bearer of France, Miles de Noyers, opened the formal proceedings by announcing that the King of France did not intend to receive Edward's homage to those fiefs in Gascony and the Agenois, which the Crown of France claimed. The Bishop of Lincoln then protested that nothing the King of England said or did was to be in prejudice of his rights as Duke of Guienne, and handed in a deed, claiming that the king's rights and possessions in Guienne were to be determined by the old treaties between England and France. Under these ominous reservations Edward tendered his homage, and the King of France accepted it; and then Edward, placing his hands between those of the King of France, Philip kissed him on the mouth. The reconciliation was not regarded as a final one on either side. Edward had not performed liege homage,—that is, had not promised faith and loyalty, and Philip's confiscation of territory was unjustifiable. Moreover, there were debts due from England and Edward to the French treasury, and a question of French rebels, whom the suzerain said that the vassal ought not to harbour, while the vassal wished them included in the peace. But the honour of France was satisfied by Edward's recognition of Philip as king, and the questions of detail pending between the two crowns were so complicated that they might well be adjourned for a time. So after several days of festivity, the two sovereigns separated on cordial terms; and Edward brought home a high report of "the great state and pageantry in France, such as no other country could carry out or essay." Plans which came to nothing were formed for marrying the king's sister Eleanor to Philip's eldest son John, and Edward's brother, John of Eltham, to Philip's daughter Mary.

Mortimer's Power.—Foreign difficulties were now set at rest for a time. But the two parties of exiles, the families of De Spenser and the Earl of Arundel, with their numerous partisans, and those who had latterly sided with Henry of Lancaster, were not disposed tamely to endure the ascendency of the Earl of March. Mortimer, however, was vigilant, unscrupulous, and well served. In a council of nobles and prelates held at Winchester, March 11, 1330, a formal charge of treason was brought against the king's uncle, Edmund the Earl of Kent. Edmund's antecedents had not been creditable. Having been sent by the last king to arrange the French difficulty in Paris, he had proved unfaithful to his mother and to the English interests. He had lately deserted the Earl of Lancaster at the critical moment of his fortunes. His household lived at free quarters in the country. He now, finding himself betrayed, made a very full statement of the plots in which he had tampered, confessing to singular folly, and exhibiting peculiar baseness. He had been told by the devil, who was raised up by a friar, that Edward II. was still alive, and in Corfe Castle. He had been incited by Sir William Clifford and by Sir Fulk le Fitz Waryn, who told him it would be a great honour to achieve,—by the Archbishop of York, who promised him £5,000,—and by a number of smaller men, whose names he gave up shamelessly. He was to fetch the king from his prison to the castle of Arundel, and there apparently to proclaim him anew; while the Scotch were to invade England from the north, the Welsh to pour in on the marches, and the exiles to come over from Paris. In all these matters the earl acknowledged that he had acted treacherously, and offered, accordingly, to come in his shirt to the Tower, and stand with a halter round his neck awaiting the king's pleasure. There can be little doubt that he had received assurance his life would be spared if he made full confession. But after he had stood shivering for a whole day, a felon from the Marshalsea, who had been bribed by a promise of life to act as executioner, led him away and beheaded him. His confederates were imprisoned, like the Bishop of London and Henry of Lancaster, or obliged to give heavy recognisances for their good conduct. Mortimer for the moment was more powerful than ever. But men noted with suspicion and distrust that some of his known creatures had been mixed up in the conspiracy which brought the earl to ruin. The order for a judicial inquiry into persons guilty of conspiracy throughout England was not calculated to appease the general alarm.

His Fall.—Mortimer, however, could not, or would not, draw back. He added to his already vast possessions by obtaining grants from the forfeitures of the De Spensers and of the Earl of Kent. He surrounded himself with an armed force of Welsh and English warriors, from whose licence no woman was safe. The king and his brother John of Eltham found themselves more and more treated as prisoners, and began to discuss the means of liberating themselves with some of the younger nobles. But there were traitors among them; and in the next Parliament at Nottingham (October 15, 1330) Mortimer summoned all present to give account of their conduct.

There was general consternation and protestations of ignorance, except from William de Montague, who answered boldly that he would give account of his conduct to any one who dared to challenge it. When the council broke up, Montague observed to the king that it was better to eat the dog than to let the dog eat you. It was resolved to seize Mortimer that very night; and while he and the queen dowager were concocting measures against the conspirators, the door of their chamber was burst open by a body of armed men, Sir Hugh de Turpyngton and Richard de Monmouth struck down, and Mortimer and his councillors taken prisoners. The queen sank on her knees before her son, and implored, "Fair son, fair son, spare my gentle Mortimer." But Edward ordered his mother to be taken into safe custody, and carried Mortimer to London for trial.

And Execution.—It was thought advisable to publish a proclamation, in which the king stated that he had arrested the Earl of March for conducting public business "to the damage and dishonour of us and our realm," and that he would in future govern himself "with aid of the common Council of the great men of our kingdom, and in no other manner." The fallen favourite was charged at his trial with usurping royal authority; with contriving the death of the late king and of the Earl of Kent; with breaking up the Parliament of Salisbury, and making war upon the Earl of Lancaster; with raising money illegally, and with embezzling the Scotch indemnity. Like all the distinguished sufferers of the last few years, he was not allowed to plead in his own defence; and no evidence seems to have been heard on either side, the peers holding that they had sufficient evidence of the facts. He was sentenced to be drawn and hanged, and some of the exiles who had returned are said to have ridden beside and insulted him on his way to the gallows. The lords then proceeded to pass sentence on Mortimer's partisans, though with a protest that their sitting in judgment on men not of baronial rank was not to become a precedent to the disparagement of the House of Peers. The justiciary, Simon de Beresford, and the double-dyed traitor, John de Maltravers, who had contrived Edward II.'s death and entrapped the Earl of Kent, were among those condemned, though the latter contrived to fly the kingdom. Thomas de Berkeley stood his trial, and was acquitted, proving that he had been ill, and absent during the last days of the late king's life. The queen was allowed to assume the dress of the sisters of the order of St Clare, and to retire to her estate at Risings. At first she surrendered her lands, and received an income of £3,000 a year in return; but after a time some of her estates were restored, and she was allowed to make changes of residence. She lived till 1357, and received a visit of ceremony every year from her son; but the people never forgave the crime of her husband's death, once known. Years later an English squire, bearing the unlucky name of Gurney, was summarily put to death by the soldiers in Scotland; and it was generally believed that Isabella had intended to kill her two sons also, and to marry her paramour.

Dispute between England and Scotland.—Edward's reign opened under the fairest auspices. The troubles of the last two years had happily freed England from some of the worst men in high place, and William Montague and Henry of Lancaster, who were now powerful in the king's councils, were men of enterprise, ability, and character. So friendly were the relations with Scotland and France, that it seemed for a time as if the young and warlike prince would find no better employment for his sword than in pacifying the English settlers in Ulster; and an expedition to Ireland was in fact determined upon (July, 1332), when the orders for collecting a fleet and army were set aside by news that order had already been restored (Aug. 4). Meanwhile an audacious enterprise of a few English nobles disturbed the political balance, and proved the beginning of wars that ultimately involved more than half Europe. It had been stipulated by the treaty of Northampton that English subjects, deprived of their fiefs in Scotland, should have restitution. In the case of ecclesiastics, where the restitution to be made was small and the actual holders weak, this had been carried out at once; but the estates of the English barons had been granted away to nobles and knights in reward for services in the field, and men who had won them sword in hand were disposed to fight sooner than give them up. Even a strong government would have found it difficult to enforce such a stipulation, and there was not the semblance of a strong government in Scotland. Robert Bruce had died almost immediately after the treaty that crowned the work of his life; his great captain, Douglas, had fallen in Spain; and Randolph, Earl of Moray, the last statesman of real authority, had died, with suspicion of poison, a little later (A.D. 1331). King David was a child ten years old, and the regent, Donald Earl of Mar, had lately been in opposition, and had corresponded with Edward Balliol, informing him of the weakness of the kingdom, and inviting him to come over. Now, it is true, Earl Donald was bound by honour and interest to a different policy; and he tried to steer a middle course, disregarding the reclamations of the dispossessed nobles generally, and the remonstrances of the English court in their favour, while he restored the lands of Henry Percy, whose power as a Northumbrian baron, and position as warden of the marches, made it unsafe to disregard him. Under these circumstances the English barons resolved to make common cause with Edward Balliol, who had lately obtained permission to live in England, and whose territorial influence was known to be great in Galloway. They were to support his old claim to the crown, and he was to give them seisin of their estates. It was a formidable confederacy, for it included the two Scotch Earls of Athole and Angus, and Henry de Beaumont, who claimed the earldom of Buchan in right of his wife, together with Richard Talbot, Ralf de Stafford, Ralf Fitzwaryne, John Mowbray, Henry de Ferrers, and Walter Comyn, and others of the high English nobility. These men between them were able to raise a force of some 2,800 men, of whom, however, less than 400 were men-at-arms. As the English Government, either fearing to pay the forfeit in which the beginner of war was bound, or not anticipating a successful issue to the enterprise, sent orders to Henry Percy to intercept the expedition its leaders embarked it at Ravenser and Hull. The fleet sailed up the Forth, and weighed anchor at Kinghorn, in Fife (Aug. 1, 1332).

Expedition of Balliol.—The landing was successfully accomplished, the English archers driving back the Earl of Fife, who had mustered the county militia to the number of 4,000, and the invaders struck across country to Dunfermline, and then marched north upon Perth. At Cartenay, probably Forteviot, in the valley of the Earn, they came upon the Scotch army, which was camped on the opposite side of the river, and learned that it was 30,000 strong, was receiving accessions every day, and intended to send a division across the water next morning. It was now certain that the hope of support from the Earl of Mar must be renounced, and Henry de Beaumont, a chief promoter of the enterprise, was loudly taxed with treachery by his companions. He replied, in a spirited speech, that they must aid themselves, and show that they were the sons of good knights. It was resolved to cross the river at night, and the passage was successfully effected. Next day the Scotch army advanced in two dense battalions to cross spears, and had nearly driven back the little English troop by sheer weight; but the English archers poured in such a storm of shot that the front files of the Scotch were struck down almost as fast as they came up, and at last wavered and fell back on the mass that pressed onwards from behind. Then the English men-at-arms forced their way in among the helpless combatants, and such a butchery ensued as, it was said, had no parallel in the annals of the wars of the time. The most moderate estimate puts the number of killed and prisoners at 16,000, and, above all, it was said that scarcely a dozen men-at-arms escaped. The Earls of Mar, Moray, and Menteith, Robert Bruce, the late king's bastard son, and Alexander Fraser, were among the slain; the Earl of Fife among the prisoners, and this nobleman alone counted 360 dead among the men-at-arms who had followed him into the field (Aug. 12, 1332).

Balliol Crowned.—This miraculous victory of Dupplin Moor opened Perth to the little English band; and, by repairing its ruined walls, they were able to hold out for a week against the new Scotch levies that had come up. The short duration of the siege is said to have been due to the want of provisions among the besiegers, to the news that the English fleet had repelled an attack, and to a report that the men of Galloway were marching upon Perth to deliver their lord. The result for Scotland was most deplorable; for Edward Balliol was now crowned at Scone, the Bishop of Dunkeld officiating, and the Earl of Fife making submission, and carrying with him the commons of two counties. This, it is true, did not materially increase Balliol's military power. He was still a mere captain of banditti, isolated in the midst of a country that disowned him, and, in spite of another gallant victory at Kelso (October 14), was at last surprised and routed at Annan, with the loss of some of his best followers, and glad to escape across the marches into England. But, as crowned king of the country, acknowledged by four earls, and by a part of the clergy and people, he had a right to treat with foreign powers; and his very first act had been to despatch the Earls of Athole and Buchan to negotiate a treaty with the English court.

Halidon Hill.—For Edward and his councillors the temptation was irresistible. They had indeed no honourable pretext for war, as the only article of the treaty of Northampton which the Scotch had failed to fulfil was that concerning the disinherited barons, whose act the English Government had formally disapproved. Nor could it be said that sound policy counselled Edward to dethrone his brother-in-law in favour of a prince who could only conciliate England by dismembering his kingdom and alienating his people. But for the moment everything was forgotten, except that the hated enemy of England had been found destitute of statesmen and generals, and that Edward Balliol had offered to become the king's liegeman for Scotland and the Isles, to pay him a yearly tribute, and to aid him at need with the whole power of his kingdom. On the first offer of Edward Balliol's homage he was acknowledged, and his cause advocated in a formal letter to the Pope. Then, when Balliol had been driven out, it was found that the Scotch forces had

trespassed with banners flying on English territory, and
the whole power of the realm was called out to avenge
the insult. By the middle of March Edward Balliol was
beleaguring Berwick at the head of a well-appointed
English army, and the King of England had joined the
camp before the end of May. The siege was soon too hot
for the garrison to endure, and they agreed to surrender if
they were not relieved within a certain time; but as the
nature of the relief to be given was not specified, the
garrison refused to open the gates when the term fixed
had expired, on the ground that a Scotch army had
passed within sight of the walls into English territory.
Edward indignantly hanged one of the hostages; and a
new compact was now made (July 16), that the town
should be given up within a fortnight unless 200 men-
at-arms should have entered the town meanwhile to
relieve the garrison. The Scotch forces under Archibald
Douglas, which had just begun to ravage England, were
compelled, on hearing this agreement, to retrace their
steps hastily, and arrived at Halidon Hill, a mile from
Berwick, on the 19th of July. They were far superior in
numbers to the English, being, it is said, two to one,—
60,000 to 30,000,—but they were imperfectly armed, and
had drawn smocks over their jacks to conceal their de-
ficiences. Their first line, instead of crossing spears with
the first English line of battle, made straight for the
second, where Edward Balliol commanded. But the fate
of Dupplin Moor was repeated. The English archers
shot with such tremendous effect that the Scotch onset
was first checked and then turned into a rout, which the
English cavalry followed up by slaying pitilessly. Seven
earls, twenty-seven bannerets, and, by one account, 36,000
men-at-arms were numbered among the slain; and of 203
knights who had been made before the battle, only five

escaped with their lives. Berwick surrendered next day on honourable conditions, and was thenceforth an English town.

French Intervention.—Several years of sanguinary warfare succeeded, during which all Scotland was repeatedly overrun, and to all appearance conquered. The English policy now was to annex a portion of the border or eastern counties, leaving the rest of the kingdom to Edward Balliol as titular king, under the bond of complete vassalage to England. But the plan met with insuperable difficulties. In the first place, Balliol's nobles were too conscious of their own power and of the Pretender's weakness to endure any real assertion of his sovereignty. The question whether John de Mowbray's daughter or brother should be preferred in the succession to his estates, broke up the whole league that had secured Balliol on the throne; one baron after another was overpowered or made terms; and within a few months of the quarrel Balliol was again a fugitive on English soil. It is true he was easily replaced on the throne by the army of his suzerain; and the Earl of Athole, whose turbulent self-seeking had been the first occasion of disorder, made his peace, and was declared guardian of the kingdom. But the appointment only inaugurated a period of worse confusion than before; Earl David using his own power against the small gentry and yeomanry, who were the saviours of Scotch independence, and whom it was said he wished to root out of the land. A fresh outbreak ended in the death of the guardian, and was in turn pitilessly repressed by an English army, under Edward himself, which carried fire and sword over the land as far as Aberdeen and Elgin (July 1336). Scotland was by this time so reduced that the king's march from Perth was made with only 1,000 men; and even these had a difficulty in finding food. Young King David had taken refuge in France, and his advisers were said to have made a treaty with the King of France by which Scotland was to be held as a fief of the French crown, and the French king was to protect his vassal against all enemies. The expectation of succour from the Continent sustained the Scotch people through the unequal contest. But Philip at first hoped to effect his purpose through negotiation, and prevailed on the Pope to join with him in offering mediation. It is said that the first ambassadors were not even admitted to an audience; but ultimately many unmeaning state papers were exchanged, Philip begging the King of England to grant the Scotch a truce, and pass over with him into the Holy Land; while Edward protested that he desired nothing better, and was only detained by the faithlessness of the Scotch, who would not accept any reasonable terms of peace, or keep any terms agreed to. Meanwhile the ships which Philip proposed to be equipping for war in Palestine, were believed in England to be destined for service in the northern seas, and English cruisers accordingly kept watch along the French coast. In August 1337 they captured two Scotch ships which had sailed from a French port, and which had on board the Bishop of Glasgow, a number of ladies and men-at-arms, the parchments of an alliance with France, and a subsidy from Philip of £30,000. So bitter by this time was the feeling between Scotch and English, that none of the men-at-arms received or took quarter, and the bishop and several ladies died of grief. Immediately after this capture war with France was finally proclaimed. It had existed some time already in fact, for French ships had ravaged the English coasts, and Philip had marched troops against Aquitaine. But the English Government had if possible to let the provocation pass by unnoticed till Scotland had been thoroughly subdued.

Results of Scotch War.—From this time the Scotch war is a mere incident in English policy. There were repeated truces, and repeated violations of truces, but Edward Balliol by himself had no chance against the whole nation, and left the country in 1339. King David came back in 1341. To Scotland the war had been a new soldering of nationality,—an additional proof that English suzerainty was another name for feudal anarchy and general devastation. To England the war had been glorious and unprofitable. The only conquests retained were the town of Berwick and the Isle of Man, which the king gave to his favourite, William de Montague. Both king and nation were well satisfied with the work done. They had wiped out the disgrace of Bannockburn and of the devastated English marches. They had proved that not only were English knights able to hold their own against the Scotch chivalry, but that English archers were more than a match for what ten years ago had been the best infantry in the world. It remained to see whether such troops, under competent generalship, could not win a nobler prize than the Scotch moors.

CHAPTER VI

THE WAR WITH FRANCE.

Power of France.—For many years past France had been the most powerful country in Europe, and had grown the more by the weakness and divisions of its neighbours. While Germany was broken up into little feudal principalities, and divided by wars of rival candidates for the Empire, the French kings were slowly annexing towns and provinces, or reducing the pretensions of over-powerful vassals. Spain was still a cluster of small kingdoms, with the Moor encamped in the southern and richer parts, and with free cities disputing the royal prerogative. Even the Popes, who had broken up the Empire, had succumbed to the audacity and intrigues of the French court, and were now settled at Avignon, in scarcely disguised dependence on the will of the successors of St. Louis. Far and wide there seemed to be no power that could hold its own against France. It is true the boundaries of the kingdom were still comparatively narrow. They did not include Provence, or Savoy, or Languedoc, with its cities of Grenoble, Vienne, and Valence; Franche-Comté, Alsace, and Lorraine, with Metz, Toul, and Verdun, were still part of the Empire; and Valenciennes and Cambrai were still in German Flanders. On the other hand, there was a French Flanders, governed by a vassal of the Crown, which included the rich towns of Bruges and Ghent, and extended along the west to the mouth of the Scheldt. It is true, also, that parts of France were held by vassals who were so powerful as to be dangerous. The English duchy of Aquitaine comprised Bordeaux, Bayonne, Perigueux, and Agen, or about the extent of the five under departments of Gironde, Landes, Basses Pyrénées, Dordogne, and Lot et Garonne. The Count of Evreux, as King of Navarre, was another independent prince of uncertain allegiance; and the Counts of Armagnac, Foix, and Albret, also in the south, were rather petty princes than mere nobles. Brittany was another province, where a nominal vassal of France governed a people who were distinct in language, tradition, and blood from their French neighbours. But when all was said, Brittany was as firmly knit to France as Wales to England, and very much more so than Ireland.

King, Nobles, and People in France.—Moreover, the French kings had been able in several instances to put their relations with their great vassals on a more satisfactory footing than in the early days of feudality. Philip le Bel constrained John II. Duke of Brittany to give up his earldom of Richmond in England, so as to be no longer shackled by a divided allegiance. He forced the Count of Flanders to renounce a marriage for his daughter, because it seemed prejudicial to the French interest. He and his successors compelled the Kings of England to do liege homage for Aquitaine, to remove the right of asylum, and to admit the right of appeal in its fullest extent to the French counts. He himself incorporated Artois by marriage with its heiress, and his sons absorbed Burgundy by similar alliances. But Philip broke down in the attempt to crush provincial franchises and establish the unconditional supremacy of the Crown.

Accordingly the French nobles possessed very different powers from those of England. Their vassals might serve them against the king, and could not serve the king against them. They might leave the campaign in which they were serving at the end of the forty days they owed, even though a battle were impending. They could not be taxed except in commutation of service. And this last privilege contributed, perhaps more than any other, to impoverish the kingdom of France. For the whole cost of a national war was borne by the cities and the peasants; or in time, as the cities purchased privileges and exemptions, more and more by the latter. Nowhere, accordingly, were the contrasts of great wealth and great poverty more striking than in France. "The French," says an old poet, speaking of the nobles, " were all curled and full of womanly airs, had many pearls and new embroideries, were brisk and mincing, and sung like syrens; they danced in halls strewn with rushes, and wore forked beards." But below these " curled darlings " was a great mass of miserable men, such as Fortescue knew and described a century later. "They may unneath (barely) live. They drink water; they eat apples, with bread right brown made of rye. They eat no flesh; but if it be seldom, a little lard or of the entrails or heads of beasts slain for the nobles and merchants of the land. They wear no woollen; but if it be a poor coat under their undermost garment made of great canvas, and call it a frock. Their hosen be of like canvas, and pass not their knee; wherefore they be gartered, and their thighs bare. Their wives and children go barefoot; they may in none other wise live." In time of war thousands of these men, unarmed except with long knives or with clubs, swelled the nominal muster-list of every French army, and died by thousands of disease or famine, or were cut down pitilessly by the enemy—not unfrequently even by their own side if they impeded a manœuvre. Their use was to stab horses and kill the wounded and fugitives, as the Welsh and Irish were used on the English side. But the Welsh and Irish were a mere handful by the side of the splendid English yeomanry, to whom a French army offered no counterpart.

Population and Wealth of France.—However, until the French power had been tested by war with a great military nation, no one understood the real weakness that arose from the degradation of the people. The population of France was at this time very great. A cautious and low estimate puts it at about 24,000,000, or at least six times the number of the English; and high as this calculation may seem, it is borne out by the statement of Froissart, that the English provinces of Aquitaine and Poitou at their greatest extent contained 1,200,000 hearths, or about 6,000,000 people. From other sources we know that the dominion was very scantily peopled, that Brittany had only some 50,000 inhabitants, and that the most densely peopled part was the large district around Amiens, where the population was even greater than now. The revenue of the French kings is not accurately known. But in A.D. 1355 the Estates granted an extraordinary supply of 5,000,000 livres *parisis*, equal to about £1,800,000 of English money, the whole of which was to be raised within a year. The greatest extraordinary grant ever made to Edward III. was of £150,000; and with all allowance for the fact that the French need was much sorer than the English, the difference in the supplies seems to show that France was relatively richer than England. Another fact points to the same conclusion. The largest number of men-at-arms that ever served together in an English army of these times does not seen to have exceeded 8,000. But Philip, in the campaign of 1337, brought 44,000 men-at-arms into the field, though at least a third of the military force of the kingdom was at that time fighting in Guienne on the one side or the other. On the other hand, as we have seen, the wealth of France was un equally divided; and the people at large did not profit by the great rent-rolls of nobles or the flourishing com merce of towns.

Political Connections of the French Court.— The power of a great state is often enhanced by alliances and by friendly relations with half-dependent princes. In all these respects France was eminently fortunate at the beginning of Philip de Valois's reign. The King of Bohemia, John of Luxemburg, who was brother-in-law of Charles le Bel, and the heir to the crown of Bohemia, had married Philip's sister. Not unnaturally King John was a Frenchman by predilection, and served in the French army at Cassel. James, titular King of Majorca, from which his uncle the King of Arragon had expelled him, only brought a royal title into the French service. But the King of Navarre was a French prince of the blood, and the Dauphin of the Viennois and the Count of Savoy were closely connected by position and interests with the kingdom. It was Philip of Valois's ambition to be the general of a new crusade, in which seven sovereign princes at least, those of England and Scotland included, should serve under his banner. The Pope encouraged the enterprise, and in October 1332 the French king thought himself in a position to fix the date for March 1334. Unluckily, in the interval came Edward III.'s acceptance of Balliol's homage, new relations of England and Scotland, and a war which Philip could not venture to leave behind him. The taxes which had been levied in France and England for the purpose of the holy war were accordingly diverted to a ruinous struggle, which drained either kingdom of treasure and blood.

English Reasons for War.—At first sight it seems wonderful that the English Government should deliberately have ventured to measure its strength with the first power of Christendom, especially while a war with Scotland was still on hand. But several causes co-operated. In the first place, king and Council undoubtedly regarded Scotland as all but a certain prize, and were loth to renounce it. Their early policy was to amuse Philip with negotiations while they secured the conquest of the north; their next to win Scotland on a French battlefield. Then the English possession of Aquitaine had for years past been held by a very uncertain tenure. It was almost certain that sooner or later the rights of England over that province must be determined by arms, and no more favourable moment was likely to present itself than the present, when Scotland was powerless to invade and the English army flushed with victory. Then, too, Philip's policy had irritated the whole English nation. By causing the Count of Flanders to break off commercial relations, and by covering the sea with privateers, he had suspended the whole commerce of the country for more than half a year, and the loss of merchants and country gentlemen was enormous. The first plan that suggested itself to Parliament was to prohibit the export of wool altogether, and turn England into a manufacturing country. But a more natural and effective revenge soon offered itself. Flanders was not more necessary to England than England was to Flanders, and the weavers of Bruges and Ghent were as profoundly dissatisfied with the anti-English policy of their court as Edward himself could be. Under the guidance of James van Arteveldt, the great brewer of

Ghent, the Flemish commons opened negotiations with Edward, intending at first only to procure a renewal of trade in return for their neutrality. But James van Arteveldt was too sound a politician to believe that the subjects of a small province of France could maintain their neutrality while the whole kingdom was in arms. Representing as he did the commercial interests of the towns against the military nobility on whom the Counts of Flanders leaned for support, he preferred an English to a French alliance. But he pointed out to Edward that the Flemings were bound in a penalty of 2,000,000 florins to the Pope not to declare war against the King of France. So long as Philip of Valois's claim was uncontested, they could only assist Edward by their neutrality. But let Edward renew his claim, and assume the title and arms of King of France, and the Flemings might then fearlessly support the lawful sovereign against "the found king."

Robert of Artois.—It so happened that Arteveldt's policy found a powerful supporter at the English court in the person of a French noble who knew Flanders well. Robert of Artois was grandson of Robert II. Count of Artois, and had claimed the country on that nobleman's death as nearest in male succession. But the reigning king, Philip le Long, had married Jeanne, daughter of Mahaut, daughter of Robert II., and claimed Artois for his wife's mother, on the ground that a living daughter took precedence even of the heir male of a dead son. The Parliament of Paris had twice decided that Mahaut's cause was good in law. But Robert III. had married Jeanne de Valois, sister of Philip de Valois, and had done more than any man in France to secure the succession of the crown to his brother-in-law and old friend. Not content with the titles and honours which Philip lavished upon him, Robert renewed his claim to the county of

Artois, and seems to have had an understanding with the king that his pretensions should be considered favourably if he could adduce any new evidence. But no genuine evidence was probable in a case which had been already twice argued. Robert accordingly had recourse to crime. The Countess Mahaut and her daughter, the dowager queen, died suddenly within three months of one another, and with strong suspicion of being poisoned. Then a series of papers was produced, containing a will by which Robert II. had devised Artois to his grandson, and a dying confession from the late Bishop of Arras, admitting that he had purloined them in the interest of the Countess Mahaut. The papers were manifestly false, and only served to provoke general indignation. The king was forced to sanction a formal prosecution of Robert, and he was condemned in his absence for the crime of forgery, banished the kingdom, and deprived of his earldom of Beaumont. From that moment Robert was a desperate man, plotting the death of his enemies, and shocking even that unscrupulous age by practices with witches against the lives of the queen and of the heir-apparent. For four years (A.D. 1334–1337) he had been a fugitive in England, when Edward (in May 1337) allowed him a pension of £800. Robert's whole influence was now thrown into the party of war; and a legend of the times represents him as sending round a heron at a royal banquet, and inviting the English king and earls to make their vows on the most cowardly of birds, since Edward's heart had failed him to claim his rightful inheritance, the noble country of France.

Edward declares War.—Nevertheless, either because the risk of war was so great, or because it was uncertain how far his people would support him, Edward hesitated down to the last moment. On the 3rd of October, plenipotentiaries were named to treat with the King of France. On the 7th Edward assumed the title of King in France, declared his intention of asserting his claim to the crown of France by arms, and appointed the Duke of Brabant his vicar-general in that kingdom. What had happened in the interval is unknown. Probably men's feelings had been roused by some tidings of hostilities in Aquitaine, and by the report of various writers in Paris of troops hired in Germany, and of vessels equipped along the coast. It seems likely that Parliament, which was then sitting, had interposed in some way, for Edward afterwards asserted that he had declared war by consent of his nobles and at request of the commons. Accordingly, the supplies granted were unusually liberal; yet they were not sufficient for the gigantic enterprise on hand, and one of the king's first acts was to seize all the wool in the country, paying for it at his own price six pounds a sack, and disposing of it in Flanders at twenty pounds a sack. As the whole amount seized in this way, or afterwards granted by Parliament, was over 30,000 sacks, the profits on the transaction were enormous. But Edward's expenses were on a commensurate scale, and were variously estimated at from 1,000 marks (£666, 13s. 4d.) to £2,000 a day. He was subsidising allies and hiring mercenaries over all the Low Countries and Germany; yet he did not even now abandon the hope of a peace with the King of France. At request of the Pope, who tried to mediate, an armistice was declared for the winter months, and there was talk of fresh negotiations on both sides. The English fleet was compelled to land troops in Flanders in order that the English wool might be sold there; and, in the first battle of the wars, the troops of the Count of Flanders were bloodily routed at Cadsand (Nov. 10, 1337). But

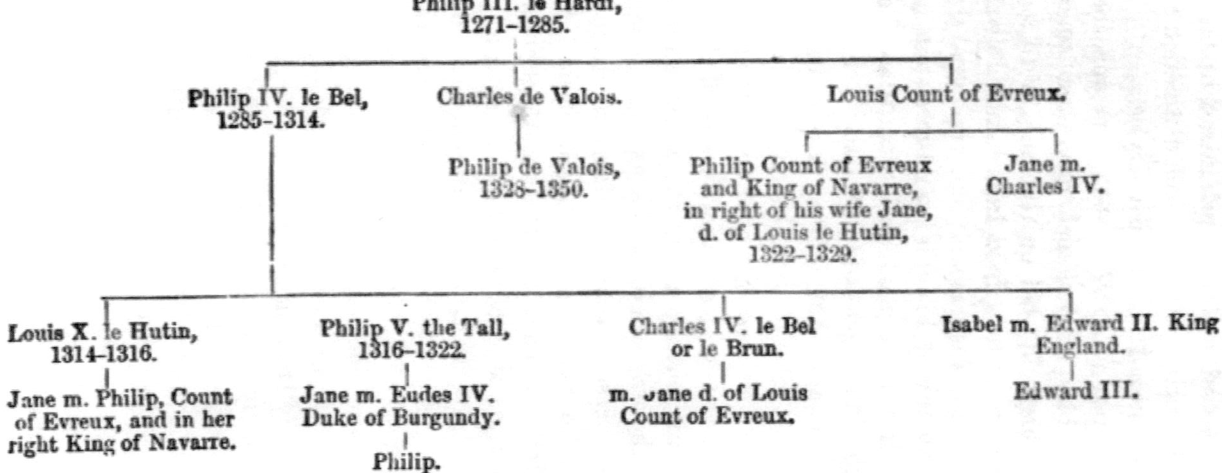

Philip III. le Hardi, 1271-1285.
Philip IV. le Bel, 1285-1314.
Charles de Valois.
Louis Count of Evreux.
Philip de Valois, 1328-1350.
Philip Count of Evreux and King of Navarre, in right of his wife Jane, d. of Louis le Hutin, 1322-1329.
Jane m. Charles IV.
Louis X. le Hutin, 1314-1316.
Philip V. the Tall, 1316-1322.
Charles IV. le Bel or le Brun.
Isabel m. Edward II. King England.
Jane m. Philip, Count of Evreux, and in her right King of Navarre.
Jane m. Eudes IV. Duke of Burgundy.
Philip.
m. Jane d. of Louis Count of Evreux.
Edward III.

Edward released his chief prisoner, a bastard brother of the count, treating him with such distinction that he soon afterwards entered the English service.

Real Causes of War.—It soon appeared that war was inevitable. No Papal mediation could persuade Philip to relax his hold on Guienne, or Edward to make peace if Guienne were held from him. Edward's title to the crown of France was probably not very strongly held by himself or by any of his chief ministers. It was not palpably bad; it was as good, for instance, as the title under which the Parliament of Paris had given Artois to the Countess Mahaut; but it was not to be weighed seriously with that of Philip de Valois, even if the will of the French Estates went for nothing. Its chief value was that it allowed subjects and vassals of France to serve Edward without incurring the worst reproach of treason. But the war of the two kings was undertaken for quite other reasons than to affirm or dispute the Salic law. Philip made war because he wished to preserve Scotch independence and to seize Aquitaine. Edward took up arms to assert his right of conquest over Scotland, and his right to retain his ancestral fiefs in France. In the moment of his greatest success, Edward renounced the title of King of France for independent possession of part of the country. His position as vassal for Aquitaine, while he was king in England, was the intolerable anomaly that made the relations of the two countries perpetually hostile in spite of diplomacy and intermarriages between the reigning families.

Edward's Alliance with the Emperor.—It was long, however, before the preparations on either side ended in anything more than a few marauding expeditions and great waste of treasure. Edward's first idea had been to secure the support of the Empire; and, in

September, 1338, he had an interview at Coblenz with the Emperor Louis of Bavaria. Louis was well pleased to be addressed as arbiter in a case involving the right to the crown of France, and had a quarrel of his own with Philip of Valois, who had refused to perform homage for the Cambrésis, Lyon, and other imperial fiefs, which had been incorporated with France. He declared Philip to have forfeited all right to the protection of the Empire, and created Edward vicar-imperial for seven years in the provinces on the French side of the Rhine. This gave the King of England the right to call out the ban of the Empire, and arm the whole population within his government against France. But the alliance of Louis of Bavaria was of doubtful value from the first. He possessed more than a full share of the pride of position, and expected Edward to kiss his feet, agreeably to the old Byzantine ceremonial, a demand which Edward indignantly refused. He was anxious to be reconciled to the church, and caught at a promise from the Pope to remove his excommunication if he would desert his new ally. At the very moment when Edward expected to be joined by the forces of the Empire, he received instead an apologetic letter, taxing the king with not having paid the promised subsidies, and renouncing the alliance. " God the Almighty Father," said Edward, "does this in every way for my good; for if the emperor came and took command of the army, and God should give us the victory, so should man always, so long as the world should last, ascribe him the victory, whosoever might be the desert. Moreover, he is under ban of the Holy Chair at Rome." This construction was the best that the case would admit; but none the less were Edward's plans for the year ruined. Nevertheless, he led his army into France this autumn in the hope of provoking Philip to fight a battle; but in this he was unsuccessful.   Philip met him between Avesnes and Buironfosse (to the north-west of Vervins, in the modern department of Aisne), and the two armies faced one another for a day.   But though Philip had the advantage in numbers, his council of war was divided in opinion whether he should give battle.   Some said that he had been warned by his cousin, King Robert of Sicily, who was a great astrologer, that he must not attack the English in any battle where Edward himself was present; but the more likely reason is, that the French lords knew they had little to gain by a victory.   Edward could not keep the field against them, and would be obliged to disband his army as soon as he had retreated into Flanders. But the honours of the campaign rested with the king, who had entered France and offered a battle which the enemy dared not accept.   Hitherto he had hung back from assuming the title of King of France on the Continent, and from quartering the arms of France on his shield.   He had even allowed those among his allies who were vassals of France to quit his standard when he entered the country.   Now he blazoned the fleur-de-lis on his shield, and addressed Philip in his letters as "Philip of Valois, calling himself King of the French."

French Fleet in the Channel.—Meanwhile the French had not been idle by sea.   The old story of the conquest of England, achieved by William the Bastard, still inflamed the popular imagination in Normandy, and as Norman sailors had an immemorial rivalry and constant quarrels with the English mercantile marine, there was no part of France in which the declaration of war was more cordially accepted, or where there was so great expectation of turning it into a profitable enterprise.   As early as March 1337, the Estates of Normandy proposed a plan by which they were to find ships for an invading army of 44,000 men-at-arms and 40,000 foot soldiers, including 4,000 cross-bowmen, paying, moreover, part of the expense, and supplying a portion of the men. During 1337 this expedition could not be got ready, or the coasts were too well watched to allow it to sail, and Edward's campaign in France had diverted the French army to the borders of Flanders during the ensuing year. But now the Norman fleet was equipped, and well-nigh commanded the narrow seas. Reinforced by Spanish and Genoese vessels, and with many outlaws from the Flemish towns in its crews, it captured five large English ships in the port of Sluys, and ravaged the English coast from Bristol to the Isle of Thanet, burning, plundering, and slaying in every direction. So great was the danger that Peter Bard, the English admiral on the southern coast, was ordered to fight the enemy wherever he could find them, and the Abbot of Sherborne was instructed to go down to the abbey estates in Dorsetshire, and undertake the somewhat unclerical duty of organising the armed force of the county. But the English sailors were forced to content themselves with reprisals on Boulogne, where they burned more than fifty ships, great and small, and an arsenal. None the less did the French take the sea next summer with an overpowering fleet of some 200 or 250 ships, of which about nineteen were of the largest size in use. The two French admirals, Quiéret and Béhuchet, were quite ignorant of seamanship, and Béhuchet was not even a soldier, but had risen in the royal service by his knowledge of finance. With them, however, was a trained seaman, the Genoese Barbanera (Black Beard), who commanded a division of forty Genoese ships. For a time the French fleet made prizes in the Channel, not respecting the flags even of neutral powers. Then, as the time came for Edward to arrive in Flanders, they took up a position to intercept him between Blankenberg and Sluys.

Battle of Sluys.—Edward had spent the last few months in England, collecting money and making preparation for a fresh campaign. But he had promised to return to Flanders before Midsummer-day, and it was of the last importance that he should be there to the time, as he had heavy debts to discharge, and the French were threatening the Low Countries. Not unnaturally, the Flemings were beginning to count the cost of the English alliance, and Queen Philippa was in some danger in Ghent. Nevertheless, when Edward proposed to sail from Orwell with only forty ships, his Council remonstrated warmly on the danger; and the primate, who was then chancellor, resigned the great seal as a last protest. Edward was at first furious, but when his admiral, Robert de Morley, and John Crab, an experienced seaman, confirmed all the archbishop had said, adding, however, that they were prepared to go before the king into any danger, the counsel of prudence prevailed, and it was determined to collect a sufficient fleet. So great were the resources of England, that within a fortnight the king's masterful energy (for Edward rode along the coast in person to quicken preparations) had brought together no less than 200 sail, and a favourable wind brought them in sight of Sluys on the very day they were due (June 24, old style). As soon as the English fleet was seen approaching, Barbanera proposed to his colleagues that they should sail out into the open sea, as otherwise the enemy would have the sun, the wind, and the tide in his favour, and would soon coop the French up so that they could neither manœuvre nor aid one another. But Béhuchet, either suspecting treachery, or more probably supposing that a defensive position was strongest by sea, as by land, declared they should take their chance where they were. " In that case," said Barbanera, " as I have no wish to be destroyed, I shall take my galleys out of this hole," and he set sail accordingly with the Genoese division, and escaped. The French fastened their ships together with cables, so that the line might not be broken, and put the largest ships in front, crowding them with soldiers and artillery. The tactics were so far successful that the English were repulsed in the first onset; but being handled by skilful seamen, retired without disorder, and tacked for a second charge. To the ignorant French captains the manœuvre seemed to be a retreat, and they instantly cut their cables, and set sail to pursue the flying enemy. They were met again almost instantly, and the English pressed thick around five of the largest ships, the " Christopher," the " Black Coz," the " Edward," the " Rose," and the " Catherine," which had been taken from themselves last year in that very port. In a few minutes the ships were boarded, the crews cut down, the banner of France torn down and trampled under foot, and the new English ensign of the leopards and the lilies displayed in triumph from the masts. Then the remaining ships fled, or were forced back, one dashed upon the other in the narrow waters. The storm of English arrows soon became intolerable. Many of the men-at-arms were drowned in attempting to land in the ships' boats; many more were cut down by the English boarders; not a few leaped into the sea. Only the reserve, composed of about sixty ships, fought well, and was not destroyed till near midnight, the battle having begun in the early morning. The smallest estimate of the French loss puts it at 25,000 men; the general calculation was that 30,000 or more had fallen. The English loss in men is variously put at from 400 to 600, including, however, only four gentlemen. Two small English ships were sunk by the heavy stones launched from the French catapults. Of the French fleet only a portion of the Genoese ships which sailed away at first, and twenty-four ships which fought their way through the English under cover of night, escaped. Besides the ships-of-war, a great number of smaller craft, transports or victualling ships, fell into the hands of the enemy. The French marine was, so to speak, annihilated; and " by Edward's victory," says a Flemish writer, "were all who speak the Dutch tongue made blythe, since the sea was now freed from pirates." Edward has been censured by French writers for allowing the French admiral, Quiéret, to be killed in cold blood, and Béhuchet to be hanged to the mast of his vessel. There can be little doubt that these acts were richly deserved reprisals for the barbarities and lawless robbery which the French crews had indulged in. The fault of Edward and of his times was rather an indiscriminating leniency to offenders of knightly rank who could pay ransom, than any mercilessness. For eighteen months past neither man's life nor woman's honour had been safe on the southern coast of England. After the battle of Sluys men were at last able to breathe freely. So highly did Edward appreciate its importance that he caused medals to be struck, with the king in a ship on one side, and on the other a cross, encircled by the legend, " But Jesus passed through the midst of them," in allusion to the manœuvre by which he had broken the enemy's line.

Truce.—But this great success could not be followed up adequately on land; though Edward was able to invest Tournai, the advanced post of the French in their own country, with an army of 120,000, 60,000 of whom were Flemings, under James von Arteveldt (July 22, 1340).

Philip watched the ineffectual siege without hazarding a battle, and when Edward challenged him to personal combat, replied by reminding the English king of the liege homage he had rendered. A small battle, won by Robert of Artois with English archers and Flemish militia, near the garrison of St. Omer, did not provoke a diversion on the French side; and bad news arrived from Aquitaine, which the French had almost reduced, and from Scotland, where the national party had taken Edinburgh, and were ravaging the north of England. Above all, Edward's expenses were enormous, and the supplies from England began to fail. The king concluded a truce for six months (September 25), disbanded his forces, and after waiting several weeks in the expectation of supplies from England, and receiving only excuses and assurances that the money raised was insufficient for current expenses in England, took ship suddenly, and arrived in the Thames before his purpose was suspected (December 1, 1340). One of the Council had sent him private information that there was gross mismanagement, perhaps treachery at work, and that only his presence could remedy the disorder. In fact, he found the Tower of London unguarded, and its constable absent, so that no one in the city knew of his landing. All the easier was it to seize those officials whom the king principally suspected. The great seal was taken from the Bishop of Chichester; the Bishop of Chester was degraded from his office as treasurer; the three chief-justices and the constable of the Tower were imprisoned. Sir John de Molyns, whose great services in the time of the seizure of Mortimer had been rewarded by full trust and large grants of land, was now an object of special suspicion, and was fortunate in being able to fly the country. The king conducted the search after Sir John's hidden treasure in person, and discovered one deposit in the Abbey of St. Albans, and another at the bottom of a well in his manor-house of Thames-Ditton. Sir John was afterwards taken and imprisoned for several years. It seems certain that he and some others had grossly abused the power committed to them.

Edward and the Primate.—But Edward's present councillors were men of doubtful character and discretion, and the king was too wrathful to be very careful about legality. It was a serious offence against the rights of the subject that he had imprisoned great officers of state on mere suspicion of malversation of trust; and the forcible entry into St. Albans was a breach of church privilege. Men saw with alarm that the king issued a commission of trail-baston, nominally to try offenders against public order, but really to extort money by something like martial law; that offences against the forests were inquired into; and that a general commission was appointed to investigate charges against the late administration. Above all, the king desired to get the primate into his hands, rather perhaps that he might make him bond for the debt in Flanders, on account of which the Earl of Lancaster was now a prisoner in that country, than because any serious charges could be sustained against one who for some time past had taken no active part in public affairs. In fact, Edward himself could allege nothing worse against John de Stratford, than that he had encouraged him to make war by assurances that the public revenue would be amply sufficient for all expenses, if the king would see that good generals were appointed, and had promised to see to the proper levying of the supplies himself. On these points the primate's answer seems satisfactory. He had not specially promoted the war, but had laboured to make peace; he had helped the king to the best of his ability with money and

credit ; and the king knew when he left England that a
great part of the taxes was already pledged in advance.
But the archbishop did not content himself with a private justification. He solemnly excommunicated all who
should violate Magna Charta, or infringe on the franchise
of the church ; and when the partisans of the king
arrainged his conduct as treasonable, he pointed out with
great justice, that he was declaring no new sentence, but
merely calling attention to penalties, that were *ipso facto*
incurred by the violators of common or church law. It
is a bad feature in Edward's case that he delayed to summon Parliament, as " inexpedient," for several months,
and that his advisers were men of damaged character like
Adams, Bishop of Winchester, the former Bishop of Hereford, or mere clerks in the chancery, or servants in the
household. When Parliament at last met it was evident
that the feeling of the Estates was with the archbishop,
and against the king. For a week there was an obstinate
conflict, whether the primate should not first answer the
charges against him before taking his seat in Parliament.
Edward first refused to attend as long as the archbishop
was in his place, and then caused him to be excluded
from the sittings. But the Earl of Warenne at last rose
in his place, and protested against the subversion of constitutional law, by which the great men of the realm were
excluded from Parliament, while men of no position in
the country were present. The feeling of the House was
so unmistakable that the lawyers and officials alluded to
at once shrunk quietly out of the chamber, and the Earl
of Arundel then carried a motion that the archbishop
should be invited to attend, and answer any charges that
might be brought against him. All Stratford had con-
tended for was the right to be tried by his peers, and not
by a Privy Council of the king's appointment. The

thirty-two articles of arraignment were read out in public, and the archbishop denied them one by one. Then the Estates interceded for him, or perhaps offered themselves as compurgators, and the king declared himself satisfied, and admitted the primate to his place.

Privilege of Peerage.—Edward's conduct, however, had raised a constitutional question of considerable importance, whether a peer, who had taken office under the Crown, lost his privileges as peer or tenant-in-chief, so that he could be tried, imprisoned, and outlawed, or punished in any other way except in Parliament, and by judgment of his peers. The prelates, earls, and barons agreed that he could not be, and their declaration has been enrolled as a statute, and is the first clear definition of privilege of peerage. It was not intended to give the baronage any exceptional privilege, for men of every class had a right to be tried by their peers; and the king's high court of Parliament only differed in dignity from the courts held by the king's deputies in the shires, and attended by the freeholders. The proceedings of this very Parliament, when a jury of twelve—four prelates, four earls, and four barons—was nominated to try the archbishop, show that the present mode of trial by the peers, when all vote, was not contemplated. But practically the statute has had two effects. It has exempted peers from the operation of the ordinary courts, and it has drawn a sharp line of demarcation between peers and their families, since the children of peers do not share the privilege. In this way it has helped to establish the important principle, that the exemptions of nobility in England are conferred by office and duty, not by birth.

Edward's Bad Faith.—Several other important statutes were passed in this session. The charters were confirmed; and it was enacted that the king's ministers should take oath to observe them; and that in every session of Parliament their offices should be resumed for a time, during which they should answer for the discharge of their functions. The objectionable commissions were recalled, and generally the king's policy was reversed. So urgent was Edward's want of money that he was compelled to submit to all these stipulations, in return for a liberal grant of 30,000 sacks of wool, estimated apparently at an average value of £5 a sack, but really bringing in more to the treasury, as the contractors who bought it of the Crown were obliged to pay a duty of £2 a sack before exporting it. It was ominous, however, that when the oath to observe the statutes was administered to the royal *employés*, the chancellor, treasurer, and some of the judges protested that they would only observe them so far as they were conformable to the various laws and usages of the realm. The meaning of this was better understood a few months later, when the king, being now relieved of his most pressing obligations, and having renewed the truce with France, sent a circular letter to the sheriffs, declaring that the late statute was contrary to law and prerogative, and that the king, therefore, annulled it by advice of his Council. He added the dangerous admission, that he had only dissembled, as was necessary, in order to avoid the dangers which would otherwise arise from no business being despatched; but the Council, he said, were of opinion that, as the statute had not received the king's willing consent, it was of itself null and void. A more shameless breach of faith, more unhesitatingly avowed, scarcely occurs in our constitutional history. His contemporaries forgave and forgot it afterwards in the conqueror of Crécy. But for a time it paralysed Edward's warlike activity. For a year he did not dare meet the Estates, and as meantime the emperor had revoked his commission of vicar of the Empire, under pretence that he had made a truce of his own authority, the war seemed likely to die out of itself. There was even truce with Scotland, though the Scotch had lately made a foray across the English border.

Question of Succession in Brittany.—Unhappily, a new question of disputed succession arose in France. Arthur II. Duke of Brittany, who died in A.D. 1312, had left descendants by two wives. The eldest son of his first wife had in course of time succeeded to the duchy as John III. But on the death of this prince in A.D. 1341, the eternal question of the times was revived, whether lame Jane, John's niece by the whole blood, and daughter of his deceased brother Guy, would carry the inheritance to her husband Charles de Blois, or whether John's half-brother, Jean de Montfort, as a male, and a degree nearer to the common ancestor, should take precedence of Jane. The barons were in favour of Charles de Blois; the clergy and towns sided with Jean de Montfort. It was probable that the king would favour Charles, who was his nephew. Jean de Montfort accordingly tried to take possession of the duchy without waiting for a royal decree in his favour, and corresponded with the King of England, with whom he had some sort of connection as titular Earl of Richmond, though the honour had been confiscated, to know how far he might count upon English support. Philip was informed of the intrigue, and summoned De Montfort to Paris to stand trial. Before the day came De Montfort had quitted Paris, and passed over, or sent envoys, into England. In consideration of his zeal for justice, and consequent promise to support Edward's claim, the King of England restored him the earldom of Richmond till such time as he should be put in possession of the earldom of Brittany (Sept. 24, 1341).

The Kings of England and France were now fully committed to contradictory principles. Edward supported the heir male in Brittany, while he claimed the crown of France from the heir female; and Philip supported the principle of female succession in Artois and Brittany, while he claimed France by Salic law. Nor can it be pleaded that he was merely punishing Jean de Montfort for premature entry upon his fief, for he told De Montfort before trial of his case that he had no right. Besides, forcible entry was punishable at most by fine and imprisonment, not by forfeiture.

English Succours to Jeanne de Montfort.—So energetic were Philip's measures, that it seemed at first as if the new war would speedily be stamped out. The Duke of Normandy and Charles de Blois entered Brittany at the head of an overpowering army, and shut up De Montfort in Nantes. Charles de Blois was a saint in the estimation of his times, wearing pebbles in his shoes, and a girdle of knotted cord round his loins, and letting vermin prey on him. But he was none the less a bad and brutal man, and by a ferocious act of cruelty to thirty knights, whom he had taken prisoners, and whose heads he caused to be shot over into the city, he so intimidated the citizens that they compelled De Montfort to capitulate. De Montfort had stipulated for his own liberty; but this article was broken as soon as Charles de Blois had entered the town, and the Count de Montfort was sent prisoner to Paris. Charles de Blois's triumph seemed to be complete. But his rival's wife, Jeanne of Flanders, went round Brittany, taking with her her young son, and encouraging her partisans. "Ah, sirs, do not be disheartened for the loss of my lord; he was but a single man. See here my little child, who, God willing, shall be his avenger, and will do well by you. I have treasure in abundance; I

will supply what is needed, and will find you such a
captain as shall bring you comfort." Animated by this
heroine, the province maintained its unequal war; and
even women did service in Hennebon, where she shut
herself up to await succours from England. Just when it
seemed that surrender was inevitable, the sails of the
English fleet rose above the horizon; and Amauri de
Clisson and Walter de Manni, who had been detained six
weeks by contrary winds, sailed into the port with a little
force of 120 knights and 1,000 archers. Next day the
English sallied out, and succeeded in destroying the great
engine that was battering the walls. "Then the countess
came down from the castle with a cheerful air, and kissed
Sir Walter Manni and his companions, one after another,
two or three times, like a valiant lady." The small reinforcement had in fact saved Brittany. The English soon
proved themselves to be more than a match for their
enemies in the open field; and after a few weeks Sir
Walter was able to return (July 7), having taken three
castles and several prisoners of importance, and concluded
a four months' truce, which the king, however, refused to
ratify.

Events in Flanders and Brittany.—The events
of the next three years are unimportant. Edward was
unable to find funds for a great expedition against France;
but there was another campaign in Brittany and Gascony,
in which the English on the whole carried off the honours
of war, and gained a new confidence in their strength.
Had there been any statesmanship in France, it is probable that Flanders and Brittany might have been
detached from the English alliance. In Flanders an
English intrigue, to induce the Flemings to transfer their
allegiance to a son of the King of England, excited so
much indignation that James van Arteveldt, who sup-

ported it, was killed in a tumult at Ghent. But on reflection, the towns dared not return to the service of their native lord, who was trying to arouse the peasants with a promise of giving them the sack of those great commercial capitals. So deputies were sent to Westminster to excuse the rash act of the men of Ghent, and propose an alliance, at some distant date, between one of Edward's daughters and the count's son, whom the Flemings kept in their hands (Sept. 1345). In Brittany the barons of the French party were alienated by the murder of the Sieur Olivier de Clisson, who had just returned from captivity in England, when he was seized at a tournament, and put to death as a traitor. Philip refused to give any explanation of the informal sentence on one of the greatest and most beloved Breton lords; and as Clisson's death was followed by that of several other Breton and Norman barons, a strong feeling was kindled against the King of France. Moreover, some of the sufferers had been avowed partisans of Jean de Monfort, and ought therefore to have been protected by the truce. It is scarcely wonderful if De Montfort's escape from prison (March 1345) was a signal for war to break out again in Brittany with greater fury than ever.

War in Guienne.—In another respect Philip was ill counselled. He was in great want of money, and could find no better expedient than to impose a tax upon salt. The discontent excited by this was great, and was not diminished when the king proceeded to adulterate the wine, and levy a duty of 20 per cent. upon all sales of merchandise. This last tax could not indeed be maintained for any long time; but while it lasted it was doubly vexatious, as it weighed very heavily upon commerce, and had to be enforced by an army of collectors. Nowhere were taxes more odious than in the English provinces, which had been retained in their allegiance to a distant and foreign sovereign by a practical exemption from all direct taxation.   Accordingly, in 1345, the men of Guienne flew to arms under Henry, Earl of Derby, the son of Henry of Lancaster, and swept a large part of the province of its French troops.   An attempt by the French general, the Count d'Isle-Jourdain, to reduce the fortress of Auberoche, was defeated in the first of those wonderful battles, which showed the full superiority of the English gentry and yeomanry to their French enemies.   With only 300 men-at-arms and 600 archers, the earl ventured to attack from 10,000 to 12,000 French soldiers, and defeated them easily (Dec. 23, 1345).   By the end of the campaign nearly all Guienne had been recovered by the English.

Edward Invades Normandy.—It was impossible that Philip could look on calmly while the King of England enjoyed the fief he had forfeited, or that Edward could refuse to succour his loyal subjects of Guienne. Accordingly, in the spring of the next year, an army 100,000 strong, under Philip's son, John, Duke of Normandy, started from Toulouse along the Garonne and invaded Aquitaine.   But the town was well garrisoned, and its garrison commanded by the Earl of Pembroke and Sir Walter Manni.   While it held out Edward had time to collect an army and invade Normandy.   The number of troops he took with him has been variously estimated; but the most probable calculation puts it at from 40,000 to 50,000, of whom, however, only 4,000 were men-at-arms, while a great many were light armed Irish and Welsh, taken probably as the least costly soldiers, and because one object of the expedition was to ravage Normandy in revenge for the mischief done by French privateers.   Edward landed (July 12) at Cape la Hogue, in

the extreme west of Normandy, having wished apparently
to disguise his route by sailing down the Channel, and
also expecting to find adherents in the parts of Normandy
that bordered on Brittany, and where Godfrey de Harcourt, a Norman exile who had advised the expedition,
had large estates and powerful connections. The plan was
completely successful. It was weeks before a French army
could be collected, and meanwhile Edward ravaged or held
the country to ransom, burning all the ships in the ports
between Cherbourg and Rouen, storming Caen, and laying
the country waste for fifteen or twenty miles inland. The
English were astonished at the wealth of the fertile province they were devastating. One of them compared its
towns to those of England, and tells us that Barfleur was
as large as Sandwich, Carentan equal to Leicester, Saint Lô
bigger than Lincoln, and Caen only below London in importance. The news of the rich plunder to be obtained
soon reached England, and adventurers flocked over in
every vessel that could be found to recruit the king's army.
Even for a portion of the Norman gentry the temptation was
irresistible, and Edward's forces actually gained in numbers
as they marched in a line with the coast towards Calais.
By the middle of August Edward had reached Poissy,
where he kept the feast of the Virgin in regal state,
sitting in his ermine furred with scarlet. Meanwhile his
marshals had pushed on almost to the gates of Paris, and
Philip could look out from his walls on the flames that
rose from the smoking suburbs,—St. Cloud, Neuilly, Petit
Boulogne, and Bourg la Reine. For a time there was a
panic in Paris, where the citizens expected daily to see the
walls stormed; but Edward was detained by the difficulty
of constructing a bridge across the Seine, and began to be
harassed by the forces that were coming up every day.
When he at last effected his passage, instead of assailing

Paris, he turned northward into Picardy. His intention probably was to invest Calais, and he calculated on having time to enclose his army in fortified lines before the enemy could come up. But he was again delayed by the Somme, and this time his position was critical, for Philip was coming up with a large army, and counted on being able to enclose the English between the river and the sea. But Philip was over-confident, and loitered on his march. In the moment of his worst need Edward lighted upon a Yorkshireman who had been settled for sixteen years in these parts, and who knew of a ford called the Blanche Taque, where the river could be crossed at ebb of tide by twelve men abreast. The place was not unknown to the French; and when the English arrived there at break of day (August 24), they found it guarded by 10,000 or 12,000 militia and a few Genoese cross-bowmen. But such a force could do nothing against a well-appointed English army, to whom victory at any price was a necessity. The French were cut to pieces, and Philip's army came up just in time to see the English in safety on the opposite bank of the river.

Battle of Crécy.—It was now too late, however, for Edward to think of pursuing his passage across country. His troops were weary with long marches, and the enemy could now pursue and hang on his rear. Neither was it in his character to avoid a pitched battle, if it could be fought on fairly equal terms. But with a curious superstition he desired to fight in his mother's inheritance of Ponthieu, the confiscation of which by Philip he esteemed one of his most righteous grounds of quarrel. He accordingly halted at the forest of Crécy, and spent a day there in fortifying a position between the village and the forest. On the 26th, when the battle was expected, the English army was drawn up on a slope, the horses placed in a park behind, and the waggons distributed on each flank as a protection. There were three lines of battle, with men-at-arms, and archers, and light-armed troops arranged alternately in each; and the knights had mostly dismounted, as there was no room for the evolutions of cavalry. All was in order by nine o'clock in the morning, when food was served out, and then "every man lay down on the earth with his arms by him, to be the fresher when the enemy should come." The vast French army, numbering at least 80,000 men, or double the English numbers, had started from Abbeville at sunrise, but could only advance slowly along the narrow roads. King Philip was advised by his marshals to delay giving battle till the morning, but his orders to halt were not attended to by the undisciplined French gentlemen, who were pressing forward to take their places in the van; and he himself could not restrain his impatience when he caught sight of the detested enemy. So the Genoese and Gascon cross-bowmen were ordered to advance and reply to the English archers, who had been thrown out as sharp-shooters in front of the first English line. The cross-bowmen were, with good reason, reluctant. They had just marched more than twelve miles in armour carrying their cross-bows, and the strings had been wetted by a thunderstorm which was only just over, while the afternoon sun was shining full in their faces. Nevertheless they came forward, leaping and shouting as they discharged their arrows, to frighten the English. But the English arrows showered so thickly upon them, that they soon lost courage, and fell back upon the French men-at-arms, trying to force their way through the ranks. Then the French, who remembered Sluys, suspected treachery; and King Philip in his anger shouted orders to cut down that rascalry, who were only blocking up the way to no purpose. A horrible mêlée ensued, and the French knights rode forward through the struggling desperate Genoese to close with the English spearmen.   The English archers retreated in good order, still raining arrows upon the foe; and some light pieces of cannon, then first used in a battle, were brought to play upon the advancing French, and caused a wild panic among the horses.   Mostly the French line was so disordered as to be powerless before it closed with the enemy; and the Welsh and Irish light-armed troops were able to glide in among the mass and stab the helpless men-at-arms, over whom their horses had fallen, or who were pinioned by the press behind and before.   Only in one place, where the Prince of Wales was present in person, the flower of the French knights struggled out into the open ground and disputed the victory.   The second division of the English was forced to come up and aid their comrades, and a messenger was sent to the king requesting that he would bring the reserve into action.   But Edward, who watched the action from a hill, knew that the field was already won, and resolved not to deprive his son of the honour.   So he sent back word that he would receive no more messages as long as Prince Edward was alive; let him win his spurs that day.   In fact, by the time the messenger returned, those who sent him had regretted their want of confidence. Yet throughout the day the English did not venture to leave their ranks or to make prisoners.   Many accordingly perished, shot down or stifled, who would gladly have surrendered themselves prisoners.   Among the slain was the blind King of Bohemia.   When he heard that the battle was turning against the French, he bade his attendants take him forward into the press of the battle, and caused his bridle to be fastened to that of a knight of Basle, Le Moine, saying jestingly to Le Moine, who

had fled at the battle of Laupen, that he should not have
the chance of flight this time. Both fell together in the
thick of the mêlée. Philip himself had almost perished
on the field. He stayed ordering the fight till it was
nearly night, till he had been wounded in the face and
one horse killed under him; and out of all the brilliant
troop that had followed him to the field, only five barons
and sixty men-at-arms remained around the oriflamme.
Sir John of Hainault then seized his bridle, and led him
away to the Castle of Broie, where Philip himself
demanded shelter in the words, "Open, open, castellan.
It is the unfortunate King of France." The emperor and
the King of Majorca also escaped from the field.

French Losses.—The loss of the French in this
battle, and on the following day, was enormous; for
next morning two large divisions of Norman men-at-arms
and militia came up, ignorant of what had happened, and
stumbled upon the English in a thick fog, with the
natural result that the greater number of them were cut
to pieces. Besides King John of Bohemia, the Duke of
Lorraine, an archbishop, and a bishop, fourteen French
counts and six of the Empire, eighty barons and baronets,
1,200 knights, and 4,000 heavy armed men, and 28,000
light armed, are said to have fallen altogether. Philip's
ferocity was not softened by the disaster. He put to
death at Amiens a number of the cross-bowmen, to whose
treachery he imputed his defeat; and afterwards, it is
said, beheaded as many as 2,000 of the unfortunate men
who had followed him to the field. Meanwhile Edward
had carried his forces across country to Amiens, ravaging
as he went in every direction; and within nine days of
the battle, had formally invested the port that had so
long been a danger to commerce and a menace to the
English coasts.

Scotch Invasion and Battle of Neville's Cross.—Meanwhile French diplomacy was taking effect in Scotland, where King David prepared to make a diversion in the interest of his ally. His natural expectation was that he should find England stripped of its fighting men, or at least with no army that could meet the whole power of Scotland in the field. His first exploit was the storm of Lidell (October 10); and he shocked even that barbarous age by putting the castellan, Walter Selby, to death in cold blood, after admitting him to his presence to sue for mercy. Then he marched upon Durham, allowing his troops the wildest licence by the way, except that he spared four towns in which he intended to take up his winter quarters. But the Archbishop of York, William la Zouche, put himself at the head of the northern nobles, and gave battle to the invader at Neville's Cross, near Durham (October 17). The Scotch were harassed by the English archers till they could not keep their ranks; and when they quitted the position they had taken up, were gradually repulsed by the English spearmen after a sharp struggle. The third Scotch line, under the Earl of Dunbar and Robert Stewart, was not even brought into action. All the more severe was the loss sustained by those who actually fought; and the number of killed is stated at two earls and 10,000 or even 12,000 of all ranks; while King David himself, with three earls, 100 bannerets and knights, and 2,000 common soldiers, were taken prisoners. The Black Rood of Scotland was among the prizes of victory. King David was taken to London, and paraded through its streets in rather unknightly fashion. Generally the captives were treated as ordinary prisoners of war, and held to ransom. But the Earls of Menteith and Fife had sworn allegiance to Edward, and were liable to be punished as traitors. The murder of Walter Selby might seem to justify reprisals. A sentence approved by the king condemned both of them to death; and the Earl of Menteith, whose crime was aggravated by the fact that he had belonged to the Privy Council, was actually hanged, drawn, and quartered. The Earl of Fife, who had the good fortune to be of the blood royal of England, was reprieved. The effect of these severities was that several captors, fearing to lose the ransoms of their prisoners, allowed them to escape on promise of payment.

Guienne and Ireland.—Crécy and Neville's Cross, though the most glorious, were not the only successes of Edward's arms during the year. Edward's invasion of Normandy constrained Duke John to break up the siege of Aiguillon; and his retreating army was pursued and attacked so vigorously by Henry II., Earl of Lancaster (late Earl of Derby), that Aquitaine was again cleared of the enemy, and the English conquests included Poitiers. Philip's intrigues had extended even into Ireland, and had been supported by the Scotch. The Irish actually took up arms, and were at first partly successful, under Brian Macmahon. But the English armed against them, and defeated the enemy in a bloody battle. By the beginning of the next year Ireland could again spare troops to the king.

Siege of Calais.—Meanwhile Edward's position was far from secure. He had entrenched himself before Calais, between the town and river, near the bridge of Nieullet, on the road to Boulogne, and had built a little wooden town, which he called New Town the Bold, which would give his soldiers better shelter than they could find under tents, and in which a market for provisions was held twice a week. His first intention apparently was to breach and storm the walls; but he provided also for a blockade, though with rare magnanimity he allowed the governor to turn 1,700 useless mouths out of the town, and even furnished them with a meal and money. It soon became evident that the fortress was too strong to be reduced except by famine, so the king surrounded it with an outwork of dykes and towers; while to lighten the cost of his army, he gave furlough so freely that sometimes scarcely 500 men-at-arms were left in the camp. The policy seems to have been a wise one, and Edward's object throughout was to spare his soldiers; but there were great murmurs at the tediousness of the operations, and complaints that Edward was thinking more of the charms of a court lady than of state matters and of war. Moreover, as the harbour had not been closed, some ships of Boulogne contrived early in spring to provision the garrison. But a naval victory, in which a convoy of eighty French barques was scattered by eleven English ships, carrying archers on board, cleared the Channel in April, and the mere sight of the English ships dispersed a second flotilla that tried to run the blockade in June. The governor of Calais made a second attempt to reduce the number of mouths within the town, and sent out 500 more. This time they were not allowed to pass, and died miserably between the English lines and the walls. On the 26th of June two skiffs, carrying despatches, tried to steal out of Calais harbour. They were instantly pursued, and the letter confided to one of them, and thrown by the captain into the sea, was washed up on the sands. It told King Philip that his people in Calais had eaten their horses, dogs, and rats, and had nothing left but to eat one another, if he did not come to their aid. They were resolved in the last resort to sally out and die honourably, hoping the king would requite it to their heirs. Edward attested this letter with his seal, and sent it on to the King of France, exhorting him, for his own credit, to bring speedy succour to his people. Philip had been for some time past assembling a great army; but he was uncertain of his strength, and resorted first to negotiations with the Flemings, who guarded the northern approaches to Calais. If they would betray their ally, he offered to procure them relief from the Papal interdict, to supply them with cheap corn, to give them a six years' monopoly of the wool exported from France, and to yield them up the three towns of Lille, Douai, and Béthune. The offers were tempting; but putting the question of plighted faith aside, the Flemings could not trust Philip's word, and besides were by this time animated with as fierce a hatred of the Calais corsairs as was felt even in England. Philip was therefore reduced to approaching Calais from the south, where his army would have an English fleet on his flank, and the terrible English archers behind earthworks and dykes in front. The chances were too uneven, and he tried to negotiate. But as he would only offer Edward the restoration of Guienne and Ponthieu, the terms could not be seriously entertained. A more tempting proposal to a sovereign of Edward's character was, that they should decide their differences by a combat of five or six knights on each side. But even Edward could not seriously propose to stake the results of a year's siege on the chances of a tournament. So the Earl of Lancaster, who conducted the negotiations, evaded the proposal by claiming that Edward, as true King of France, must arrange the details of any such fight; and ended by suggesting that the English would demolish their defensive works, if the French would give them battle in their present position. This the French council of war decided not to do, and the French host disappeared suddenly after three or four days, and was broken up at Amiens (August 2).

Surrender of Calais.—There was now no alternative for the garrison except to surrender, if they could obtain terms, and the governor, Sir John de Vienne, hung out a flag of truce. Sir Walter Manni and Sir Simon Basset were sent to discuss terms, and demanded that the garrison and citizens should surrender at discretion. There seems no reason to doubt that Edward intended to put the townsmen to death, though he might perhaps have spared the men-at-arms. " Calais," says an Italian writer of those times, " was a refuge of corsairs, and a den of thieves and sea-pirates." It was no uncommon incident of war, as then practised, that the population of a town should be massacred ; and even Sir Walter Manni had lately been in danger of his life from Philip, who had seized him treacherously, for no better reason than that he was the king's greatest enemy. Fortunately, the heroic defence of Calais had redeemed the character of its people in the eyes of many. The two cardinals who had just been negotiating on Philip's behalf interposed their intercession, and Sir Walter Manni and many other captains objected that it was a bad precedent if men were to suffer death for fighting well, as it was certain that the French would take reprisals. The king yielded to their arguments, but insisted that the form of the surrender should be unconditional, and that six of the leading burgesses should come out in their shirts, and with halters round their necks, to receive sentence. On report of these conditions in the town, there was general consternation, till Eustache de St Pierre offered himself for the dangerous embassy. His example was followed by five other rich burghers. They were ushered into the presence of the King of England, who at once gave orders that the executioner should be called. A scene ensued, which, if not arranged beforehand, had certainly been anticipated. The barons and knights present implored the king to show grace, and at last Queen Philippa threw herself on her knees and added her entreaties. The king professed to give a reluctant consent; and the six burghers were taken to the queen's chamber, where they were fed and received a present in money, with a safe conduct through the army. The mere fact that they were admitted to Edward's presence seems conclusive against the idea that he meant to put them to death. Even Edward I., who was of much sterner mind, made it a rule never to refuse grace in such cases. Practically, the six deputies were much better off than their fellow-citizens, who were driven out of the town with no more than they could carry upon their backs; and some of whom, it is said, were tortured to make them disclose where they had buried their treasure. Eustache de St Pierre afterwards returned, and was naturalised as an English subject. Edward would not listen to the Flemings, who wished the rival port to be utterly destroyed. He introduced an English population, made it the depôt for English merchandise, and secured it by a strong garrison.

English Successes in Brittany.—The capture of Calais was not the only success of the year for England. Sir John Dagworth, a gentleman of Suffolk, had been sent to command in Brittany, and had won some successes in the previous year. This summer as Charles de Blois was besieging Roche-Dernien, in the north-west of Brittany, Sir John with a small Breton and English force surprised him in the early morning (June 20), and aided by a sally from the garrison inflicted a signal defeat. Charles de Blois himself was among the prisoners, and though every effort was made to rescue him was brought over safely into England. The long series of disasters shook even

Philip's pride, and he was glad to negotiate a truce till Midsummer next year, by which each party was to retain its actual possessions. On the English side, it was granted that the Scotch might be included in the truce if they wished; and the French consented that their Flemish partisans should not be allowed to return to Flanders. Edward now sailed for England. He found the country in a state of unparalleled prosperity. Commerce flourished, the harvest had been good, and there was general content and confidence in the government. "For there was not a woman of any family who had not something from the spoils of Caen, Calais, and other cities beyond sea. Dresses, furs, cushions, and household utensils; table napkins and necklaces, glass and silver cups, shawls and linen, were seen scattered over England in all people's houses."

Appearance of the Black Death.—But within a few months the most tremendous visitation, perhaps ever witnessed in the world, had changed England into a land of mourning and death. For some years past (A.D. 1333–1348) the most fertile regions of the East, and especially China, had been visited by a combination of drought, famine, floods, earthquakes, and pestilence. In A.D. 1347 Europe was reached. The accounts of the time say that a dark stinking mist came up from the East, and spread over Italy, affecting men wherever it came with languor and debility. It seems certain that at the same time earthquakes were frequent and violent, and coincided with pestilence in various countries, probably because the course of rivers was disturbed and morasses formed. Thus a great earthquake in Italy (January 25, 1348), Greece, and Carinthia shook down many castles, houses, and churches, and swallowed up whole villages. In England there was a slighter shock in the early part of 1349, which was sufficient to shake men to the ground; and here also it was noticed in some parts, that the earthquake coincided with a visitation of pestilence. But the Black Death, as it was called, had entered England in the previous year. It first visited Southampton, Dorchester, and Bristol, brought no doubt by merchant ships from the Mediterranean, and seems to have been first observed in August. It reached London in about three months, but had excited no alarm on November 22, when a Parliament was summoned to meet at Westminster in the month of January. By the 1st of January it had become necessary to adjourn the Parliament till April; and in April (April 28) it was prorogued again for the same reason without further appointment. The constant rain which fell in England from Midsummer to Christmas 1348, was, no doubt, a predisposing cause of sickness. The plague seems to have travelled shortly over the whole of England, reaching Yorkshire, where it was very deadly, in the summer of 1349. In December of that year it was still ravaging the country with such severity, that there was danger of a general exodus to the Continent, under pretence of pilgrimage to Rome, and Edward issued orders to stop persons emigrating at the ports. The end of winter seems at last to have checked the progress of the malady.

Character of the Plague.—There is little doubt that the Black Death is the disease that was afterwards known as the Plague. It began sometimes with fever and dysentery, sometimes but more rarely with pains in the head and sleeplessness, or perhaps heavy sleep. Before the end of the disease, if it lasted any time, the lungs were affected, and there was spitting of blood. Buboes or black spots and boils, especially under the shoulder, and in the arms or legs, were unfailing signs. In its beginnings the disease was more deadly than it proved afterwards, and persons often dropped down suddenly in the streets.   Towards the end the disease often ran a course of two or three days, and there were some recoveries.   The medical science of the times was at first powerless; but latterly the expedient of opening or cauterising the buboes was resorted to with some success. The mortality was beyond anything that has been known in later times.   The lowest account says that a fifth of the population perished; one estimate declares that only a sixth remained alive.   Where we have any data for calculation, the numbers seem to point to a mortality of at least two-thirds.   This was the proportion among the clergy in Norfolk, Suffolk, and in the East and West Ridings of Yorkshire.   In Meaux Abbey, forty-two out of fifty-two died; in St. Albans, forty-seven out of less than a hundred; in Croxton Abbey, out of more than twenty, only the abbot and the prior survived.   In Leicester nearly 1,500 persons died in three parishes alone; in Yarmouth 7,000 died out of perhaps 10,000; in Norwich nearly 60,000, or probably nearly the whole population, was cut off suddenly; and in London 100,000 deaths are said to have been reckoned.   Bristol was another great town that was almost desolated.   With every allowance for the facts that we certainly hear most of the exceptional cases, that the clergy may have suffered unduly from their obligations to visit the sick, and that some parts of England may have escaped altogether, it is difficult not to suppose that from a third to a half of the population was actually cut off.   In fact, some towns, such as Norwich and Yarmouth, seem never to have recovered the blow, and it is doubtful if the country generally retrieved its numbers for three centuries.   We do not know in what spirit the visitation was taken, or what moral effects it produced.   In France and Scotland,

and probably in England, there was great fear of nursing
the sick, who were often in consequence left to die un-
tended, the contagion being so virulent that it was
believed a mere glance from the eyes conveyed it. In
Florence, during the worst times, when death seemed inevitable, there was general recklessness, and men devoted
their last days to pleasure. But in England and the
north generally, the prevailing surmises seem to have
been that the black death was a deserved chastisement for
sin. The Scotch regarded it as God's judgment on the
English for their unrighteous wars of conquest, and invaded the northern counties, to profit by the general prostration, till they were in turn scourged back by the
breaking out among themselves of the "foul death of the
English." 5,000 died in a short time, and the broken
remainder, chased back by English troops, carried the
fearful pestilence into Scotland. In the Low Countries
a sect of Flagellants sprung up, who scourged themselves
publicly in expiation of the sins that had provoked God's
anger. Some of them visited England, and excited much
curiosity, but they do not seem to have found followers.
The feeling in England seems to have been partly religious, partly political. The churches were crowded with
worshippers, and the shrines of saints thronged by pilgrims, who of course spread the contagion throughout
the country. But as prayers seemed to be unavailing,
the opinion grew up that the black death was God's
judgment on the pride and profligacy of the upper classes,
on the piracies and cheatings of merchants, and on the
corruptions of the clergy.

Effect on Labour. — The black death had been
attended by a murrain among beasts. It was followed
by deficient harvests (1352–1353), the natural consequence of the great mortality among labourers. But corn

was imported from abroad, and on the whole the poor
benefited by the many gaps in their ranks; for so imminent was the dread everywhere lest the country should
be deserted, that landlords were obliged to compromise
with tenants, and lords with serfs, to keep them on their
estates. "But the world," says a chronicler of the time,
"was never able to return to its own estate."

CHAPTER VII

SUBJUGATION OF FRANCE.

Weakness of England.—From the time of the black death Edward's conduct of the French war assumed a different character. He was no longer the arbiter of Europe. In A.D. 1347, it was a question for a short time if he should not accept the Imperial crown which envoys from Germany pressed upon him. Fortunately, he had learned enough of German politics to be aware that those electors who favoured him only desired an ally and a paymaster, if they were not even the tools of the French court, which wished to entangle him in a war with the rival candidate, Charles of Moravia. Edward prudently rejected the glittering bait. Only three years later (A.D. 1350) he was compelled to fight for very existence against a Spanish fleet equipped by the cities of Biscay, that was committing piracies in the Channel, and threatening to ravage the English coast. Never was Edward more thoroughly the knight-king than in this battle of Winchelsea, where he and his son, the Black Prince, saved themselves and their crews only by boarding Spanish ships in the very moment when their own vessels were foundering. But the mere facts that the king and two of his sons and the whole baronage fought on this occasion in the kind of battle that knights generally disliked; that the English fleet was inferior in its own seas, and only gained the day by the desperate courage of its crews; and that not more than twenty-six ships at most were taken from the enemy, show how greatly the English power had declined. A year later the Spanish cities concluded peace on their own account with the seaports of Aquitaine. It is true A.D. 1350 was a year of exceptional calamity. The spirit of the nation soon revived, and proved itself capable of any sacrifice of money or blood. But it was simply impossible for Edward to enlist such an army again as had fought at Crécy, unless he recruited his ranks from foreigners. For a time he was anxious, accordingly, to conclude peace, the more so as his bitter enemy, Philip of Valois, was now dead (A.D. 1350). But Philip's successor, John, inaugurated his reign by granting away Aquitaine to the Dauphin of Vienne; and when Edward tried to negotiate on the basis of regaining his own fiefs Guienne and Ponthieu, with none or with only nominal dependence on the French crown, the treaty was suddenly broken off, either from the strong repugnance of the French nobility to dismember France, or, as another account states, because Edward would not abandon his allies in Brittany.

Renewal of War.—The war, therefore, began again, and was waged in a new way. Edward and his son made descents with small English armies upon different points of France, and trusted to their prestige as generals, or to the treasure which the English Parliament lavished liberally, to enlist adventurers from every part of Europe, but especially from Germany, where the ravages of the black death had been small. For a time it seemed probable that France would be divided by a civil war. Charles the Bad, King of Navarre, had just cause of complaint against his second cousin, King John of France, who withheld several fiefs and some large sums of money that were due to him.   It is said Charles visited England (**A.D.** 1355); it is certain that he concluded a treaty of alliance with Edward.   But he soon returned to his natural allegiance, and was repaid for his treachery to the King of England by being seized and imprisoned next year by King John.   At the same time, the Count of Harcourt, who was in his company, was arrested and put to death.   The excuse for these acts of violence was that Charles had opposed the levying of the gabelle or salt tax in Normandy.   Some years before the king had put the Count of Eu to death without trial, on a vague suspicion that he intended to surrender Guines to Edward as part of his ransom, or because, as some said, the count had spoken too favourably of the English.   King John thus carried out the principle he more than once expressed: " I will have no man but myself master in France."   But his treacherous and cruel policy alienated the hearts of the people.

Plan of a Triple Invasion.—In the end of **A.D.** 1355 both kingdoms prepared for a decisive war.   The French Estates granted a sum of more that £1,600,000. The English Parliament gave the king a wool tax of fifty shillings the sack, calculated by the defective statistics of the time to produce £250,000 a year, and really bringing in about £80,000.   Edward, accordingly, carried three armies into France.   But the news that the Scotch had surprised Berwick forced him to return hastily to England (November 1355).   His eldest son, however, was sent into Aquitaine, and Henry Duke of Lancaster into Brittany. Next summer, when the kinsmen and partisans of the King of Navarre, and of the dead Count of Harcourt, came to solicit English aid, Duke Henry was ordered to transfer operations to Normandy.   King John took the field in person, and easily drove the English force to the farthest extremity of the province. But while he was besieging Breteuil, he received intelligence that the Prince of Wales, who had last year ravaged the south of France, was now carrying fire and sword over the fertile midland districts. John instantly marched south, and succeeded in crossing the Loire at five several points between Orleans and Saumur, while Edward was wasting time on the siege of Romorantin. A chance encounter between the English van as they were moving southward, and the French rear who had outstripped them, apprised both parties of their position.

Prince Edward Intercepted.—Nothing so far could have been worse than Prince Edward's generalship. He had advanced without support and without plan into the middle of a hostile country, and had taken no pains to inform himself of the neighbourhood of an enormous army. He himself said afterwards that he hoped to meet his father and the Duke of Lancaster, but he evidently took no care to learn whether his father had sailed. It was too late now to return back into Aquitaine, or advance forward into Brittany. If he could not fight his way through an army six times his own in number he was lost. His army was not even provisioned, and the French army might have starved him into a surrender by remaining quiet.

Battle of Poitiers or Maupertuis.—But the chivalrous ideas of the day saved the English in their extremity. King John would not seem to decline battle with superior forces; the English were resolved to offer it. Negotiations were indeed opened by the intervention of two Papal legates, who had been charged to mediate a peace; but though the Black Prince was willing to restore all the spoil of his expedition, booty, prisoners, and fortresses, and to pledge himself not to bear arms for seven years against France, John naturally insisted that the Prince himself should surrender with a hundred knights, and to this Edward would not listen. Nor did he wish to protract negotiations, for his own men were in want of food, and reinforcements were coming in to the French. Nevertheless, the English made good use of the time given them, and threw up dykes to strengthen the position they had taken up on the rising ground overlooking the plain of Maupertuis. In France they could only be attacked by a narrow lane between hedges and through vineyards, just the position in which the English archers were most formidable. On the flank and to the rear they were comparatively exposed, but the Prince guarded himself on his side by a reserve of 300 armed knights and 300 armed archers. Altogether the English numbered 2,000 men-at-arms, 4,000 archers, and 1,500 brigands, or men armed only with knives. The French advanced to the attack in three great divisions, 16,000 strong each. The first, headed by the marshals of France, Arnoul d'Audeneham and Jean de Clermont, was preceded by 300 horsemen, who were intended to scatter the English archers. But they were shot down as they advanced, and their horses, rearing, stumbling, and falling, added to the confusion of men pressing forward into a narrow road, harassed by shot, and unable to reply. Before long, the first battle came back in confusion. In doing so it got mixed with the second battle of the Duke of Normandy, which was advancing to take the English in flank. Before order could be restored the English mounted reserve charged, and the French wavered and gave way, many of the second division at once unloosing their horses and riding in all haste from the field of battle. There was a general panic, and the king's three sons and the Duke of Orleans were among the fugitives. King John himself, at the head of the third battle, awaited the attack of the English, who now descended upon the plain. But though inferior in numbers, the English had the advantage in cavalry, and their furious charges broke up the French ranks, while the English arrows fell thick upon all who remained standing. Before long there was a hopeless rout, and the English were following up the enemy to the very gates of Poitiers, which were closed upon the unhappy fugitives. Among the last to yield was King John, who fought desperately with a battle-axe, and saw the oriflamme trampled down at his side, before he handed his right gauntlet, in token of surrender, to an outlawed knight of Artois, Denis de Morbecque. For a few minutes the king's life was in danger, from the eagerness of all around to claim a share in his capture. But the Prince of Wales, alarmed at the general confusion, had just hoisted his banner on a small tree, as a sign of rendezvous to his followers, and as news came of the important capture, the Earl of Warwick and Sir Reginald Cobham were sent to save the illustrious prisoner.

French and English Losses.—The slaughter at Poitiers was fortunately not very great; on the French side, two dukes, one of whom (the Duke of Athens) was Constable of France, the Bishop of Châlons, sixteen barons, and more than 2,400 knights and squires were numbered among the dead; while King John and his son Philip, the Archbishop of Sens, eighteen counts and viscounts, twenty-one barons, and more than 1,900 knights and squires, were taken prisoners. The light armed among the slain were estimated at 6,000. The loss of the English cannot even be guessed,—one contemporary account placing it at only sixty, of whom four were men-at-arms, while another puts it at 1,900 men-at-arms and 1,500 archers. As, however, it was remarked that former battles

were often decided by three or four, or at most six, dis-
charges of arms, while in this battle cool shots emptied
their sheaves, and were at last reduced to hurling huge
stones, as at Inkermann, we may probably assume that
the English loss was severe for their small numbers. The
English received great credit for their courteous treatment
of the prisoners, many of whom were dismissed on parole
when the terms of ransom had been arranged. The Black
Prince, in particular, got great praise for refusing to seat
himself at table with the King of France, and for
endeavouring to console him by a well-deserved tribute
to his personal courage. But Edward had shown traces
of lower qualities during the battle. He had an old
quarrel with the family of Talleyrand of Périgord, who
had taken the French side in Aquitaine, and was not
unnaturally incensed when some of the cardinal's household fought at Poitiers, though their master had been
sent by the Pope to mediate. Finding the cardinal's
nephew dead on the field, he sent the body to his uncle
with a mock message of salutation; and soon after, taking
one of the household, the castellan of Amposta, would
have struck his head off, if Sir John Chandos had not
interceded. Yet it proved afterwards that the cardinal
was quite innocent in the matter.

Unimpeded March of the English.—Next to the
miracle of the battle of Poitiers, it may seem wonderful
that the English should have been able to carry their
captives and spoil into Gascony. Either of the two
divisions that had left the field unbroken might probably
have effected a rescue, had there been a general to rally
and head the troops. But a great fear had come upon
the French. It seemed hopeless to meet the English in
the field; and knights and squires scattered over the
country amid the curses of the people. It was hardly

safe for a gentleman to show himself in a town.   So the
little English army of the south made its way safely to
Bordeaux, where the spoils of Poitiers were soon wasted
in every kind of extravagance; while the army of the north,
which had followed King John at a distance, in the hopes
of taking part in a battle, but had not been able to
force a passage across the Loire, withdrew again when they
heard of the victory.   As the two countries were by this
time thoroughly exhausted, a truce for two years was
arranged in the following spring, and Prince Edward
carried his royal captive to England.   There were great
rejoicings in London, where the streets were lined with
trophies of bows and arrows, and more than 1,000 citizens
rode out to escort the conqueror.   The French king was
mounted on a white horse, well caparisoned; the Prince
rode by his side on a little black pony.   King John
bore misfortune better than he had borne prosperity, and
behaved with a quiet dignity that conciliated public
opinion in his favour.

Brigandage of the Free Companies in France.
—Meanwhile France was suffering severely from the long
war and from the loss of its king.   The rich country was
preyed upon by adventurers from every part of Europe,
who called themselves English or French indifferently,
and whose whole thought was to plunder.   In Normandy
Sir Robert Knolles, having amassed the almost royal
treasure of 100,000 crowns, kept a little army in his pay,
and stormed castles and sacked towns on his own account.
A Welshman, Griffin, emulated him in the country between
the Seine and Loire; and a Frenchman, Sir Arnold de
Cervolles, a kinsman of the Talleyrands, who was nicknamed "the arch-priest," took Provence as the field of
the operations, held Avignon to ransom, and with grim
humour compelled the Pope to ask him to dinner, and

grant him pardon for his sins. A Fleming, Lord Eustace
d'Ambreticourt, commanded a body of 700 men in the
neighbourhood of Compiègne, and took twelve fortresses;
it was said that all who served under him were enriched.
The great object of these adventurers was to sack a town
or to hold the nobles and gentry of a district to ransom.
They were sometimes not unpopular in the cities which
they made their headquarters, and where they spent their
money; the women of Montauban joined them on one
occasion in a street fight against the French troops. But
in the country districts the presence of these marauders,
foraging and living at free quarters, was a source of unmixed
misery and demoralisation. It is true the peasants dug
trenches round their villages, fortified their churches, and
kept a watchman in the hill-tower to give notice of the
approach of a "company;" but what could men armed
with stakes and knives hope to do against the soldiers
who had conquered at Crécy and Poitiers. In the parts
watered by the Loire, it was customary to pass the night
in islands or in boats; in Picardy they took refuge
underground in vaults, which had originally served for
an asylum from the Norman sea-rovers. Meanwhile
their patience became a byword—"Jacques Bonhomme,"
it was said, "has a broad back, and can bear everything."

The Jacquerie, or Peasants' Rising.—Accidentally,
too, the very measures that were taken to restore order
and peace did but increase the general misery. The truce
between England and France threw many thousand disbanded soldiers upon the country. The efforts of the
middle class in Paris under Marcel, provost of the
merchants, to procure a reform of the government, kept
the city in a ferment, and obliged the Duke of Normandy
to keep his troops about him at headquarters. Meanwhile

the King of Navarre, whom the popular party had set
free, organised a civil war in Normandy, and ravaged the
country to within a few miles of Paris.   At last the
wretched peasants could endure their miseries no longer.
Towards the end of May 1358 there were small risings in
the country north of Paris, about Amiens, Beauvais, and
Soissons.   "They said that the noblemen of the realm of
France, knights, and squires disgraced the realm, and
that it would be doing a great service to destroy them all,
and each of them said it was true, and they all said as
with one voice, 'Shame be to him that doth not do his
endeavour to destroy all the gentlemen of the realm.'"
Unhappily the first insurgents, though armed only with
stakes and knives, succeeded in storming several castles,
and were accordingly joined by thousands, who only
waited to compute the chances of success.   Men who had
grown up in misery, had endured every wrong, and were
now engaged in a war where no quarter would be given,
were not likely to use their victory with moderation; and
"the companies of the Jacquerie," as they were popularly
called, committed atrocities that can scarcely be paralleled
in the world's history.   At one castle "they slew a knight,
and afterwards put him on a spit and roasted him at the
fire, in the sight of the lady his wife and his children;"
and after grossly mishandling the lady, "made her, by
force, eat part of her husband, and then they put her and
all her children to a cruel death."   Altogether they burned
and destroyed more than 100 castles and good houses in
the country between the Marne and the Somme.   Ladies
everywhere fled to the towns for shelter, and the towns
were in constant dread of attack and storm.   Altogether
it was said that 100,000 men were engaged in the
Jacquerie

Its Defeat at Meaux.—Such a rising threatened the very existence of society, and knights and gentlemen flocked in from the neighbouring districts of Flanders and Germany, and executed stern justice on the insurgents. The King of Navarre killed more than 3,000 in a day near Clermont. But the most decisive defeat they sustained was at Meaux, where a number of ladies had taken refuge, trusting to the protection of two English partisans, the Count de Foix and the Captal de Buch, who had just returned from the crusade against the pagans of Prussia. These nobles had only sixty men-at-arms in their company, and the peasants numbered 9,000 strong, and were supported by some of the townsmen, who opened the city gates to them. But the steel-clad soldiers were irresistible; and the wretched serfs fled in disorder, and were cut down pitilessly or drowned in the Marne, to the number, it was said, of 7,000. Then the knights set fire to the town, to punish the citizens for their sympathies. From that day forward the insurrection was virtually at an end. The "king of the Jacques," as their leader was called, tried to negotiate for assistance with Charles of Navarre; but was seized treacherously and put to death, with a red-hot crown of iron forced upon his brow. The French gentlemen took stern vengeance for the revolt. Before Midsummer more than 20,000 had perished; and it was said that the English themselves could not have worked so much mischief as did the nobles of the country.

Restoration of Strong Government in France. —The defeat of the Jacquerie assisted the Duke of Normandy to retrieve his power in Paris. The Provost Marcel had gone so far as to send troops to aid the peasants in storming the castle of Ermenonville. He was now left with no support outside Paris except the alliance

of the King of Navarre; and Charles the Bad, who saw
the regent every day gaining troops and prestige, while
Marcel was discredited by his connection with the serfs,
was at last inclined to purchase peace by a private treaty
for himself.   He negotiated by turns with the regent,
from whom he demanded a sum of money; and with the
English, whom he invited to divide France with him.
Marcel suspected his treachery, but knew also that the
regent was determined to put himself to death, in revenge
for the murder of three of his court.   In despair, the
great popular leader, who had seemed at one time to rival
the Arteveldts, determined to enlist Charles on his side,
by offering him a greater prize than any other party could
bestow—the city of Paris itself.   The King of Navarre
caught eagerly at the bait.   But Marcel had miscalculated
his own power.   One of his own captains, Jean Maillart,
assembled a company of citizens, and cut down the provost at the very moment when he was about to unbar the
gate of St. Antoine (July 31).   Two days later the regent
entered Paris again, and found himself absolute master of
the city.   The late troubles had consolidated his power.
The revolt of the serfs, the treason meditated by Marcel,
had shown men of all ranks that the country had no
hope at present but in a strong single rule.   Charles, too,
had learned experience and moderation in the danger and
embarrassments of the last two years.

King John's Treaty Rejected.—In the spring of
1359 (May) the French envoys returned from England,
bringing with them a treaty which King John had
signed.   The exact terms are not known, but it is supposed that they included the absolute cession of Normandy, Anjou, Maine, Touraine, and Poitou, together
with the actual English fiefs in Aquitaine.   In one
sense the demand was not wholly unjust.   The countries

had all at one time or other been possessions of the English Crown, and wrested from it by force of arms, often against the will of the inhabitants. Edward III. in fact aimed at restoring the kingdom of Henry II., without that feudal allegiance which had been found impracticable. But times had changed. Except in Aquitaine, the English rule was nowhere desired by the population. Nor could any Frenchman endure calmly that the whole sea-coast from Calais to Bayonne should be alienated from France, as would have been the case by this treaty, which provided separately for the independence of Brittany under the De Montforts. Besides, the ransom stipulated for King John was enormous, amounting to 4,000,000 crowns; and the surrender of Normandy, which was still unsubdued, would have been a base desertion of that gallant province. The Duke of Normandy lost no time in summoning the States General, and laying the disgraceful terms before them. All agreed without much deliberation that they would sooner bear their actual misery than thus impair and despoil the kingdom of France (May 25). It was a generous, and, as the event proved, a wise resolve. But to the captive and despondent king it seemed so perilously rash that he imputed it to the intrigues of Charles the Bad.

Anger of Edward III.—There was no ground for this belief, though Charles of Navarre, constrained by public opinion, and alarmed by the capture of Melun, consented not long afterwards to make peace with the regent on easy terms. But the event almost justified King John's fears and compliance. For King Edward, when he learned that the Estates would not ratify the treaty, vowed to enter France before winter was over, and remain there till he had conquered the country or extorted a peace. Edward, indeed, had strong reason to be exasperated. He had intercepted a correspondence in which King John, probably desiring to conciliate his subjects, declared that he had never intended to yield a foot of French soil. Moreover, the Parisians, when the disgraceful compact was first reported, had murdered all the English they could find in the city, many of whom had been naturalised by long residence. Then the Count of Flanders was again powerful in the Flemish towns, where the English merchants were expelled, and the English partisans massacred. In spite of some chivalrous courtesies between lords and gentlemen, the feeling of bitterness between the two races was now one that admitted neither justice nor mercy.

Invasion of France—Successes of the English. —Edward resolved this time to make his preparations for war on a scale of unexampled magnitude. He could trust to his name to attract adventurers, and long before an English army was ready to sail for France, Calais was filled with Germans in such numbers that they caused a famine in the place. Late in October Edward himself arrived. His intention in choosing winter for the time of his operations probably was to intimidate the nation at large by an unusual force of war, and to follow up his threat that he would never leave France till he had won peace. His commissariat was on a gigantic scale—6,000 waggons, it was said, following him; but so vast was the army, which some numbered at 100,000, and so dire the distress of France, where parts had not been tilled for three years, that the English were compelled to divide their forces, and even so, suffered severely, except where the king commanded. Even in Edward's force, the plenty enjoyed was mainly due to a high-handed invasion of the district of Cambrai, a country which held of the Empire, on the ground that the inhabitants had assisted the

French. Edward's wish was to take Rheims, no doubt
that he might be crowned King of France; but the gallant
defence of its archbishop foiled all efforts of the besiegers;
and after a siege of more than six weeks, the English
army broke up its encampments (Jan. 11, 1360), and
marched into Burgundy. At Tonnerre and Flavigny the
invaders found wine and food; and the king fixed his
headquarters at Guillon on the Serain, feeder of the
Yonne, and amused himself with hunting and hawking,
while his troops ravaged the country in every direction.
The Burgundian nobles were not so French in feeling
that they were disposed to make great sacrifices for the
regent's policy; and their young duke, Philip the Bold,
was easily persuaded to send ambassadors and sue for
peace. It was Edward's interest to divide France; and
he readily promised to withdraw his troops, and grant a
truce for three years, in return for a payment of 200,000
gold pence of the gold called " moutons," from the stamp
of a sheep, a sum equal to about £14,000 of English
money. Scarcely had this treaty been concluded when
Edward received intelligence that the French fleet had
landed troops at Winchelsea, who had killed unarmed
men, and outraged and carried off women with some
circumstances of peculiar barbarity. The king was furious
at the insult, and probably a little alarmed at the possible
consequences of an expedition which had, in fact, forced
the English Government to make great levies at once
throughout the kingdom. So the royal banners were
turned northward again, and the English troops ravaged
up to the very walls of Paris, where the last French army
lay, forced to decline a pitched battle, and foiled in all
small enterprises by English strategy. Edward's intention was to distribute the bulk of his army in fortresses
round Paris, to spend the summer in Brittany, and to

return in the time of vintage and besiege the capital. When his intentions were known, the French Government gave way. All hopes of effecting a diversion on the English coast were at an end, for even the raid on Winchelsea had ended in the repulse of the French, with more loss than they inflicted; and by this time the country was in arms, and a large fleet at sea, making stern reprisals. The Duke of Normandy reluctantly resolved to treat. Edward, it is said, refused at first to hear of any terms by which he was not acknowledged King of France. But the Duke of Lancaster mediated, and a great storm of thunder and hail, " as if the world had come to an end " (April 13), swayed the king's superstition to counsels of peace, and would, under any circumstances, have enforced a suspension of arms, as many men and more than 6,000 horses perished in it. After seventeen days' negotiation, a treaty, known as the Treaty of Brétigni, was concluded (May 8, 1360).

Treaty of Bretigni.—By it both parties yielded some of their pretensions. The English renounced the old pretensions of the crown, Normandy, Touraine, Anjou, Maine, Brittany, and every right that might be pretended over Flanders; and France consented to cede Gascony and Guienne, Poitou, and sundry outlying districts, including the Limosin and Rouergue in independent sovereignty; as also in the north, the county of Ponthieu, the town of Montreuil, and Calais, with all the adjoining territory. King John was to pay a ransom of 3,000,000 crowns, equal to about £500,000 of English money, and to be released in exchange for hostages. King Edward was to renounce all claim to the crown, title, and arms of France. The question of Brittany was to be decided by judgment of the two kings, an article which was really meant to leave the question open, as neither France nor England

could honourably desert its candidate. The French were
to renounce their treaties with Scotland, and to abstain
from giving any aid to the Scotch in their English wars
for the future, and in like manner the King of England
was to renounce his Flemish alliance. Free intercourse
was to be restored between France and England, so that
the subjects of either country might study in the schools
and universities of the other as before. Lastly, by a separate treaty which Edward negotiated, the King of Navarre was reconciled to the King of France.

Treaty and Peace.—The terms of the treaty of Brétigni cannot be considered extravagant, and it was no doubt
intended to form the basis of a permanent peace. It was
fortunate for England that the article relating to Flanders
was more than excused by the late defection of the Flemings, who had made terms with their earl during the
Black Death, on the condition of remaining neutral in the
war, and had lately, as his influence increased, driven
every English trader out of the country. In fact, Edward did not sacrifice an ally, for a special article stipulated that he should determine the succession to the
Harcourt estates in Normandy, no doubt, in order that
his own partisans in the family might not be unfairly
treated. To France the terms were perhaps as good as
could be expected. Enormous as the ransom demanded
for King John undoubtedly was, it was less than the cost
of six months' war would have been. The cession of
feudal suzerainty over the English fiefs in Aquitaine and
Ponthieu only removed a constant cause of difficulty, and
the cession of Calais was unavoidable. The surrender of
Poitou was the costliest and most bitter sacrifice. There
nobles and cities were passionately French, and had made
heroic efforts during the war against the foreign enemy
who was now to receive their allegiance. The sailors of

Rochelle, in particular, had fought the English by sea wherever they could be found; and wrote to King John in remonstrance against the treaty, saying that they would sooner pay half their substance a year than become subject to the English. The king could only exhort them to comply, and reward their loyalty with a grant of commercial privileges; but the city gates were closed against the English for more than a year; and when they were at last opened, the burgesses vowed among themselves that their hearts should remain French.

War with Scotland.—Scotland, fortunately for itself, had made peace before France was reduced to extremities. There had been an attempt in 1355, when the truces with England had expired, to renew the war on a great scale, and the Scotch had obtained the aid of a small body of French troops, and had sent soldiers into Ireland, who joined the native tribes in a descent on the English pale. In Ireland the invading army was almost instantly defeated with great loss by the Englishry. In England, the town of Berwick had been taken, but the success had gone no further. So exhausted was Scotland that the Scotch could not defray the cost of their allies, even during the few weeks that might be required to reduce the castle of Berwick; and when the French contingent had left, and it was known that Edward had returned, vowing vengeance on those who had marred his French enterprise, the Scotch army scattered, every man to his own home, leaving a small garrison in Berwick, which could only surrender the town on the first summons (Jan. 13, 1356). Edward's indignation was great when he found that the greater part of the city had been burned or otherwise destroyed during the siege; and he seems for a time to have cherished the idea of reasserting English sovereignty over the unruly Scotch people.

He accepted, in presence of his court at Roxburgh (Jan. 23), the surrender of Edward Balliol's title to Scotland and estates in Galway, which had been matter of negotiation for some weeks past.

Burned Candlemas.—Then he summoned William Douglas to come to his peace, and on his refusal marched through the Lothians, killing and burning with such energy that the time was long remembered in Scotland as " Burned Candlemas." Even churches did not escape the havoc of the English army; and the church of the Franciscans at Haddington, and the church of White Kirk near the coast, fell victims, with many others, to the soldiers and to the sailors of the fleet. Thus far the English navy had accompanied the army in its progress; but a storm, which popular superstition ascribed to the vengeance of the Virgin of the Holy Cross at White Kirk, blew the ships out into the deep, and wrecked the ship whose sailors had plundered the shrine. The want of provisions forced Edward to return; and a Scotch army soon took the field again, and drove out the unwary English settlers who had entered into Galloway. Later on in the year a Scotch contingent, under William Douglas, was present at Poitiers, and escaped from the field, though with some loss of men. It was now matter of certainty that the Scotch could not expect aid from France, and Edward's hopes of a French crown were so dazzling that he could afford to intermit his Scotch wars. Besides, David Bruce had become popular at the English court during his captivity. A treaty was accordingly concluded by which the Scotch Estates were allowed to ransom their king for 100,000 marks (Sept. 26, 1357), and David went back to his people accordingly. A little later several of the Scotch prisoners were allowed to pay short visits to their country; and Scotch students received licence to

CHAPTER VIII

THE LOSS OF THE FRENCH CONQUESTS.

Government of Aquitaine.—The first viceroy whom King Edward appointed in Aquitaine after the peace was Sir John Chandos, the descendant of an old Norman family founded by Hugh the Ass, under the Conqueror, in Herefordshire. No better man could have been selected to fill the office. Chandos was probably the best general in Europe. He had fought with distinction under Edward in the battle of the Downs, and had been the prince's right-hand man at Poitiers. When he died some years later, his English companions-in-arms predicted that they should lose Guienne, since they had lost the man who won it for them, and the presage was speedily verified. But Chandos was much more than a mere soldier. He was reputed the wisest and most moderate among English statesmen. "All nobleness was found in him," says Froissart, and "in a hundred years after there was not a more courteous man, nor one possessed of more noble virtues and good qualities among the English." Thoroughly unselfish and patriotic, Chandos was something more than a mere patriot, and throughout his service in France tried to mitigate the horrors of war, and to cause the king's French subjects to be governed with a righteous regard for their own interests. He seems to have been the only Englishman of high position who kept himself free from

the hard and insolent tone which the Duke of Lancaster
and the Black Prince in particular adopted towards their
inferiors, and especially towards the French subjects or
aliens.   Nevertheless, the barons and gentry of Aquitaine,
who had known Prince Edward only as a comrade in war,
a successful leader, and a brilliant host, were anxious that
a province so large and populous and rich as England
should be administered by the prince in person.   Not
only would Bordeaux thus have its court, but if Prince
Edward, as seemed certain, should one day succeed to the
English crown, his old connection with Aquitaine would
certainly be remembered to the advantage of the province.
The king readily granted the petition, and invested his
son with the principality, to be held as an English fief by
the yearly payment of an ounce of gold (July 19, 1362).
The prince had just married his cousin, Joan, daughter
of Edmund Earl of Kent, whom Mortimer had beheaded,
a lady of such beauty that she was known as the Fair
Maid of Kent, and of so little discretion that she had
married the Earl of Salisbury, being already the wife of
Sir Thomas Howard.   She followed her husband into
Aquitaine, and he inaugurated his rule by bestowing
many of the vacant fiefs and offices on Englishmen.   For
the time, however, there was no open discontent, as the
prince kept royal state, and entertained his new vassals
courteously.

Free Companions.—For some years, the English
dominions in Aquitaine were the only part of France
that enjoyed peace and good government.   The English,
German, and Gascon soldiers of fortune, whom the war
had left unemployed, were ravaging France in every
direction, and defeated a royal army under Lord Jacques
de Bourbon, in a pitched battle at Brignais, near Lyon
(April 6, 1362).   King John thought for a time of

enlisting them under his banners for a crusade. But before he could collect funds for the expedition, he was warned by the princes of the blood-royal, who were in England as hostages for his ransom, that they were weary of their banishment, and intended to gain their liberty as they best could, by surrendering their castles and fiefs to the King of England. This disloyal menace induced John to surrender himself again, and he did it (January 1364) with such alacrity, that he was suspected of finding life in the court of England pleasanter than the cares of government. Fortunately for his country, the incapable king died three months after his return (April 8). His successor, Charles V., was a sickly and unwarlike prince, with the tastes of a scholar, but also with the capacity of a statesman. Trained in the rough school of defeats and rebellions, Charles abhorred the splendid disorders of the French court that had left the sovereign dishonoured and powerless; and without much regard for the chivalrous point of honour, indeed with some taint of dissimulation and faithlessness, was careful to restore public credit and to respect the laws.

Bertrand du Guesclin.—His favourite and ablest general was a man after his own heart, Bertrand du Guesclin, "the ugliest man from Rennes to Draort," as an old poem calls him, was a soldier of such distinction that the best captains of his day were willing to serve under him. But he was also at least as ready to employ stratagem as force, and had none of that foolish punctilio which induced many captains of his time to accept a battle against odds. His hatred of England was not so inveterate that he could not serve with Englishmen as brothers-in-arms. None the less, he kept before him as the great purpose of his life to drive the foreigner out of France.

Battle of Auray.—The first war in which Du Guesclin

commanded for his new king had an unprosperous issue. He was sent into Brittany with 1000 lances to support Charles de Blois, and encountered De Montfort and Sir John Chandos at Auray. The army of Charles de Blois was the flower of French chivalry; that of De Montfort was chiefly composed of 400 English under Chandos, a body of free companions under Sir Robert Knolles, and some Navarese and Breton troops. Even Chandos's influence had failed to draw any number of Gascon soldiers into a war against their French countrymen. For a time it seemed as if terms would be made between the two leaders. But Charles de Blois had promised his wife to agree to no peace that did not give him the duchy; and the English soldiers, who had everything to lose by peace, threatened to kill the negotiator, and persuaded Chandos that he was in honour bound to give them a battle. So the two armies advanced against one another (September 28). De Montfort had the advantage of position, but was inferior in numbers. The French troops, dismounted as at Poitiers, advanced in such close array, that an apple could not have been thrown among them without lighting upon a helmet. The English arrows bounded back from the coats of proof. But the archers flung away their bows and arrows. and dashed fearlessly into the French ranks, seizing he axes out of their foe's hands. The heavy armour, which saved its wearer from arrow point or sword stroke, made the soldier · slow to move, and helpless when he was overthrown. Gradually De Montfort's force gained upon the enemy, chiefly through the good conduct of Sir Hugh Calverley, who kept the reserve well in hand, and brought his men up to every point where there seemed signs of disorder. At last Charles de Blois was left with only a few knights and squires, who would not desert him in his extremity.

It was understood on both sides that no mercy was to be shown to either commander, so that the cruel war might at last end, and Charles de Blois died more honourably than he had lived, leaving the inheritance of Brittany to his rival. Charles V. wisely agreed to invest the conqueror with the disputed fief, and Jean de Montfort made some compensation in lands and money to the widowed Jeanne de Penthièvre. Edward III., whose daughter Mary, De Montfort had married, and to whom he owed everything, was consulted throughout the negotiations for this peace of Guérande. The fact that he recommended the terms agreed to, is proof that he honestly desired the restoration of peace in France.

Pedro the Cruel.—Yet the French had real cause of complaint against England. Half the "Free Lances" who were still ravaging France were either Englishmen or Gascons, and the Captal de Buch and Sir John Joël, two English subjects, had lately been defeated at Cocherel in Normandy, in a pitched battle against the royal forces. Edward III. indeed offered to take the field in person against the marauders; but the French naturally shrank from accepting the services of so dangerous an ally, and believed that a simple order to withdraw, if it were enforced by confiscations and legal penalties, would be effectual against all who had any stake in England or Aquitaine. Meanwhile it was necessary to rid the country of its tormentors. An attempt to draw them off through Germany in the service of a crusade, failed through the stubborn good sense of the people in Alsace, who rose in arms and drove the Free Companions back when they attempted to enter the province. An opening in another direction seemed to promise better. Pedro the Cruel, King of Castile at this time (1350–1369), had earned his title by a series of murders, which dated from the time he was sixteen years old, and comprised his wife, his stepmother, two of his half-brothers, and a great number of the chief nobles of his kingdom. He was on bad terms with the pope, for he was the friend of Moors and Jews, and had plundered bishops and monasteries; he was hated in the court of France, for his murdered queen was the king's cousin, Blanche de Bourbon; he was at war with the King of Arragon. Instigated by this monarch and by the King of Navarre, the eldest of Pedro's half-brothers, Don Henry of Trastamare, who had been serving for some time with the Free Companions in Languedoc, conceived the idea of uniting them in a grand enterprise against the kingdom of Castile. Charles V. approved the project, and lent money and his best captain, De Guesclin; Pope Urban V. contributed his blessing and money; and the Free Lances eagerly embraced a scheme which promised them the plunder of a new country. Edward III. and his son disliked an enterprise which, if it succeeded, would place an ally of France on the throne, and ordered their subjects not to join it. Sir John Chandos, who had been offered one of the chief commands, was in consequence obliged to decline; but many English and Gascons of inferior rank joined the expedition. It succeeded without bloodshed. The people rose to welcome it, and Don Pedro was forced to escape through Portugal, and take ship hastily at Corunna. Don Henry was crowned in his palace at Burgos (April 1366).

His Alliance with Prince Edward.—In his distress Don Pedro applied to the Prince of Wales for support. There was no reason why England or Aquitaine should be mixed up in Spanish politics. Both countries required rest after an exhausting war. There were many reasons why Pedro should not be supported. It was under him that Spanish ships had committed piracies in the

Channel and fought the Battle of the Downs against our English fleet, commanded by the king in person. His name was infamous in Europe for the many murders he had committed; "and what is worse," says an old chronicler, "he had loved a Jewish woman." Only a bloody war could force him again upon subjects who detested him. But Pedro was a skilful diplomatist. He bribed the Prince of Wales by a promise to cede the province of Biscay; and tried to bribe Chandos with the town of Soria. He made lavish promises of lands and money to the nobles and knights who stood high in the prince's council and court. Chandos used his whole influence to oppose the expedition; but the prince inclined to it. Descended himself from William the Bastard, he considered the cause of all kings and king's sons at stake if Don Henry, who was a natural son, should be allowed to rule by the people's voice. Nevertheless, he so far deferred to the strong feeling of his council as to consult his father. Edward III. wrote back approving the expedition. There were certain old alliances, he said, between himself and his cousin, the King of Castile, which obliged him to give aid if he was required. The treaties unhappily cannot be denied. They had been concluded as lately as 1362, probably with the object of securing Edward's French dominions on the side of Spain; and they bound the contracting parties to assist one another at need against any enemy. In so exceptional a case as the present, the opinion of Chandos, who heard that Don Pedro had put himself out of the pale of humanity, might well have satisfied a scrupulous conscience. But if public faith required that aid should be given, it certainly ought not to have been sold. The treaties by which Pedro ceded the cities of Bermejo, Bilbao, Lequeytio, and Castro Urdiales, forming, with their territories, the best part of Biscay, while he left his three daughters hos-

tages for the performance of the compact, are evidences
that the Prince of Wales was not actuated by purely honourable motives.

Battles of Vittoria and Navarette.—There was
little hope that King Henry could resist such an army
as the Black Prince led into Spain (A.D. 1367). The best
soldiers of the day flocked to fight under his banner,
and the Lord of Albret, whose contingent was reduced
from 1,000 to 200 spearsmen, never forgave the insult
and supposed injury. Altogether, the prince's army,
when it crossed the Pyrenees, numbered 24,000 horse,
and innumerable archers. Bertrand du Guesclin advised
that they should not be met in the open field, and
had this counsel been followed, there is little doubt
that the English host, which suffered severely from
cold and dysentery, might have been worn out and
compelled to evacuate the country, or even to capitulate.
But the Spaniards were 60,000 strong, and their pride
recoiled from the idea of avoiding battle with an enemy
of only half their numerical strength, though really the
disproportion was against themselves, as only 7,000
of their men were heavy armed, the archers were far
inferior to the English, and a part of the troops
were only armed with slings. As it happened, the first
encounter was in favour of the enemy. The Duke of
Lancaster, a bad general, allowed himself to be surprised
by the king's brother, Don Tello, and was completely defeated, with great loss of killed and wounded, in a battle,
near Vittoria, that would have been a rout but for the
heroic courage of the soldiers. As it was, the prince was
obliged to manœuvre for several days and at last force a
battle by crossing the Ebro near Logroño, and threatening
to march upon Castile. When the two armies at last met
for a decisive battle at Navarette, the English men-at-arms

are said to have numbered only 10,000. The battle-field was a broad treeless plain, with the Ebro at the back of the Spaniards, and the Najerilla river behind the English. The first shock of battle between the French Companions, under Du Guesclin, who led the van, and the English van, under Chandos and the Duke of Lancaster, was rather to the advantage of the Spaniards; and the Spanish slings did some execution. But the English archers were now again among men, whose armour had not been specially prepared to keep out English shafts; a strong body of Spanish horse, under Don Tello, fled in a panic, leaving the flank uncovered; and the English centre, under the Prince of Wales, coming up broke through the main line of the Spanish, and scattered them in every direction. Last of all, Sir Robert Knolles brought up the reserve of "the grand company," and completed Chandos's victory. King Henry fled, after leading three charges in person, and escaped into France. Du Guesclin and the Conde de Denia, a Spanish prince of the blood, were among the prisoners. The slain among the Spaniards were estimated at from 5,000 to more than 8,000, besides many who were drowned in the Ebro; the prisoners do not seem to have been numbered. The English loss was put at 1,600.

Disastrous end of Campaign.—The tactical skill of his officers and the bravery of his troops had again saved the prince from the defeat his bad generalship had deserved. He had made no proper commissariat; had suffered his van to be surprised; and had provoked battle by leaving the enemy in force between himself and the Pyrenees; but Chandos and the English yeomen had carried him through everything. For a moment the pres-tige of England stood higher than ever, and city after city opened its gates to Don Pedro, till the country lay at his feet. Then came disappointment. The prince demanded performance of the promises Don Pedro had made, and proposed to stay in Spain till they were acquitted. There is no reason to charge the Spanish tyrant with wanton treachery to his imperious but very useful ally. He paid the prince all the money he could lay hands on, £40,000 in all, giving him even the crown jewels, and putting many of his subjects to death that he might seize their property. He sent commissioners to hand over the promised towns in Biscay, and found that even the news of Navarette had not quelled the courage of the stubborn Basques, who closed their gates, and vowed that they would not admit the English. At last, having given Edward the city of Valladolid as his quarters, Pedro went off to Seville, as he said, to collect money; probably to be free anyhow from his importunate guest. For some months Edward vainly awaited the performance of his ally's promises. Then, as his troops were wasting away with dysentery and other diseases caused by the strange climate, till it was said scarcely a fifth remained alive, Edward resolved to remove into Aquitaine, which Don Henry was attacking, and was glad to find that the passes of the Pyrenees were left open to him by the Kings of Arragon and Navarre (August 1367). It was the last tribute to English prestige that no advantages of number or natural position emboldened an enemy to attack the wreck of the unconquerable army.

Results of the English Policy.—The results of Edward's mischievous policy soon became evident. All he had achieved in Spain was almost instantly undone by Don Henry, who crossed the Pyrenees a few weeks only after Edward had left Spain (Sept. 1367), recovered his kingdom in the course of the next year, and captured and killed Don Pedro a little later (March 1369). The whole power of Castile, which was far from being contemptible at sea, was then thrown into the scale against England. Meanwhile the Black Prince, after sacrificing the ransom of his prisoners, and even his plate, to pay the troops he had enlisted, was compelled to dismiss them with fair promises, and bid them shift for themselves outside Aquitaine. The Free Companions, who were still 6,000 strong, were well disposed to quarter themselves again upon France, and readily crossed the border. Great was the indignation in France when the "host of England," as it was now called, recommenced its ravages. King Charles was not yet able to declare war, for he had not even an army which could face the Companions. But he prepared for it by detaching some of the chief supporters of the English interest, such as Clisson, in Brittany, and the Lord of Albret, in Gascony, binding the latter to him by a marriage with his own sister-in-law.

Disaffection in Aquitaine.—Before long, the Black Prince was involved in new difficulties. The extravagance of his court, which had not its equal "in all Christendom," could not be supported with a bankrupt exchequer. He convoked the states of Aquitaine, and proposed an extraordinary tax, to last five years, of a franc on every hearth. It was calculated that this would bring in 1,200,000 franks, or £200,000 a year, from the populous province. The great commercial cities were disposed to consent, if the prince would covenant not to tamper with the coinage for seven years,—a stipulation which shows to what desperate expedients the English Government had resorted. But the lords and knights of the marches, on whose poor tenantry such a tax would have weighed very heavily, pleaded that they had always been exempt from taxation, and that the prince had sworn to maintain their privileges. In fact, Aquitaine,

as a distant and uncertain possession, had always been
treated by the English crown with exceptional lenity, and
owed its prosperity very much to its privileges. Chandos
knew the state of public feeling, and warned the prince
that it was unsafe to persist in his project. But the
prince judged everything from an English standard,
believed that whatever was done in Yorkshire could be
carried out in Gascony, and scarcely concealed his con-
tempt for his foreign subjects. Chandos, finding it useless to advise, and not wishing to be mixed up in the
coming political crisis, got leave of absence, and went
into Normandy. The Gascon baronage demanded leave
to withdraw for a time from the parliament and consult.
Having obtained a prorogation, they proceeded to lodge
an appeal with the King of France, claiming protection
from him as their suzerain.

The French resolve upon War.—By the treaty of
Brétigni, Charles had no more right to entertain an appeal
from Aquitaine than from England. Nor could the
argument of the Gascon lords that the king could not
deprive his old subjects of the right of appeal without
their own consent, weigh seriously against the fact that
Charles had undoubtedly undertaken to do so, had been
partly compelled by Gascon arms, and had received no
remonstrance from his Gascon subjects on the matter.
But it might still be a question whether the treaty of
Brétigni was still binding. It had stipulated that the
King of England should formally renounce his claim to
the crown of France within a fixed term; and though
Edward had abandoned the use of the title of King of
France, there seem to have been delays and difficulties
in executing the treaty, and the formal documents of
renunciation had never been exchanged. Indeed, the
arms of France were still quartered on the great seal of

England, though, perhaps, only as heraldic distinctions. Above all, Edward had bound himself to "nourish perpetual peace and love" towards his "brother of France," and here the country was being ravaged by English troops but lately serving under the Prince of Wales. The French baronage decided that war was justified and expedient (June 30, 1368). Charles lost no time in sending ambassadors into Spain to negotiate an alliance with King Henry. But he waited till he was assured of support, before sending a formal summons, ordering the Prince of Wales, as a vassal, to appear in Paris before the Peers, and answer to the complaints of the Gascons against him (Jan. 25, 1369). Prince Edward was furious at the insult. "Sirs," he answered the two envoys, "we will gladly go to Paris to our uncle, since he hath thus sent for us, but I assure you that it shall be with our bassinet on our head and 60,000 men in our company." Some of the courtiers advised that the ambassadors should be put to death for their pains. The Black Prince was not brutalised to the point of sanctioning such an outrage upon the law of nations; but, on second thoughts, he caused them to be pursued, learning that they had left Bordeaux without a passport, and threw them into a prison, from which one of them never came out alive. It can only be said in extenuation of this barbarity that the prince was now suffering from a disease contracted in Spain, and believed by his physicians to be dropsy, and was wanting his best counsellor, Chandos. Charles V. resented the outrage becomingly. Some months later, when he sent a formal despatch to the King of England, he caused it to be delivered by a servant of his kitchen.

Commencement of Hostilities.—Fortunately for France, the country had recovered their great general. Du Guesclin was popular among the English, and a favourite

with the Black Prince, to whom he had surrendered at
Navarette, and who offered him his liberty and 10,000
francs if he would engage never to make war upon England.
The Breton captain rejected the tempting bait, and was
allowed to name his own ransom, against the opinion of
Edward's council, who were for keeping him prisoner.
He fixed it in magnificent self-respect at 100,000 Spanish
doubloons, about £23,000. The result showed that he
had not over-estimated his popularity. King Charles
advanced 30,000 doubloons; the Princess of Wales herself, it is said, subscribed 10,000 francs; and the merchants of Bordeaux found the remainder. Bertrand's
first use of his liberty was to join King Henry in Spain.
Having followed his Spanish master's fortunes till the
war was practically ended by Don Pedro's death, Du
Guesclin returned to France, where hostilities began in
earnest about summer (1369). Charles's policy was to
attack England at as many sides as possible; to provoke
Scotch invasion, or Welsh revolt; to ravage the English
shores with a fleet; and to attack Ponthieu, Poitou, and
Aquitaine, while the King of Castile put a fleet to sea to
prevent succour from being sent. The gigantic plan
broke down in several of its parts. Castile was kept in
check by an alliance with the King of Arragon; and the
Captal de Buch was propitiated by a transfer of Edward's
unreal sovereignty in Biscay. The Scotch were easily
induced to conclude a fourteen years' truce; and precautions were taken against a rising in Ireland. An expedition from Calais under the Duke of Lancaster, compelled the French King to resign all thought of invasion,
and confine himself to the defence of his own territory.
But the issue was none the less prosperous to the French
under the wise tactics of the King and Du Guesclin, who
disbanded their armies, and let a princess of the blood be

paraded prisoner before their eyes, sooner than fight a
pitched battle, and yet never ceased to harass the enemy.
Fortress after fortress was taken on either side, skirmish
after skirmish lost or won, and the English, for a time,
seemed to be holding their own gallantly. But though
their losses in battle were never great, the loss of 700 or 900
men was felt now very sensibly, and before the end of the
year almost every strong place in Poitou and Querci had
opened its gates to the King of France. The greatest
loss of all was that of Chandos, who was killed in leading
on his men at Pont de Lusac in Poitou; with him departed the last hope of English ascendancy. It is probable he was the one great general of his time, the man
to whom the Prince of Wales owed Poitiers and Navarette.
It is certain he was the one man under whom the undisciplined English nobles and the disaffected Gascon
baronage were well contented to serve. Had he been
confirmed Captain-General of Aquitaine, or had the Prince
of Wales followed his counsels, it is probable that Edward's reign would have closed in unbroken peace.

Massacre of Limoges.—In an evil day, for his own
good name, the prince achieved one last victory. The
defection of the town of Limoges had been particularly dis-
pleasing to him, as he had singled the bishop for especial
confidence, and "he sware by his father's soul, whereby
he was never forsworn, that he would recover it, and
punish the traitors." The Prince could not muster more
than 3,200 men; but, in the general decay of France,
these were enough to invest Limoges for a month. As
the town was too strong to be stormed, he took it by
mining, and was carried in a horse-litter to witness the
general massacre which he commanded. Men, women,
and children implored mercy on their knees; but the
Black Prince was pitiless, and the only mercy shown was

to some of the captains of the garrison, and to the Bishop, who owed his life to the Duke of Lancaster's intercession. "There was not so hard a heart within the city of Limoges," says Froissart, "if he had any remembrance of God, but that wept piteously for the fate of the citizens, for more than 3,000 persons were slain that day. God have mercy on their souls, for I think they were martyrs." Perhaps, for real wickedness, the massacre of Limoges falls short of the war in Spain, waged to replace a tyrant, and costing infinite lives; but there can be no doubt that the moral sense of the times was more outraged by the slaughter of unarmed men and their families, though guilty of rebellion, than by any carnage of soldiers on a battlefield.

Departure of the Black Prince.—Fortunately it was Prince Edward's last exploit. His physicians recommended him to return to his native air; and as his failing health unfitted him for business, and the death of his eldest son had cast a gloom over Bordeaux, he determined to renounce public life, and transferred his government to his brother the Duke of Lancaster (Dec. 1370). With the Prince's departure the last hope of retaining a portion of our French conquests vanished. He was probably not a great captain, and certainly not a conciliatory statesman ; but in both capacities he was far superior to his successor, and he had the prestige of Poitiers and Navarette. One by one the brilliant com pany of English soldiers was dying out. Henry of Lancaster and Chandos were dead. Sir Walter Manni was now too infirm for war. One consummate soldier, Sir John Hawkwood, was still, it is true, in the English service. But as a mere gentleman of Essex, he seems to have wanted influence to push him after the death of his patron, the Earl of Oxford (1371); and having in some way incurred the royal displeasure, transferred himself to more profitable service with the White Company of Free Companions in Italy, among whom he had already seen service.

Invasion of France by Knolles.—The want of a capable leader of high birth was severely felt by the English during this very year. Sir Robert Knolles, a soldier of fortune, who had lately been endowed by the king with estates in England, and who is said to have engraven on his helmet—

"Qui Robin Canolle prendra C mille nobles il ara,"

was appointed general of an army of invasion, which started from Calais about the middle of the summer. For a time the success of the expedition was brilliant, and a little force of 12,500 men traversed the country at pleasure, and burned the suburbs of Paris. But one of Knolles' officers, a Welsh gentleman, Sir Thomas Mynsterworth, took umbrage at the strict discipline of the commander, who forbade the troops to scatter, and persuaded a large party including one of the generals, Sir Thomas Grandison, to separate from the main body under the old moss-trooper, as he nicknamed Sir Robert Knolles. Knolles, seeing the danger, withdrew into Brittany, and before long, Bertrand du Guesclin had surprised and defeated Grandison's division at Pont Valaint, with the loss of their general, who was taken prisoner. Mynsterworth escaped, and accused Knolles at the English court of deliberate treachery in not having remained to support his colleague. The charge was so far entertained, that Sir Robert's English fiefs were sequestered, and he was compelled to fine that he might be restored to the king's favour. But further inquiry showed that the real blame lay with Mynsterworth, a factious and worthless man, who had embezzled the public money.

He fled the country, and was declared a felon, with forfeiture of his estates. Some years later he was taken in Pampeluna (1377) and brought to England, where he was drawn, hanged, and quartered.

Naval Defeat off Rochelle.—The next year (1371) was marked by no event of importance except a little victory at sea which the English fleet won over some French and Flemish ships that were bringing back salt. It was an unlucky battle, for it served to irritate the Flemings, whose men appear to have accepted battle readily, but who were not the less indignant that their neutrality had not been respected. In 1372 a much more important naval battle turned to the disadvantage of the English. A small body of men was sent, under the Earl of Pembroke, to reinforce the garrison of Rochelle, and convoy a large sum of money. At the entrance of the port the little English squadron was assailed by a powerful fleet of Spanish ships that had long been lying at anchor to intercept them (June 23). So fiercely did the English fight that the battle lasted nearly two days. But the odds were too uneven; the Spaniards grappled the English barks, and flung down great stones and bars of iron and lead from the high decks of their galleons. Four ships closed round the vessel which held the Earl of Pembroke, and never left it till its crew had been overpowered by mere dint of numbers. The people of Rochelle looked on with covert exultation, and refused to assist their English masters, on the ground that they were not practised in naval war; but an English governor and three Gascon knights of the English party went out in four ships, hastily equipped, and shared the universal disaster. By the evening of the second day the English fleet was all taken or destroyed; and the Spaniards spread their sails and departed, " making great noise of trumpets and other minstrelsies ; and with long streamers waving in the wind with the arms of Castile, and with other pennons and standards." This defeat was fatal to English ascendancy. The reinforcement of soldiers was sorely needed, and the 20,000 marks taken could ill be spared from an empty treasury ; but greater misfortunes still were the loss of prestige, the captivity of the Earl of Pembroke, a young soldier and statesman of high promise, and the certainty that Spain was now to be reckoned with as a dangerous enemy. Moreover, the Spaniards declared that they had found written orders upon the Earl of Pembroke, instructing him to seize 10,000 of the chief inhabitants of Guienne, and ship them to England as hostages. It is highly improbable that the English court ever issued orders of the kind ; but the fable is said to have been believed, and turned the affections of people in the old hereditary province from their English masters. Later on in the year (August) King Edward and the Black Prince put to sea with a large fleet destined for the relief of Rochelle. The whole English nobility had embarked, and the expedition is said to have cost £900,000. But contrary winds kept the ships back till the news of the surrender of Rochelle, or the lateness of the season, made it useless to proceed.

Duke of Lancaster's Ride across France.—Next year the Duke of Lancaster led an English army from Calais across France. He had started from Calais in good time, and might have inflicted great damage upon the country. But the French amused him with proposals of peace till the harvest had been gathered in, and then resorted to the old tactics of declining a battle, and hanging upon his march to cut off stragglers. Some ravage was of course done, and some districts were constrained to ransom themselves, but on the whole the English passage through Normandy to Auvergne, and so to Bordeaux, was disastrous only to themselves. Almost all the horses perished in the hills of Auvergne, and a third of the force was destroyed by famine or dysentery. It would seem that the Duke had horsed his whole force, and perhaps taken spare horses in the expectation of mounting Free Companions. The loss was enormous, and the English were so dispirited, that next year when the French offered battle an army could not be mustered to meet them in the field. Moreover, the Duke of Lancaster, who had married the eldest daughter of Pedro the Cruel, and called himself in her right King of Castile, governed Aquitaine without waiting for instructions from the English council, and was generally suspected of aiming at the crown of England. Nothing could prosper under such a rule ; and when the Duke returned to England in the summer of 1374, Bayonne, Bordeaux, and a few fortified places in the south, with Calais in the north, were all that remained under English sovereignty. Next year a twelve months' truce was negotiated (June 27, 1375), and this was afterwards extended for another nine months. The old King of England died just in time not to see the English coast ravaged by a combined French and Spanish fleet.

Rumours of Great Persons Poisoned.—The short interval of cessation from foreign war was crowded with intrigues and political combinations. It is characteristic of the changed temper of the nation, that the death of a great man was now constantly ascribed to poison. In 1368 the Duke of Clarence, Edward's second surviving son, died soon after his marriage at Milan to Violante, daughter and heiress of Galeazzo Visconti. The death was ascribed to poison. In 1369 the Earl of Warwick died of dysentery on his return from a plundering expedition along the coast of Normandy. It was remembered that he had quarrelled with the Duke of Lancaster and the Earl of Hereford, who were then in command at Calais; and when the Earl of Hereford died suddenly, more than two years later, there were not wanting men who declared that he had been found guilty of poisoning Thomas de Beauchamp, and had been hanged at night-time by the king's orders. In 1375 the Earl of Pembroke died on his return from Spanish captivity; again there was a story of slow poison administered by his Spanish captors. That the Prince of Wales had been poisoned in Spain was matter of current belief, though he lived nine years after Navarette. Now, when his death was only a question of time, men saw with alarm that the crown would devolve on a boy only ten years old; and gloomy predictions were current that the Duke of Lancaster would find means to remove the one obstacle between himself and a crown. His own conduct increased the suspicions against him. He was making a party for himself of a few nobles and soldiers of fortune, was leagued with some of the bishops, and seemed to have a secret understanding with the religious reformers of the day; but, above all, he courted the favour of Alice Perrers, who governed the old king with almost absolute power.

Alice Perrers.—It is probable that several of the charges against this lady are false or exaggerated. Her position as maid of honour to Queen Philippa almost proves that she was not of low origin; her favour at court certainly began six years before the death of her royal mistress; and, as she married an officer of high rank and distinction, Sir William de Windsor, who had been lieutenant of Ireland, there is some presumption in favour of her reputation. She once at least employed her influence at court in favour of one of the best men of the time,

William of Wykeham, Bishop of Winchester, who seems
to have thought it not improper to solicit her mediation.
Still, when some allowance has been made, it remains
certain that Alice Perrers acquired estates in at least nineteen counties during her connection with the court, obtained a grant of the late queen's jewels, and scandalised
public opinion by appearing in courts of justice that she
might influence the judges in cases in which her own interests were concerned. Her power over the old king
was so unbounded that it was ascribed to sorcery; and
he treated her with the honour due to the first lady of
the land. In 1374 she presided as Queen of the Sun
over a great tournament in West Smithfield that lasted
for seven days.

The "Good Parliament."—It was the interest of
Alice Perrers, and scarcely less of the Duke of Lancaster,
to surround the king with unworthy ministers, their own
creatures, and to postpone the calling of Parliaments. For
more than two years (November 1373–April 1376) the
Estates were not consulted. But government by the
worst men of the country meant disaster abroad and embarrassment at home. When "the Good Parliament" at
last met (April 20, 1376), it was evident that men generally were eager for reform, and that the knights of shires
would be supported by a majority of the great earls,
under the direction of the Black Prince, who was gradually dying, but still able to advise.

Disposition of the Nobles.—The earldoms of
Pembroke and Oxford were held by minors. The Earls
of Devon and Angus were too aged to take much part in
public affairs, though the former, an old soldier, seems to
have been a partisan of Prince Edward's. The Earl of
Salisbury, whose first wife was now Princess of Wales,
his brother-in-law, the Earl of Suffolk, and the Earl

of Arundel, a young man, were probably not unfavourable
to the Duke of Lancaster.   But the Earl of March, who
had married the daughter of the Duke of Clarence, and
whose wife could therefore claim before John of Gaunt,
was a large landowner, held the office of Marshal of England, and was a man of ability and character.   He had
the ardent support of the Earl of Warwick, who perhaps
partly ascribed his father's death to the duke; and the
Earl of Stafford, by marriage with a sister, was pledged
to the same cause.   Among the great barons, Lord Percy
and Guy de Brian were in the prince's party; and Lord
Neville sided with the duke.   Altogether the party of
the prince had a decided, though not a great, majority ;
but several of its members, such as Lord Stafford and
Lord Percy, were of doubtful loyalty, and did not care to
go to extreme lengths against a prince of the blood who
might one day be king.   What the Parliament might
effect, therefore, depended on the term of life that remained to the Black Prince.

Impeachments of Latimer and Stury.—The war
of parties began with the impeachment of the royal
chamberlain, Lord Latimer, by Sir Peter de la Mare, who
was steward to the Earl of March.   A strong case of em-
bezzlement was established against the late favourite, and
he was committed to the Tower and fined 30,000 marks.
But it was resolved to follow up the minor charge with
one of treason for betraying the king's council, and here
the prosecution, having it would seem a weak case, failed
to establish anything.   Certain merchants of London, who
had been concerned with Latimer in cheating the Treasury
by fictitious debts, were next proceeded against; Sir
Richard Stury, a Lancastrian, and suspected of heresy,
was put out of the Council and imprisoned ; Lord Neville
was called to account for disorders committed by soldiers

in his pay; and Alice Perrers was threatened with banishment if she ever promoted suits at law again, and was forced to swear that she would not venture again into the king's presence. But there were signs that the reforms carried in Parliament would be short-lived. Lord Latimer defied his judges by the riotous state he kept during his short captivity in the Tower, and, being a fluent speaker, procured his release on bail in a few weeks. Sir Richard Stury seems to have been equally fortunate, and had the audacity to visit the Black Prince on his deathbed. Prince Edward, with unabated fierceness, told him to come and see the sight he desired, adding, that he should certainly have been brought to trial and punishment if the prince had been spared to live a little longer.

Death of the Black Prince.—Not long after, the prince died (June 8). To the nation at large the loss seemed irreparable. He had been "the flower of English chivalry," "the Hector," "during whose life the English feared no invasion, under whose leadership they faced any enemy." It had been his singular fortune to win two of the greatest battles of the century, and carry off the highest honours in the third; the skill of his captains and the courage of his men making up for his own deficiencies in generalship. He risked his life as fearlessly as any common soldier, and was nearly cut down at Crécy. His last days brought him forward in England as the head of a popular party and the champion of national rights; but as soldier, statesman, and man, the Black Prince was of very vulgar mould. The same fault of attempting great strokes with inadequate means, which nearly proved fatal to him at Poitiers and at Navarrete, inspired him in the fatal policy of the Spanish war. The pride of birth that made him side with Pedro the Cruel, because his rival was a bastard; the pride of race that led him to treat his

Gascon allies as inferiors, and persist in taxing a privileged community; and that worse pride of a vindictive mind, which led him to order the murder of prisoners in cold blood at Poitiers and at Limoges, and to command a general massacre, are the most distinct traits of a character that made him detested in Aquitaine, and would probably have provoked revolt in England had he ever come to the throne. He was religious after the fashion of his times, a devotee at the shrines of popular saints, and gave freely to monasteries. But his piety never induced him to spare an abbey in his line of march; and his advice to the Free Companies that they should gain their livelihood by ravaging France was as faithless as barbarous. Though not a vulgar profligate like the Duke of Lancaster, he was a man of low morality. Altogether, England could scarcely have found a more fatal leader than the Black Prince; uniting, as he did, the dazzling qualities of a knight-errant to the lust of war for its own sake, and to the ferocity that make conquest doubly accursed, and the retention of foreign dominion impossible.

Last Reforms of the Good Parliament.—Among Englishmen of the day, however, reverence for the dead hero was stronger than any other sentiment; and the Good Parliament never lost the consciousness of strength and reforming impulse with which the prince had inspired it. John of Gaunt sounded the Estates with a proposal to declare himself next heir after Richard of Bordeaux, to the exclusion of his brother Lionel's daughter, the Countess of March; in other words, to introduce the Salic law into England. The Estates not only refused, but requested that the young prince might come before them, so that the Lords and Commons might see and honour him as the real heir-apparent of the kingdom. The formal presentation took place accordingly (June 26). The

popular victory was followed up by a measure intended
to assure it. Early in the session it had been represented
that the king's council was too small, and not sufficiently
composed of persons of high rank; and the King had
agreed that ten or twelve earls, prelates, and great barons
should be added. These were now appointed in Parliament. The Archbishop, and the Bishops of London and
Winchester, the Earls of Arundel, March, and Stafford;
Lords Percy, Brian, and Beauchamp, and the three chief
ministers for the time being, who were then Sir John
Kryvet, the chancellor, Sir Robert Ashton, the treasurer,
and Roger Beauchamp, chamberlain. This list did not
include the name of the Duke of Lancaster, but it is probable that he and the Earl of Cambridge always sate in
council in virtue of their rank. It is more noticeable
that, except the Primate, who could not well be omitted,
it did not include the name of a single Lancastrian, unless
the Earl of Arundel might be considered one. That the
Earl of Warwick's name was omitted, was probably due
to an outrage lately committed by his tenantry, who
having a quarrel with the Abbey of Evesham, had attacked
it, killed some of the dependants, and ravaged the park
and demesne lands as in time of war. The earl was
known to have encouraged this gross outrage upon public
order, and his guilt served to discredit the whole party of
reform. Still, with two Beauchamps in the council, the
family interest was well represented. Not content with
the mere change of ministry, the Estates petitioned that
for the future Parliament might meet once a year. This
was no new demand; for the right had been recognised
under Edward II. and in the beginning of the present
reign. The king replied, accordingly, that "there were
statutes and ordinances made which should be duly kept
and observed." To these successful demands for constitu-

tional safeguards, more than two hundred other petitions were added, embracing every variety of grievance, from unjust taxation, papal usurpations, and oppressions by royal officers, down to the unjust demands of labourers for higher wages, and the use of unlawful engines in fisheries. These were variously entertained according to their subject, but generally received a gracious, though sometimes an evasive, answer. Then the Parliament was dissolved.

Change of Ministry.—Within a few days all its measures were reversed. The trial of strength came on the question of appointing a governor in Ireland, where the natives for some time past had been very formidable and where William de Windsor, the husband of Alice Perrers, was king's lieutenant. The council determined to supersede him by Nicholas de Dagworth, who had served in France, and had been sent a year before into Ireland to inquire into its financial administration. To Alice Perrers it was a matter of the greatest importance that her husband should not be superseded by one whom she regarded as his personal enemy, and who had probably reported unfavourably upon him. As the Duke of Lancaster declined to interfere in the matter, she again forced herself upon the old king, and procured the withdrawal of Dagworth's commission, after it had been already made out. From that day everything returned to the old disorder. The new lords of the council were informed that the king had no need of their services, and Lancaster governed with a council composed of creatures of his own. Lord Percy was bought over, Lord Latimer restored to favour, and though the great officers of state were continued for a time, they had no real power. Richard Lyons was pardoned and restored in full. The Earl of March, ordered on foreign service, thought it safer to resign his

post as Marshal of England, than to go on an expedition
in which the chances of assassination would be added to
those of war. Sir Peter de la Mare was thrown into
prison. The Bishop of Winchester was deprived of his
temporalities on pretence of misconduct in the council,
and forbidden to come near court. So infatuated was
the old king, that he was not ashamed to transact public
business with Alice Perrers seated at his bedside, and
interposing remarks or giving orders. But the general
business of the country was no doubt transacted by the
duke in council.

The Packed Parliaments.—By the end of the year
Lancaster felt strong enough to meet Parliament again,
and writs were accordingly issued for a new election
(Dec. 1). So cleverly was it manipulated that only twelve
members were returned on the popular side. As soon as
the result was known, the acting chancellor, treasurer,
and chamberlain were replaced by men of more pliant
politics ; and when the Estates actually met, twelve of the
duke's most powerful partisans were nominated a standing
committee to advise the Commons in matters of state. It
is noticeable that John of Gaunt had many partisans
among the high clergy, so that in spite of an ordinance
issued in 1371 that churchmen should not be appointed
to great offices of state, the Bishops of Worcester and St
Davids were now chancellor and treasurer. Others among
his supporters were John Gilbert, Bishop of Hereford, in
whose diocese the duke was very powerful, an eloquent
but dishonest man ; and Ralf Ergham, of a Yorkshire
family, who was almost as unpopular as Latimer. Among
the Lancastrian earls, Warwick and Stafford were now
reckoned, the former being probably at the king's mercy
for his misconduct in Warwickshire. The barons were
the renegade Percy, and three old soldiers who had served

with the duke in France, Fitz-Walter, Ros of Hamlake,
and Basset of Drayton.   Under such guidance, the Commons were easily induced to revoke all the acts of their
predecessors.   They coupled a grant of money with a request that Alice Perrers, Lord Latimer, Richard Lyons, and
all the other offenders who had been condemned by false
suggestions and without due process of law in the last
Parliament, should be restored to their houses and estates.
The request was, of course, cheerfully granted.   But a
petition of the clergy of Canterbury for the Bishop of
Winchester was decisively put aside; and the great
churchman owed his restoration, on payment of a heavy
fine, to the mediation of Alice Perrers some months later.

Trial of Wycliffe.—Yet a small circumstance showed
how insecure John of Gaunt's power was.   The day after
Parliament was dissolved (Feb. 23, 1377), the Primate
and the Bishop of London held a court of inquisition in St.
Paul's, under instructions from the pope, to investigate
certain charges of heresy against Dr John Wycliffe.
Wycliffe, an Oxford man by training, had been employed
by the crown in diplomatic matters, touching the pope's
right of presentation to benefices, and the relations of
France and England.   Like most graduates of Oxford,
Wycliffe had a strong feeling against the mendicant friars;
as an English clergyman he disliked the rights which the
pope claimed over the English Church; and as a patriot
he was offended at the undisguisedly French feeling of the
pope and cardinals.   In all these matters he had a strong
party at his back.   The very last Parliament had legislated
against the pope's interference with benefices.   A large
party of officials was prepared to support any churchman
against his order; and the Duke of Lancaster was Wycliffe's avowed patron.   The Primate, his principal judge,
was certain to temporise; but the Duke of Lancaster and

Lord Percy thought proper to assist in person at the trial
in sight of the interest they took.   An altercation began
by Percy's ordering a chair to be placed for Wycliffe, who
was an aged man.   The Bishop of London declared that
it was against all usage for an accused person to sit in his
judges' presence.   The duke instantly struck in, and at
last told the bishop, who was a Courtenay and allied to
royalty, that he trusted in his kinsmen, who should have
enough to do to defend themselves; and wound up with
a threat that he would drag the bishop out of church by
the hair of his head.

Riot in London.—These outrageous words were the
signal for a riot which terminated all the proceedings. The
duke left St Paul's, and the bishop succeeded in calming
the people, who were inclined to follow John of Gaunt to
the Savoy Palace and burn it over his head.   But they
tore down his arms and hung them up reversed in the
market-place, killed a priest who told them that Sir Peter
de la Mare was a traitor, and then, hearing by accident
that the duke and Percy were dining with a rich merchant,
rushed to the house and would have killed them if they
had not hastily taken boat and fled for shelter to the
Princess of Wales at Kensington.   It seems certain that
no religious question was involved in this disturbance.
No charge of false doctrine, except in relation to the pope's
power, was brought against Wycliffe; and a little later
the people of London were among his warmest supporters.
They sided with their bishop because his father and himself had favoured the legislation of the Good Parliament;
their first thought was to release Sir Peter de la Mare;
and their anger was entirely directed, not against Wycliffe
or his followers, but against the duke and his supporters.

Death of Edward III.—Nevertheless, there was
peace in England till the old king died. The Lancas-

trians dared not provoke further resistance; the Reformers were content to bide their time. Edward had been gradually sinking for months, and was left in his last days altogether to the care of Alice Perrers and her daughter. She is accused of keeping the clergy from him, of cheating him with hopes of restoration to health, and, when she found him actually dying, of drawing the rings from his fingers and leaving him. It is probable that, in fact, she was jealous of other influences, and she may have fled when the news of his death might occasion a riot directed against herself; but her interests were so entirely bound up with the king's life, that she may be credited with having discharged the duties of a careful nurse. One priest was present at the last, heard the king murmur the name of Jesus, held the crucifix before him for his last kiss, pronounced absolution, and closed his eyes in death (June 21, 1377). "It is goodly to believe that he obtained mercy, although he was seduced, or rather overcome with certain vices; yet the affection of his gentle mind, the great innocence which he used since his mother's womb, his mercy and abundant contrition before his death were accounted to him for health or salvation." "He excelled in a singular graciousness," says another chronicler, "and was of such stoutheartedness that he never turned pale for any danger he might be in. He was a father to the fatherless, suffering with the afflicted, grieving with the wretched, raising up the oppressed, and succouring the needy. Liberal above all men in largess; mixing as an equal with his inferiors, and showing himself chief among princes. Curious and careful in architecture. He was well-shaped, and of middle height, with a face like an angel's, more venerable than belongs to human mortality. Down to the time of his old age he governed his kingdom vigorously, wisely, and greatly; and it seemed to his subjects as if to live under his rule was to reign." " A merciful king, of peace conservator," says an old English version of his epitaph, and quaint as the praise may sound for him who began the hundred years' war, it expresses the feeling of the times, that under him England was safe from insult.

CHAPTER IX

THE RESULTS OF FOREIGN AGGRESSION.

Resemblance between the Policies of Edward I. and Edward III.—Nothing can seem more opposed at first sight than the lines of policy pursued by Edward I. and Edward III. The first was willing to resign his possessions in France that he might consolidate Scotland and England. The second renounced his claims upon Scotland that he might carry the war with France to a successful conclusion. Yet in fact Edward III. did but adopt and develop under changed circumstances the policy of his grandfather. He also desired primarily to reduce Scotland, and was well content to hold Aquitaine under the old conditions. His pretensions to the crown of France were a mere afterthought of policy, devised partly in retaliation for the arrogant interference of Philip of Valois. He long hesitated to quarter the arms of France; he renounced them without reluctance. It is the great justification of his French wars that they were forced upon him by the pretension of a foreign prince, his ally, kinsman, and suzerain, to prescribe the boundaries of English territory. At last, when it became a question not only of conquest in Scotland but of self-respect and independence in England, the king ventured to draw the sword against a power five times as great as his own.

The anxiety with which the most remote alliances were at first courted, the Emperor bought over, and the weavers of Flanders treated on an equal footing, shows how little Edward and England were aware of their real strength. But a few years changed this feeling of diffidence. Wherever Englishmen met an enemy, by sea or by land, it might almost be said on whatever terms of inferiority, they conquered as certainly as if victory were the birth-right of the English race, or Englishmen what they have since been called " the hereditary nobility of mankind." Naturally enough, a new change came upon the English people. The industrious, unwarlike race, whom French-men not a century ago vaunted as cowards, were gradually transformed into the knights-errant of the world; and the dreams of conquest and plunder on the Continent replaced the statesmanlike though disastrous policy which had led the first Edward to attempt the incorporation of Scotland with England. But it must always be borne in mind that the change came gradually. Edward I. desired to effect Scotch vassalage by process of law not by armed conquest; and it was long before his people seconded his later and warlike policy with any heartiness. At the beginning of his French campaigns Edward III. would have renounced his claims and his prospects across the channel for a secure and honourable peace; and as late as 1344 the Bishops, Lords, and Commons requested the king to bring the war to an end either by battle or by a suitable treaty if he could negotiate one. But it is the curse of war that it engenders war. Dunbar and Falkirk led up to Crécy and Poitiers, and these in turn to Navarette, and so on through a hundred years of miserable bloodshed.

Effects of the Scottish War.—The practical ob-jects aimed at by Edward I. had been to secure the service of Scotch troops in war, and perhaps to gain some slight accession of revenue from the fines for justice paid to the English courts. These hopes were destroyed for ever by that very battle of Dunbar which appeared to reduce Scotland from the position of an almost independent fief to that of an English province. Scotland was now an active enemy, connected by the closest alliance with France. Not even during the short period when it was nominally subdued, did it ever add to the strength or treasure of England; whenever England was threatened with foreign war it became necessary to watch the Scotch frontier, and at times the Scotch felt strong enough to challenge their neighbour to war unsupported. Nor was the political separation of the two countries the only evil. In the reign of Edward I. the Scotch could not be distinguished from their southern neighbours by dialect, and it was their habit gradually to adopt the laws of England and the explanation of English lawyers. The difference of language and law, which proved so great a barrier to union in later centuries, dates from the English attempt to enforce suzerainty. In one respect, undoubtedly, Scotland gained by its war of independence. Its people were welded into an unconquerable race, with a national history and honourable traditions, and with a half foreign civilisation, which in some respects was higher than England could have imparted. But if we set against this the miserable havoc of war, the destruction of towns, and the desolation of the country, the bitter war between the Scotch patriots and the English partisans, on the borders or in Galloway, or that inveterate hatred of Scot and Englishman which made either nation at times attempt to exterminate the other, it is difficult not to regard Edward I., great though he be as legist, general, and statesman, with feelings in which reprobation and horror predominate.

IIis best excuse must be that he probably believed himself to be enforcing a just claim; his punishment would perhaps have been sufficient if he could have seen a century and a half later what the results of his policy had been.

The English lose their Hold on Ireland.—For not only did the Scotch war sever Scotland from England, but it broke our power in Ireland. The mere invasion by Edward Bruce, unsuccessful as it at last proved, would not have done this. But the hundred years' war did it effectually. Ireland had been the colony, so to speak, into which the surplus English population emigrated; and during the 13th century the tide of English settlement poured steadily into it, and Dublin became an important commercial city with a university (1320). Ulster was really subject to an English earl, and the subjugation of Meath and Connaught was several times attempted during the reign of Edward I., and was a mere question of time. In the first years of Edward III. Ireland brought in a large sum, £30,000 a year, it was said, to the royal exchequer. As late as 1310 we hear of fresh arrivals of colonists, whom the Irish designate "the black English." But England, drained by war, was in no condition to spare population to Ireland, and the scanty English and well-affected Irish tribes were constantly called to supply recruits for Edward II.'s and Edward III.'s campaigns. In other respects Ireland was left pretty much to itself during the greater part of Edward III.'s reign, and there was almost constant war between English and Irish, or between the great Irish chiefs. As the English settlers conformed to the habits and espoused the interests of the natives, a distinction grew up between the English born in Ireland, "Irish dogs," as they were called, and the "English hobs" (or ponies) who were born in England, and whom the government at Dublin marked out for special favour.   In 1340 Edward III. went so far as to direct that all Irish and all English who had intermarried with the Irish should be removed from office, but a convention at Kilkenny forced him to rescind this impolitic order.   Nevertheless, the Duke of Clarence, four times lieutenant in Ireland (1361–1367), having conceived a profound distrust of the Irishry, signalised his last year of office by passing a statute at Kilkenny, which was equivalent to a declaration of war against the native race.   By this, which was partly based on an English statute ten years old (1357), the English were again forbidden to intermarry with the Irish, to make them nurses or sponsors, or to sell armour to them, under penalty of high treason.   Englishmen speaking Irish or adopting the Irish dress, were to be treated as Irishry, and Englishmen using Brehon law were to be accounted traitors.   No Irish were to be admitted to benefices.   The Englishry were to practice warlike exercises, to abstain from civil war, and only to war with the Irish by leave of the Council.   It is noticed incidentally that "the common (English) labourers were for the greater part absent, and fled out of the said land."   This statute did not strengthen the English power in Ireland. Two years later (1369) the English of Munster were defeated "with indescribable slaughter," and Limerick, one of their oldest strongholds, was taken from them and burned.   In 1375 the English of Downpatrick were defeated with the loss of several of their leaders.   It was necessary to apply to England for aid, and a royal brief to the king's subjects in Ireland complains of the heavy and intolerable expenses of the war lately waged there. How completely our sovereignty was lost will appear from a single fact.   The Duke of Clarence was heir, in right of his wife, to the estates of the earldom of Ulster.

But neither he nor his son-in-law, the Earl of March, could ever recover the property. It was seized by two kinsmen of the De Burgs, who renounced the English name and governed in their own right.

Character of Edward III.'s Foreign Policy.— Abroad, Edward's policy was unfortunate, though not always by his own fault. The war with France was forced upon him, and though his own attack upon Scotland was undoubtedly the first occasion of it, it is certain that the conduct of the French king was everywhere high-handed and violent, and that France provoked the struggle which so nearly ruined it. Of Edward's conduct throughout the first thirty years of the war as statesman and general, it is difficult to speak too highly. He cannot be blamed for the attempt to ally himself with Germany, costly and useless as it proved, and having once learned by experience of what stuff his imperial ally and the German princes were made, he showed a wise caution in severing the connection promptly and for ever. But throughout the contest he retained the sympathies of all who spoke the German tongue, except the House of Luxembourg and its dependants. Thrown on his own resources, he created allies in Artois, Flanders, and Brittany, never turning back any who had a common purpose with himself. His support of Pedro the Cruel was undoubtedly the fatal mistake of his reign. Having fought for his life against a Spanish fleet at the battle of the Downs, and being next neighbour in Aquitaine to the kingdom of Castile, he rightly appreciated the importance of a Spanish alliance, and he perhaps knew enough of Pedro's undoubted ability to believe that he would triumph over any rebellion. Probably Edward was influenced by the counsels and wishes of the Prince of Wales. But

though the enterprise deserved to fail because it was
unjust, was undertaken with insufficient resources, and
was based on no certain knowledge of the country. it
merits attention, as it shows the grasp of Edward's policy.
He was at the same time treating for the marriage of
his son Lionel to the heiress of the Duchess of Milan,
and the King of Navarre was professedly his ally. By
the union of the Basque provinces all danger from a
Spanish fleet would be at an end; by the alliance with
Castile, Navarre, and Milan, the English duchy of
Aquitaine would be secure against all attacks from
France. Bertrand du Guesclin understood well, when
he led a second army into Spain, that he was fighting
the English quite as much as their treacherous and
discarded ally.

Relations of England and Flanders.—In judging
Edward's relations with the Flemings, it must be borne
in mind that there were in fact three parties in Flanders; the party of the count, embracing nobles and
knights; the party of Ghent, representing the strongest
popular feeling of the times; and the party of Bruges
and other towns, which sometimes sided with Ghent and
sometimes turned to the count. Ghent was the real
stronghold of English influence, and the death of James
van Artevelde, who claimed relationship with Queen
Philippa, was a heavy blow to the alliance. Nevertheless, the Flemings, having indeed a common cause
with England against the French pirates, behaved with
signal loyalty till the capture of Calais. They were not
well pleased when Edward decided to keep that town in
his own hands. A little later, when the truce between
England and France exposed them to bear the sole brunt
of the war, they sent an embassy to England to learn
what assistance they might expect. Edward replied

that he would help the Flemings as they had helped him ; and finding that they misunderstood his answer to mean that he would support them with his whole power, explained that he would furnish troops, but that they must defray the expenses of the war. There was great indignation when this answer was reported in the Low Countries; and it probably influenced the determination of Bruges and other towns to make terms with their count. Ghent was divided, but so far English that it required to be reduced by an armed force. The Earl of Lancaster was sent over to negotiate a treaty by which Flanders was to remain neutral during the war. It was probably the best possible termination to an alliance which had served the ends of both parties, giving Edward Calais, and securing the Flemish towns in their franchises. From that time, accordingly, Flanders, fortunately for itself, enjoyed peace till the end of Edward's reign, though the old political parties were not extinct. In 1358 the French party drove out the English merchants, and in 1367 a conspiracy was formed in the English interests, for which several burgesses of Tournay, Artois, and other places suffered death. But neither these incidents nor the naval action in 1372 were allowed by statesmen to disturb a peace which was equally profitable to both countries. Moreover, the Flemings had imbibed a profound respect for English courage, which seems to have survived the long series of our disasters in France.

The King's good faith towards France.—By an article in the treaty of Brétigni, Edward reserved to himself the right of creating the province of Aquitaine into a kingdom. It is not improbable that he contemplated some such policy in favour of a younger son, and could it have been carried out, England would have gained the loss of a costly dependency, while France, for a time at least, would have been dismembered, and perhaps would have split up, like Germany, into a number of hostile principalities. On the other hand, by retaining Calais, England gained a valuable commercial entrepôt, a guarantee against French piracies in the Channel, and a point from which invading armies might start. It is not to be wondered at if the king and baronage were determined at all hazards to defeat this policy. Against Edward himself they had no tolerable cause of complaint. Even if it be true, as a French chronicler asserts, that Edward never executed the renunciations provided for by the treaty of Brétigni, it is certain that English commissioners were appointed for this very purpose, and probable that they were only withheld from carrying it out by diplomatic difficulties ; certain that Edward renounced the obnoxious titles in practice, and certain also that this argument was never seriously urged till long after his death. In all other respects Edward was punctiliously honourable. It was very much through his counsels that the civil war in Brittany was brought to a close. He could not by any mere command recall the adventurers who were ravaging France, and whose profits from brigandage were greater than any sentence in Edward's courts could outweigh, but he offered to take the field in person against them. On the other hand, Edward's French adversaries behaved with signal dishonour. Philip de Valois aided Scotland, and prepared for an invasion of England, while he was still nominally at peace. King John wrote privately to disown the covenants he proposed to enter into at Windsor ; and spent the last months of his life in England in importuning Edward for a remission of his ransom, and in secretly exporting arms and specie to be used in the next war. Both he and his son entertained appeals from Aquitaine after they had renounced the right solemnly; and Charles negotiated a treaty of conquest with Henry of Castile, while he was lavishing protestations of friendship upon the English court. The only charge of bad faith that attaches to the English Government is from the conduct of the Prince of Wales in sending his army out of Aquitaine, in the certainty that they could only quarter themselves upon France, and perhaps with the advice that they should do it. Such an act, though disavowed by Edward III., who denounced the penalties of treason against offenders, amply justified the French reprisals. But in fact there could be no sure peace between nations whose struggle had been so bloody and intolerate, while one was still encamped as a conqueror in the fatherland of the other. "Paix n' arez jà s'ilz ne rendent Calais" was the burden of a French song a few years later. And the English hatred of France was no less deep-seated. "The English-men have hated the realm of France more since the peace than they did before," say the French Estates, when King Charles consults them on the question of venturing again into war.

Chivalrous Sentiments of the Times.—It is some-times believed that the horrors of the hundred years' war were so mitigated by the spirit of chivalry, that English and French were like brothers-in-arms, and parted from the battlefield with no more rancour than from a tour-nament. It is true that Edward III. was more than any of our kings the knight crowned. Not incapable of great political combinations, he loved adventure for its own sake so passionately that he would risk kingdom and life for it, and at times fought like a common soldier in the ranks, or disguised himself that he might contend on equal terms in tournament. How he valued knightly punctilio; how he scorned the cruelty of the French kings and disdained to take reprisals; how he loved music and architecture and all that refines the taste, has been variously recorded.   Nor can it be doubted that there were many among his courtiers and soldiers, from Chandos downwards, who were like-minded with himself. But the boasted courtesy of the times will not bear examination.   It was confined pretty much to English and French; Spaniards, Germans, and Scotch were confessedly governed by rougher and sterner codes.   In its greatest extent it only modified the practice of war between gentlemen of fortune.   It was still a principle that the life and fortune of a prisoner were at the mercy of his captors; only in the case of rich men it became customary to accept a reasonable ransom, partly to avoid reprisals if no quarter were given, and chiefly because most men preferred enriching themselves to shedding blood.   But those from whom no ransom could be expected, received, as a rule, no quarter; and even nobles and knights were often refused mercy, or even killed in cold blood after surrender.   At the skirmish of Olivet, for instance, "none were taken to ransom."   A French knight who served in the Scotch army that took Berwick (1356), bought several English prisoners from his Scotch companions-in-arms, and killed them with his own hand to revenge his father's death.

Du Guesclin's Murder.—At the siege of Montcontour (1372), an English knight, to whom Bertrand du Guesclin owed money for the arrears of a ransom, thinking with some justice that Du Guesclin had no business to be in the field, reversed his scutcheon, and hung it from a gallows on the rampart.   Du Guesclin was so enraged at the insult that, on taking the town, he hanged his unlucky creditor from the same gibbet.   The conduct of the Black

Prince at Limoges has received its due meed of blame. But it was not unprecedented. When the King of Navarre and Sir Robert Knolles took Compiègne, they massacred a great part of the population for the crime of sympathising with the Jacquerie; and a body of 1,600 English troops, having shut up more than 600 peasants in a house at Longueuil St. Marie, were preparing to burn them alive, when they were defeated and driven away by a sally of the half-armed but desperate men.

Captain Marant.—After the surrender of Calais (1347) a few French ships that were in the harbour sailed out into the Channel, under a Captain Marant. They encountered a little flotilla of English transports, and, finding that they could not carry off the whole number as prizes, scuttled five of the ships, and cut the throats of seventy-five of the crews. Even ladies of rank were not safe from insult at the hands of regular soldiers, though King Edward and his captains did their best to protect them. Of the misery endured by peasants, the Jacquerie is conclusive proof. When the French troops came as allies to Scotland their habits of license were so intolerable that the people killed all stragglers, and the Estates forced them to make compensation in money.

Increase of Brigandage in England.—England itself suffered from the demoralisation of its people, who brought back the license of camps. In 1354 the Prince of Wales attended with an armed force to protect the judges on circuit in Cheshire, and it was thought necessary to renew the provisions of the Statute of Winchester (1285), by which the gates of towns were kept shut at night, strangers travelling after sunset arrested, the highways cleared 200 feet on either side, and the district made responsible for all robberies committed within it. But stringent as these regulations were, they were only effectual for a time, and in 1376 Parliament decreed a general arrest of vagrants, who, under the name of staff-stickers, went about in companies of three or four, and plundered the country people. It would seem that the prisons were crowded accordingly, for three years later the clergy obtained a general pardon for all escapes of felons out of the church gaols, kept by bishops and abbots. The poem of " Piers Ploughman " represents the plough-man's first enemy as the "Waster," who was "not wont to work," who recked " little of the law," and would have his will of the peasant's flour and meat. Calais was a notorious depôt for their goods. Nor were highwaymen or sturdy vagabonds the most dangerous disturbers of the peace. There was a general growth of lawlessness among soldiers and the retainers of great men, who hoped to earn pardon by their services, or to be secured by their masters' rank. Edward III. was far from blameless in his enforce-ment of the law. He celebrated the battle of the Downs by issuing pardons wholesale for various felonies, from robbery and conspiracy to murder, which his soldiers or their retainers and friends had committed (1350). Some years later (1355), Thomas de Lisle, bishop of Ely, who seems to have been a high-handed, violent man, and un-popular in his diocese, was fined £900 in court for some houses which, it was said, some of his men had burned on the property of the Lady Blanche Wake. The bishop's apologists say that he could not obtain justice in the king's court, because Lady Blanche was daughter of the king's cousin, the Duke of Lancaster. What is cer-tain is, that before the bishop's appeal could be decided his own chamberlain had committed a foul murder on one of Lady Blanche's squires; and a jury impanelled from the district found the bishop guilty of harbouring the assassin. Whatever the real merits of the case, as regarded Thomas de Lisle, may have been, it presents a curious spectacle of disorder. A bishop accused of sanctioning arson and murder, juries accused of conspiracy and perjury, public riots, and the king publicly declaring, " I take the quarrel into my own hands," and, it is said, charging the bishop as "an open liar" in Parliament. The attack on Evesham Abbey by the Earl of Warwick's retainers (1376) was a crying scandal of the time, and excited the king's special displeasure, yet no worse punishment than a fine, quite insufficient to make good the losses sustained, was imposed upon the powerful offender.

Frequent Parliaments.—There is no doubt that Edward III. was constrained, by the necessities of his policy, to summon Parliaments very often; so that as many as seventy met in the fifty years of his reign. Nor are signs wanting that the rights and privileges of all classes gained on the whole during the reign.

Statute of Treason.—All subjects, but especially the nobles, received a new security from a Statute of Treasons, which had the merit of defining, with something like precision, what offences against the king's person and dignity really were. Till this time the law had been so loose that almost any crime against the peace might be interpreted as an assumption of royal power; so that one man had been found guilty of treason for imprisoning a private enemy, and another for killing the king's messenger. By Edward III.'s statute (1357), treason against the king was limited to the compassing or imagining the death of the king or queen or of their oldest son and heir; to offences against the honour of the royal family; to levying war against the king in his realm or assisting his enemies; to slaying the king's judges; to counterfeiting his seal; or to the passing false money. Offenders in all these cases were to be attainted on probable grounds for open deeds by persons of their own rank ; a provision which was intended to exclude convictions for mere seditious talk or by common informers. As at this time the jury often gave evidence, it was added that no one bringing a charge of treason should be allowed to serve on the inquest. Besides this important guarantee of their lives and liberties, the peers obtained a recognition of their right to be tried only by their own order (1341), which does not seem to have been affected by the formal repeal of the statute two years later. These were solid advances in constitutional right. Several other laws were passed for a time, and afterward abolished or allowed to fall into disuse, which no doubt had a certain influence on public opinion. Of such kind are the law that "Parliament must be summoned at least once a year" (1330) ; the law that ministers were responsible to Parliament (1341) ; the ten times repeated confirmations of Magna Charta and of the Forest Charters ; and the frequent regulations against purveyance and other forms of unjust taxation. But these statutes are at least balanced by complaints, which show that the commonest rights of the subject were still insecure. Thus, in 1347, the Commons complained of customs' duties imposed by the king's council without consent of the Estates, and seem to have received no better answer than that it had pleased the king, the prelates, the earls, and other great men. Next year complaint was made of an ordinance respecting serfs, which the council had passed by their own authority and in violation of the common law. This time the reply was that the business should rest till the king's council had been better advised.

Influence of the Crown in Parliament.—After Crécy and Calais, Edward felt himself strong enough to disregard the Commons. Mixing freely with men of all classes, who were conciliated by his charm of manner, the king seems to have understood with rare tact precisely how far he could go in his encroachments on popular liberty. His power was for the most part great or small, as his foreign policy was successful or disastrous. In the Lower House the knights of counties seem to have been the really independent section; and in one session the presence of the burgesses can only be inferred from a casual entry in the Rolls of Parliament (1351). But the knights were a fluctuating body, and easily swayed by the court. The lawyers among them were accused of drawing up petitions for their private clients, which they caused to be included in the list of grievances presented to the king for redress. It was accordingly ordered on one occasion (1372) that they should not be returned as knights of the shire. Nothing, perhaps, better illustrates the real dependence of the Commons upon the court than the history of the two Parliaments of the last two years of Edward III.'s reign. Disaster abroad, bad administration at home, a corrupt court, an insolent church, and general distress, had produced a ferment in the country that might easily have become an armed rebellion. Supported by the Prince of Wales, and by more than half the peers, the Lower House actually succeeded in changing the ministry, and bringing the chief offenders to trial. But the death of the Prince of Wales left his party powerless. John of Gaunt, unpopular and incapable, but having entire influence over his father, succeeded in packing a Parliament that reversed almost every act of its predecessor; and the acts of this were in turn upset when a new king ascended the throne a few months later.

Increased Power of the Nobles.—A period of great wars is generally favourable to the growth of a nobility. Men who equipped large bodies of troops for the Scotch and French wars, or who had served with distinction in them, naturally had a claim for reward at the hands of their sovereign; and accordingly, though the earldom of March was forfeited in 1330, and though the Earls of Hereford died out in 1372, there were even more English peers of the first rank at the end of Edward's reign than there had been at the beginning. The number of barons summoned to Parliament averaged from forty to fifty during his reign; but, if anything, rather dwindled towards the end. This gradual diminution in numbers had been going on for a long time, as families died out from the want of heirs male. That it should be so slight in the reign of Edward III., when war and pestilence reduced the population in general by one-half or two-thirds, can only be explained by the fact that many new families had risen to baronial fortunes and rank. But the feeling of the times did not allow mere soldiers, however distinguished, to become barons of England. Sir John Chandos, the greatest soldier of his time, though member of a baronial family, and invested at one time with the highest office under the crown, never sat among the English peers. His military services and rank did not even protect him from insult and insubordination at the hands of the soldiers who served under him. The Earl of Oxford insulted him publicly; the Earl of Pembroke refused to obey his orders; and Sir Hugh Calverley could hardly be induced to take the post Chandos assigned him at the battle of Auray. This strong feeling of caste among the English nobles was undoubtedly one of our great weaknesses during the French wars. Even the king himself and the Prince of Wales could not secure obedience to their orders. Berwick was lost in 1355, because its governor, William de Greystock, chose to leave it that he might join

Edward III.'s march into France ; and a little later the
Earl of Oxford deserted the Prince of Wales in the march
that ended in the battle of Poitiers.   The expedition of
1370 broke up disgracefully because young men of family
would not obey Sir Robert Knolles, "the old moss-
trooper," as they nicknamed him.   This sentiment of caste
has left its mark on the legislation of the reign in a land
intended to promote entails, by repealing the statute of
Edward I., which only allowed a year and a day for
appeals against a fine levied in court ; that is, against a
public act of alienation of landed property.   The excuse
was that nobles and gentlemen engaged in the wars had
not time to look after their property, the real object
and effect to keep land in families.   The 13th century
had broken up estates all over England and multiplied
families of the upper class ; the 14th century was
consolidating properties again, and establishing a broad
division between a few powerful nobles and the mass of
the community.

Profits of War to Gentry and Yeomanry.—
But if the gentry, as an order, lost a little in relative
importance by the formation of a class of great nobles,
more distinct than had existed before, the middle-classes
of England, its merchants and yeomen, gained very much
in importance by the war.   Under the firm rule of the
" King of the Sea," as his subjects lovingly called Edward
III., our commerce expanded.   Englishmen rose to an
equality with the merchants of the Hanse Towns, the
Genoese, or the Lombards, and England for a time over-
flowed with treasure.   The first period of war, ending
with the capture of Calais, secured our coasts ; the
second, terminated by the peace of Brétigni, brought the
plunder of half France into the English markets ; and
even when Edward's reign had closed on defeat and

bankruptcy, and our own shores were ravaged by hostile fleets, it was still possible for private adventurers to retaliate invasion upon the enemy.   Picard, who entertained four kings; Philpot, who fitted out a fleet at his own charge; Exton who quarrelled with the lord chancellor, and put in two earls as sureties; Walworth, who distinguished himself against Wat Tyler; and John de Northampton, whose seditious practices provoked a special parliament, are a few of the merchant princes who ranked only second to barons in their day.   Nor were the chances for power then less glorious.   Sir Robert Knolles began life as "a poor valet of mean extraction;" Sir John Hawkwood is said to have been a tailor; Sir Robert Salle was "no gentleman born."   Froissart tells us that "two thousand who had ten or twelve horses of their own would shortly have been obliged to go on foot, if they had made no more war."   These freebooters were in great measure cleared off during the last years of the war. One of Froissart's informants told him that he knew of few besides himself that had not perished.   But their memory remained for good and for evil.   The romance of foreign conquest, of fortunes lightly gained and lightly lost, influenced English enterprise for many years to come.   And to men who remembered how the shafts of the English yeomanry had mainly won the day at Crécy, Poitiers, and Navarette, and on a hundred battlefields besides, the interval between knight and yeoman could not any longer appear immeasurable.

Depressed Condition of the Lower Orders.— The change to the lower orders during the reign arose rather from the frequent pestilences, which reduced the number of working men and made labour valuable, than from any immediate participation in the war.   In fact, English serfs, as a rule, did not serve in Edward's armies.

They could not be men-at-arms or archers for want of training and equipment; and for the work of light-armed troops and foragers, the Irish and Welsh seem to have been preferred. The opportunity of the serfs came with the Black Death while districts were depopulated, and everywhere there was a want of hands to till the fields and get in the crops. The immediate effect was unfortunate. Landowners, who were compelled to lower their rents in the land they farmed over, were not disposed to let the labour of their serfs slip from them; and the indifference of late years, when men were careless if their villans stayed on the property or emigrated, was succeeded by a sharp inquisition after fugitive serfs, and constant legislation to bring them back to their masters. The Bishop of Ely is said to have kept troops outside Norwich that he might arrest a runaway, and suits to reclaim bondsmen became part of the history of every monastery. On the other hand, some of the largest employers tempted men into their service by high wages, and protected them from pursuit. Under these circumstances, Parliament interfered again and again to protect the small gentry; and two Statutes of Labourers were passed (1349–1350), compelling workmen to offer their services, and fixing the rate of wages. These ordinances were added to and confirmed in three later Parliaments (1357, 1361, 1368), but down to the end of the reign the complaints of " valiant beggars " and of bondsmen declining labour were little abated. The leading idea of the legislator was that the labourer, whose work had doubled or trebled in value, was to receive the same wages as in years past; and it was enacted that he might be paid in kind, and, at last, that in all cases of contumacy he should be imprisoned without the option of a fine.

Effects of the Black Death.—It is curious that a

few years after the Black Death, in 1362, an attempt was
made to fix the stipends of the inferior clergy, who were
demanding and receiving higher pay.   They were a
privileged class, and their new salaries were determined in
convocation.   The rate was so inadequate, that it is
said many were forced to take to stealing.   Yet the worst
paid priest, who was properly not a married man, received
about as much as a skilled artisan.   It seems probable,
therefore, that the wages decreed by the Statutes of
Labourers were insufficient as they were certainly unsatisfactory.   Almost a worse grievance was that the lords in
many parts of the country claimed the right to exact again
the labour services, which it had been customary to exchange for rent.   In this way a part of the population was
practically brought back into serfdom, and constrained
to labour by irons and imprisonment.   Indignation and
resentment prevailed largely among the injured people,
who seemed to be all the more miserable for the false
splendour of the reign.

Commercial Relations to Italy and Germany.—
The French war contributed in many ways to heighten
the feeling of English nationality.   Our trade, our language, and our church received a new and powerful influence.   In the early years of Edward III.'s reign,
Italian merchants were the great financiers of England,
forming the taxes, and advancing loans to the Crown.
Gradually the instinct of race, the influence of the Pope,
and geographical position, contributed with the mistakes
of Edward's policy to make France the head, as it were,
of a confederation of Latin nations.   Genoese ships
served in the French fleet, Genoese bowmen fought at
Crécy, and English privateers retorted on Genoese commerce throughout the course of the reign.   In 1376 the
Commons petitioned that all Lombards might be ex-

pelled the kingdom, bringing amongst other charges against them that they were French spies. The Florentines do not seem to have been equally odious, but the failure of the great firm of the Bardi in 1345, chiefly through its English engagements, obliged Edward to seek assistance elsewhere; and he transferred the privilege of lending to the crown to the merchants of the rising Hanse Towns. In 1348 the Commons complained that all the tin of Cornwall was bought up and mostly exported by a German merchant. The relations with the Hanseatic and Prussian merchants were not always tranquil. They were a hard-fisted, practical race, apt to make reprisals if they were ill-treated; but their need of England, and England's need of them, prevailed in the long run, and a rupture ended in a new treaty of commerce with mutual concessions (1388). But this definite transfer of English commerce from Spain and Italy to Germany is the only certain result of Edward III.'s policy upon trade. Neither he nor his Council had any clear theory of promoting commerce, except by keeping the seas clear, and the legislation of one session was often repealed in the next. In 1364 perfect freedom of trade was authorized, and, in particular, the wine trade with Gascony was declared open to Englishmen and aliens alike. In 1368 it was confined to aliens, and in 1369 was again opened to such Englishmen as were large importers. By the end of the reign, however, all trade with France was practically at an end; the staple of wool was transferred from Calais to various English ports; and even the old trade with Flanders was embarrassed by the growth of the French party in every town except Ghent.

Disuse of the French Language, and General Use of English.—It is more easy to trace the steps by which the French language was discarded from our speech

and literature. It had come slowly in during the 12th
and 13th centuries; had been introduced into the law
courts in the reign of Richard I., and became the language
of official documents only under the first Edward. As
late as the second Baron's War it was the mark of a
foreigner not to be able to speak English. As, however,
French was the language in which our kings conversed
and our peers debated; the language of law, commerce,
and romance literature, it rather strengthened than lost
its hold with time. Roger Bacon tells us that in Henry
III.'s time, English, French, and Latin were currently
known, and Robert of Gloucester said in the next reign—

> "For but a man ken French one telleth of him lit (little)
> And low men holdeth to English as to their own tongue yet."

Under Edward III. the practice of schools was to teach
first French, then Latin, and English little, if at all.
Children in gentlemen's families were taught to speak
French, says one writer, "from the time that they be
rocked in their cradle," and at school were compelled "to
leave their own language and to construe their lessons in
French." The result was that many French phrases and
words strayed into the language even of the lower orders;
the ploughman went to his work with the song of "Dieu
vous sauve Dame Emme;" and the beggar implored alms
"pour sainte charité." Still there were always many who
never cared to acquire what after all was a strange language. The writer of the romance of Arthur and Merlin
says that he had seen many nobles who "could say no
French;" and Rolle, who died in 1349, says that he
wrote for laymen who understood nothing but English.
Nor was the French actually current; "French of Norfolk," as some called it; French "after the school of
Stratford-le-Bow," as Chaucer terms it; the language of
Paris or even of Bordeaux. At its best it was an anti-

quated dialect, mispronounced and interpolated with
foreign words. As spoken, it often "turned into English," to use the phrase of a French master. There
was therefore every reason for giving it up, and the
English war with France supplied the motive. Men had
been proud to speak the language of their Norman conquerors; they scorned to copy the conquered people. In
1362 the chief-justice, Sir Henry Green, opened Parliament with a speech in English, and a formal enactment
was passed that all pleas should henceforth be pleaded in
English and enrolled in Latin; the reason assigned being
that the French tongue was much unknown in the realm.
In spite of this statute the rolls of Parliament and other
proceedings still continued to be kept in French. But
the feeling which the ordinance expressed told upon
school teaching, and two schoolmasters, Cornwall and
Penkridge, having substituted English for French about
this time, or a little earlier, the change was introduced
everywhere within about thirty years. It is doubtful if
Edward III. knew English. His son certainly spoke it,
but not habitually. But Henry V. wrote letters in good
plain English. Naturally the change told last upon the
court. It is very noticeable in literature. Gower had
made a reputation by his French and Latin poems, when
the success of Chaucer as an English poet induced him to
attempt the great work by which he is chiefly known.
The popularity of the writings of Wycliffe and his followers
no doubt contributed also to familiarise the upper class
with their own language.

**Increased Power of the Church under Edwarp
II.**—The reign of Edward II. had been very favourable
to the power of the clergy. The mortmain laws, forbidding the alienation of land to the church, were constantly
set aside by special authorisations to purchase in favour

of particular monasteries. In the autumn of 1316 Edward II. was at York, and seems to have held an informal Parliament of nobles and clergy. The clergy took advantage of the absence of the Commons to get the royal assent to a series of decisions on disputed points of jurisdiction. The mischievous rights of church sanctuary to felons were extended again ; the spiritual courts got jurisdiction in matters concerning the clergy ; and it was enacted that no distraint should be levied within the old estates of the church. The church was not to be hindered by the state from excommunicating the king's subjects ; and in return, clergymen employed by the state were to be exempt from residence in their benefices. Altogether, more mischievous provisions than these " articles of the clergy," as they are called, could scarcely have been framed. Presently a new concession of great consequence was made. The pope, at the instigation of the King of France, had ordered an inquiry to be made into the conduct of the Knights Templar. This order of knighthood, founded to defend the Holy Sepulchre, had become generally odious from the pride and grasping character of its members, was flagrantly immoral, and was said on good grounds to be tainted with infidelity. After a process of some years, the pope thought it better to dissolve the order (1312). It now became a question in England what was to be done with the rich estates which the Knights Templar possessed. The king and nobles held that they ought to revert to the families of the original donors, since the order to which they were given had ceased to exist, and the judges being consulted, declared this to be their opinion also. Such a transfer would have been very useful in several ways; for the crown revenue was insufficient, the church lands on which military service could not be increased were already too numerous, and the day

for monastic and knightly order had quite gone by.   But
the pope and the English clergy disliked the precedent
of giving back church lands to the laity, and insisted that
the possessions of the Templars ought to be transferred
to the other crusading order of St. John of Jerusalem.
For eleven years Edward refused to carry out this bull,
though he seems to have given the Hospitallers (as the
Knights of St. John were sometimes called) temporary
possession of their rivals' lands in cases where the crown
was interested.   But in 1323 the De Spensers, who had
probably been bribed to support the claims of the Hospitallers, procured the passing of a statute by which the
transfer was formally decreed, and though it was not
thoroughly carried out till the next reign, the precedent
was in this way established that church lands could not
be forfeited for any abuse, or secularised again under any
circumstances.   Accordingly, though the numerous estates
of alien princes were repeatedly sequestered during the
French wars of the third Edward and his successors, they
were only kept in trust for the church, and either restored
in time of peace to their original possessors, or applied to
pious purposes in connection with English foundations.

National Church Favoured.—Under Edward III.
the clergy seemed to maintain their ascendancy.   Thirteen
churchmen of eminence were chancellors fifteen times,
while only four laymen rose to that dignity, and these
were forced on the king by Parliament.   The list of royal
treasurers shows that that office also was commonly held
by a bishop till during the last years of the reign.   The
reason of this strong preference for churchmen is uncertain.
Edward and his eldest son had their full share of superstition, and made frequent offerings to shrines.   Possibly,
when so many gentlemen were engrossed by war, it may
have been difficult to find laymen who were qualified for

the highest posts. But, as the king's predilection was
certainly not shared by Parliament, which petitioned in
1371 against the employment of clerks as not "justiceable,"
that is, as not answerable to law for their conduct, it is
probable that the king's real intention was to put law and
revenue under the conduct of pliant and unscrupulous
ministers accountable only to himself. The policy, however, had an effect which was not designed. Churchmen naturally recommended churchmen for employment,
and a number of tonsured officials grew into importance in the royal service, and came to regard the king
as their proper master. Now, the policy of the popes who
were living during the whole of the reign at Avignon,
and were mere creatures of the King of France, was
naturally French in the extreme. Whether it were David
of Scotland, or Philip or John of France, who wished to
embarrass English policy, he could always count upon the
support of the pope. It was the pope who contrived that
the heiress of Flanders should marry the Duke of Burgundy instead of the Earl of Cambridge. Whenever
France was hard pressed, cardinals came forward to mediate in the interests of humanity; and when fortune turned
against England, the interests of humanity seemed to be
forgotten at Avignon. At Calais, at Poitiers, and at
Brétigni, Papal nuncios were conspicuous by their regard
for French policy. Moreover, the pope, claiming to be
arbiter over princes, pronounced Edward's claim upon
France to be bad, and would not sign any document in
which the title of King of France was given to him. It
was a proverb in England after our victories, that the pope
had turned Frenchman and God English. Accident
brought about a formal rupture for a time. The Bishop
of Ely, Thomas de L'isle, whose quarrel with Lady Blanche
Wake has been mentioned, finding that the Primate took

the king's part, fled into France, and lodged a complaint against Edward at Avignon. The pope took the matter up warmly, and cited the English judges to appear before him. Some of these citations were actually brought into England in spite of the king's writ forbidding them, and were fastened to the doors of churches in the district of Ely. But none of the persons cited paid the smallest regard to them. Thus sentences of excommunication were promulgated, and the body of one who had died unabsolved was dug up and thrown outside the churchyard. This only increased the indignation in England, and the next papal emissaries who were captured were committed to Newgate, and died there of the severe treatment they sustained, or, by one account, on the gallows (1358). Thomas de L'isle dying, the matter was finally adjusted by diplomatists. But the victory rested with king and people ; and it shows the changed state of feeling in England that the king made no submission, though the pope went through the form of absolving him.

Popes unpopular under Edward III.—Under these circumstances, it is not wonderful if the legislation of the reign, though favourable to the native church, was hostile to its foreign head. The jurisdiction of the church in England was fenced round with additional securities ; so that the clergy, on proof of their orders, were exempted from punishment by the secular courts for any crime but treason. But when, in 1366, Pope Urban V. claimed the arrears of the yearly tribute of 1000 marks—granted by John in sign of vassalage, discontinued for seventeen years by Edward I., paid up by Edward II., and now disused again for thirty-three years—Parliament set the matter at rest for ever, by declaring that John had no right to bind the kingdom without consent of the Estates. Pope Urban had threatened process at law in his own court ; the

Estates replied that they would support the king in his resistance. So the disgraceful tribute was blotted out. But the connection with Rome was shown in other ways. The pope claimed the right of investing bishops, not only with the spiritual office, but with the lands and property of their respective sees. The crown habitually met this by forcing the bishops to sign a renunciation of the clauses in question. But the pope also claimed the right of appointing to bishoprics and private livings throughout England, by special deeds of grant, which were called provisions. This interfered with the rights of cathedral chapters and of lay patrons ; and as the papal nominees for benefices were often foreigners excused from residence, many parishes in England were deprived of their pastors, and many English clergymen of the preferment they might naturally have expected. As early as 1343, an Act was passed forbidding papal provisions to be brought into England ; and, by a statute of the next year, offenders were to be punished with outlawry or perpetual imprisonment, or were to abjure the realm. In 1353, these penalties, with forfeiture of goods, were extended to anyone who appealed from the king's courts to the pope's ; and, in 1364, all the legislation on the subject was consolidated and enlarged, with penalties against the persons presented and against their aiders and abettors. Like most laws of the time, these were not carried into effect at once. Edward even agreed, in 1375, to remit the penalties imposed by the statute ; but this was only an arrangement with the pope in favour of persons already presented, who could not decently be sacrificed. The Act remained in force, and was renewed under Richard II. (1390), and slightly added to under Henry IV. (1401). Before the end of the century it was so thoroughly established that the universities (1399) complained of the loss of the patronage, which the popes had often bestowed on deserving students. Yet the general effects of the measure were good; it freed parishes from absentees, took away from the clergy the inducement to look to Rome for reward, and made the Church of England more thoroughly national. For many years after Edward III.'s death, the popes were not men to whom patronage in any part of the Church could safely be entrusted.

Quarrel between the Universities and the Friars.—In connection with these statutes of Provisors, or Præmunire, as they are sometimes called from the first word of the royal writ for enforcing them, we may notice an ordinance (1366) requiring the Mendicant Friars to abstain from procuring bulls against the universities of Oxford and Cambridge. This had reference to a quarrel of long standing. The friars used every method to entice students into their orders; and many parents were accordingly afraid to send their sons to the universities. It was said the number of students had declined four-fifths in 1357; and if we allow for the effects of the Black Death and the war, a great falling off will appear probable. The universities, however, ascribed the decline chiefly to the friars, and ordered that they should receive no scholar of the university in future into their order till he was eighteen years of age. The restriction seems reasonable; and it is difficult to understand why the king repealed it, unless he hoped to re-establish peace by cancelling all changes that had been made during the quarrel. The result of his interference was, that the feud between the university and the orders was embittered, and that the friars got fresh confidence, and presently removed their applications to Rome for support. All the more did opinion in Oxford favour reformation in the church, and condemn the popes.

CHAPTER X

THE MINORITY OF RICHARD II.

Accession and Coronation of Richard II.—
Richard of Bordeaux came to the throne in a time of great
national peril.   A combined French and Spanish fleet
invested the coasts, ravaged the Isle of Wight, burned
Hastings, and obtained the fortress of Ardres, near Calais,
by the treason of its German commander.   In Aquitaine
the last English army sustained a ruinous defeat under
Sir Thomas Felton, and the general and many gentlemen
of the province were taken prisoners.   There was war
again on the Scotch borders, and the town of Roxburgh,
then held by the English, was burned, with the slaughter
of all its people.   It was impossible to attempt any
reprisals, for the treasury was quite empty, and it seemed
inexpedient to summon Parliament while the harvest was
still out, and the coasts still in danger.   During eight
years of peace the receipts of the English exchequer,
swelled by ransoms and other occasional sources, had
averaged £140,000 a year.   No economies had then been
made, partly, perhaps, because there were old arrears to
discharge, but chiefly, no doubt, because Edward III.
delighted in the magnificence of a sumptuous court, and
was a patron of the arts, and a liberal giver.   The habit of
expense lingered on even when the state of the country
demanded instant retrenchment; and the young king's

coronation was a scene of costly profusion. In October
the Estates met to consult on the public needs.

Balance of Parties in the Government.—The
first reform that the country desired was unquestionably
a change of government. There seemed every reason to
anticipate it. John of Gaunt had abated his old pride,
shown himself the most courteous and affable of men in
public, and was known to meditate leaving England to
vindicate his title to the crown of Castile. Sir Peter de
la Mare was released from prison, and was again elected
Speaker of the Commons. When it became a question of
naming a committee of peers to advise with the Commons,
the names were selected evenly from both parties; and
the Duke of Lancaster took advantage of the interim to
vindicate himself from the charges of treason that had
been brought against him in the Lower House. But
though the Commons excused themselves, and pointed
out that they had asked him to advise them, they recommended the nomination of a council, on which only two
out of nine were Lancastrians. The duke was strong
enough to disconcert this arrangement, and the list actually
selected was taken evenly from the two parties, comprising the Bishop of Salisbury and Lord Latimer among the
Lancastrian six. So, too, the Lancastrians retained a full
share of the great offices of state, the Lancastrian chancellor being retained, and an old official, the Bishop of
Exeter, made treasurer. Nominally, little was done in
the way of reform. But the Commons were allowed to
appoint two commissioners to receive and disburse the
money from the new taxes; and they punished Alice
Perrers for her malpractices by banishment and forfeiture. Her husband afterwards succeeded in getting
the sentence of exile reversed, and a part of her lands
restored.

Unpopularity of the King's Uncles.—It was soon evident that the Duke of Lancaster was still the real ruler of the country. As soon as the season for warlike preparations approached, he succeeded in getting complete control of the finances, under the excuse of fitting out a great expedition. But party feeling ran so high that the nominal division of power between the two factions only served to paralyse the English arms. When Thomas of Woodstock, the duke's younger brother, engaged a Spanish fleet, a portion of the English crews positively refused to assist him, in spite of the urgent remonstrances of their commander, Lord Fitz-Walter. But for this mutiny, it was said, the whole Spanish fleet would have been destroyed. A disaster of the same kind occurred again when the Duke of Lancaster's fleet put to sea. Sir Hugh Courtenay engaged the Spaniards with the vanguard, and was overpowered and taken prisoner, through the fault, it was said, of John of Gaunt, who did not come up in time to support him. When the duke at last put to sea, he was beaten back disgracefully at St Malo. Nevertheless, fortune this year, on the whole, favoured the English. The King of Castile was involved in a war with Portugal; the French coasts were ravaged, and Cherbourg occupied; and the Scotch were beaten at sea, and induced to conclude a truce. Everything seemed to show that the nation had lost none of its warlike genius, when its enterprises were conducted by nobles or gentlemen, and not interfered with by John of Gaunt. An unhappy accident added to his unpopularity.

Hawley and Schakel.—Among those who followed him from England, to assist the invasion of Spain by the Black Prince, had been a Lincolnshire gentleman, Robert Hawley, who had distinguished himself in the French wars by taking the Castle of Havre. Hawley and a

brother-in-arms, Schakel, were lucky enough to capture a
Spanish prince of the blood, the Conde de Denia, at the
battle of Navarette, and agreed to take Alfonso, the eldest
son of their prisoner, as a hostage for the father's ransom,
which seems, later on, to have been fixed at the enormous
sum of 75,000 Spanish doubloons, or about £46,000. It
was always a question whether the crown might not claim
an important prisoner ; but, in this case, Hawley and
Schakel arranged, in 1376, that they should receive £3000
for expenses, should pay the Prince of Wales 5000 doubloons, and should give the king a third of the remainder.
So matters stood till the accession of Richard, when John
of Gaunt thought it desirable for his own interests in
Spain, or, as he said, for the kingdom's, that a prisoner of
such importance should not be allowed to return. He
tried to buy the young count of his captors, but offered too
small a price, and they, imagining, it would seem, that he
only wanted money, were willing to give him £1000 for
a passport to take the prisoner out of England. Certain
persons were then induced to set up a claim in the king's
courts to a part share in the prisoner, and Hawley and
Schakel were ordered to produce him. They concealed
him, and were committed to the Tower by Parliament
(Oct. 1377). After a captivity of some months, during
which the young count could not be traced, the prisoners
seem to have been brought out again for trial in court, and
contrived to knock down their guard and escape to the
sanctuary at Westminster. The Duke of Lancaster was
just then at St Malo, but the council took up the matter
warmly, and commissioned Sir Ralf Perrers, an official of
long standing, and Sir Alexander Boxhull, the governor of
the Tower, to take a company of fifty men-at-arms and
bring away the fugitives. Unhappily, the cause of the
two men was popular; the right of asylum was prized;

and the men-at-arms, fearing a rescue, and enraged at
Hawley's gallant resistance, slew him on the steps of the
altar, and killed one of the church servants who remonstrated at his side. Schakel surrendered, and was taken
back to prison. There can be no doubt that Hawley was
foully murdered. But when the archbishop and five
bishops excommunicated all who had counselled or abetted
the violation of the mischievous rights of asylum, only
excepting the king, the king's mother, and the Duke of
Lancaster, though they did no more than public sentiment
demanded, they did enough to alarm and irritate statesmen.
Though the duke had been out of England, it was thought
he had been consulted in the matter, and it was certain
the measures taken had been in his interest. When
he returned to England he spoke sharply against his
old enemy the Bishop of London, who had refused to
confer with the council before publishing the sentence of
excommunication, and said that, if the king desired it, he
would ride to London and bring back the malapert bishop
to answer for himself before the council, in spite of the
London rabble. It was said he meditated a general attack upon the church at the next Parliament, the imposition of heavy taxes, and the abolition of mischievous
privileges.

Support of Wycliffe by Government.—Other
circumstances favoured this supposition. The prosecution
of Wycliffe had been renewed in the early part of 1378,
and a number of fresh charges had been brought against
him, still bearing more, however, on church government
than on church doctrine. In fact, the two were inextricably connected in Wycliffe's mind. Ardently disliking
the papal rule, he embraced every opinion that undermined
it; declared that laymen might arraign the pope; that
he could not excommunicate any who were not cut off

from Christ by their own acts; that the church might be
deprived of its temporalities if it failed to discharge its
duties; and that the secular power was bound to despoil
a corrupt church under pain of damnation. These views
were not likely to be acceptable in the highest quarters.
But in England it was well understood that Wycliffe held
others which were even more offensive to a large portion
of the clergy. He carried his doctrine of church endowments to the conclusion that parishioners might refuse to
pay tithes to a parish priest of notoriously bad life, and
divert them instead to private charity. He considered
that temporal lords also held their lands by service to
God, like fiefs from a suzerain, and forfeited them by dis-
loyalty of any kind, whether it were immoral life or false
doctrine. It is possible that Wycliffe himself meant little
more by this than that property had its duties as well as
its rights; but it is certain that in a time of ferment his
teaching might be made the excuse, as it in fact was, for
a general attack upon property. He held other views,
also, that were unsound by the teaching of the times. He
regarded Scripture as the only rule of faith; taught that
the consecrated host in the eucharist was not changed
into Christ's body, though Christ was present in it; and
was accused of believing the eternity of matter, and the
doctrine of predestination, and of explaining Christ's
nature as a second Trinity. Above all, he hated the
friars with absolute intensity, declared their teaching blas-
phemous, and suggested that all Christian men should
unite to stone them, or at least suppress them, and confis-
cate their possessions. There is no question that Wycliffe
was a man of singular power and honesty, devoting
himself to reform abuses, and teaching much that has since
been accepted as true by Englishmen. But there can be
no doubt, also, that he was violent in his language, and

fond of putting subtle distinctions of no real importance
into an epigrammatical form that attracted attention.
Hence he has been accused of dishonesty, so inadequate
have his explanations appeared to those who do not study
his writings. For instance, he taught that God himself
could not give civil dominion for ever, and explained it to
mean that civil dominion would naturally pass away at
the millennium. In the same way, he, or his followers,
taught that God ought to obey the devil; meaning, as
two of them explained it, that God owes the devil the
obedience of love, by which he loves and punishes him.
As a teacher, Wycliffe's influence throughout England
was enormous, and in 1377, when the Pope sent orders
to Oxford to imprison him, the chancellor dared not execute them, and was obliged to ask Wycliffe to consent to
a nominal restraint. For years past he had been labouring on a translation of the Bible into English, and had
probably by this time brought out the Gospels, as well as
many sermons and controversial tracts. Then, again, he
had instituted an order of Poor Priests, recruited largely
from Oxford, clad in russet dresses that reached down to
their heels, and going about barefoot to preach and minister in neglected parishes. It is probable that they also
heard confessions, though this cannot have been regular;
and they were licensed in the large diocese of Lincoln, by
its bishop, John Bokyngham. Not unnaturally, therefore, Wycliffe had a large party in the country, at Oxford,
and among the parish clergy, because he opposed the
friars; and among laymen, because they did not yet understand that Wycliffe's doctrine of property threatened
the selfish landlord as well as the corrupt priest. Nor
can it be doubted that most of the religious earnestness of
the times was among Wycliffe's followers. Yet his
doctrine was so manifestly heretical, that it must have

been condemned by the council of Lambeth (March 1378), in spite of the warm partisanship of the Londoners, if the Princess Dowager of Wales had not sent down Sir Louis Clifford to forbid the bishops to proceed. With people and court against them they dared not disobey. The interference has often been ascribed to the influence of John of Gaunt, who had patronised Wycliffe on his first trial. It was probably the act of the collective council. Wycliffe had been repeatedly employed on matters of state affecting the pope's claims, and only seven months ago had given a written opinion, at request of the council, to the effect that it was lawful to forbid the export of money collected for the pope. Government could not afford to sacrifice the ablest of its partisans, and John of Gaunt no doubt concurred with the council, and was perhaps well inclined to Wycliffe personally. But there is no reason to suppose that the duke ever held or inclined to Wycliffe's opinions. His own special friends or confessors were friars; some of his strongest partisans were bishops; in his private character he was a profligate and superstitious man; and he afterwards turned decidedly against the reformers. For a time, however, he certainly enjoyed the credit of sharing Wycliffe's views, and men anticipated that the second Parliament would witness a concerted attack on the church.

Parliament of Gloucester.—But though the precaution was taken of summoning the Estates to Gloucester (Oct. 20, 1378), where they would be under the influence of the king's uncles, who had great property in those parts, the church and, for the time, Westminster sanctuary escaped untouched. The scandal of Hawley's murder seems to have saved the abbey; and churchmen and laymen took advantage of the distance from London to lay the burden of taxation upon the merchants as the richest

class.   The court was strong enough, however, to procure
the re-enactment of Edward I.'s statute (1275) for punishing those who devised or spread false news against the
great men of the realm.   It is noticeable that in this Parliament the custom of appointing a committee of Peers to
sit with and assist the Commons, which had been introduced in the last three Parliaments, was abandoned; and
the old practice was resumed, by which the various Estates
named committees to confer together.   The Parliament
broke up quietly, and we learn, incidentally, that the
cloister-green of St Peter's Abbey, in which the Estates
were lodged, was ruined by men wrestling and playing
tennis.

An Intermission of War.—During the next two
years fortune seemed to be more propitious to England.
The French arms were distracted by revolts in Brittany
and Flanders; our English army, under the Earl of
Buckingham, penetrated as far as Rheims; and Berwick
was taken back from the Scotch, who had surprised it.
A defeat of the combined Spanish and French fleet, off
Kinsale, in Ireland, cleared the English seas of pirates for
a time (July 20, 1380).   Above all, the death of Charles
V. (Sept. 16, 1380) freed England from its most dangerous
enemy, and his successor, Charles VI., was a boy only
ten years old.

The war accordingly languished between France and
England, and would, perhaps, have died out altogether
had there not been a schism in the church (1375), in
which France supported a Frenchman, Clement VII., and
England the Italian, Urban VI.   But both countries were
so thoroughly drained by this time of money and men,
that even the call to a new crusade met with little response
among the two rival peoples.

Imposition of a Poll-Tax.—Meanwhile trouble of a

new kind was coming upon England. The device of the
Parliament of Gloucester for throwing all taxation upon
the merchants could not be carried out, probably because
the merchants could not export wool with an increased
duty. It became necessary, therefore, to provide some
additional taxation for 1379, and the plan of a poll-tax,
which had been first approved in 1377, was revived.
Then fourpence a-head had been levied from every person
in the country over the age of fourteen, and not "an honest
beggar"; now a graduated tariff was drawn up to adjust
the payments to rank and fortune. An earl was to pay four
pounds; a baron or baronet, two; a knight, one; a ser-
geant of the law, two; an ordinary barrister or a great
merchant, one; a small squire or merchant, six shillings
and eightpence; and labouring men and women, fourpence
each. The clergy taxed themselves separately, but in proportion, the bishops ranking as earls. This tax was unquestionably on a fairer principle than the first poll-tax;
and it had the advantage of varying the burden of taxation, which, for some time past, had weighed much too
heavily on a single class. But small as the sum asked
from the poorest class was, it was more than many could
afford, and serfs murmured with justice that they, who by
law could not even own property, were required to pay
taxes. The evasions, accordingly, were so numerous, and
the expense of collecting so great, that the Treasury only
received £22,000, when it had calculated, perhaps un-
reasonably, on obtaining £50,000. The returns appear to
show that the population had not yet recovered the Black
Death, and was still little over 2,000,000. At first, Parliament seemed inclined to renounce the unpopular tax,
and to throw the blame of the national bankruptcy on the
king's ministers (Jan. 30, 1380). But a change of administration produced so little effect that before the end of

the year the Treasury was still in debt to the amount of £160,000, much more than a year's income. In sheer despair, the Estates resolved to revert to the poll-tax, and to treble the assessment; leaving it, however, to the towns to rate themselves as they chose, provided no one paid less than a groat, and no one more than sixty. The burden would thus fall chiefly on the country people. As the harvests for some years past had been good, it was perhaps thought that they could bear more taxation. Probably the higher payments for the rich were retained in some degree at least, as we know that priests were taxed six shillings and eightpence. But the rates for the richer classes do not seem to have been raised in proportion to those imposed on the lower, and these last were exorbitant. Twelve pence to a farm labourer represented a fortnight's work in haying-time.

Insurrection of the Commons.— Accordingly, when the returns from the tax-collectors came into the Treasury, it was found that no more had been collected now the tax was a shilling, than two years ago when it was fourpence. Evidently there were great arrears somewhere, and John Leg, a royal official, with a partner, proposed to the Treasury to pay a sum of money down for the amount still due in Kent, Hertfordshire, and the eastern counties, provided the royal justiciaries might be instructed to assist him in collecting it. The collectors now employed acted with intentional brutality, in the hope of forcing people to pay up the tax. There was thus a general excitement; and when one Thomas Baker, of Fobbing in Essex, who had been himself a collector on the first occasion, was summoned before the justiciary to show his accounts, he easily persuaded his neighbours that a new tax had been imposed, and headed a riot before which judges and tax-gatherers fled precipitately. Before long

5,000 men were in arms in Essex alone, and while some went into Hertfordshire to rouse the country, the greater number crossed the river into Kent. The time (May 30, 1381) was very favourable to an insurrection, for the Earl of Cambridge had taken one army into Portugal, and another small force had gone northwards to escort the Duke of Lancaster, who was commissioned to conclude a treaty with Scotland. Moreover, men's minds were fired by the partial success of a popular insurrection in Flanders, where the men of Ghent were waging war against all nobles and gentlemen. The men of Kent had special cause for complaint, as the seneschal of Dover Castle, otherwise hated for his pursuit of a fugitive bondsman, had lately been reviving unpopular rights of jurisdiction with the support of the Duke of Lancaster. They rose so instantaneously and in such numbers that the king's mother, who had just been visiting the shrine of St. Thomas of Canterbury, drove in a day from Canterbury to the Tower; but though she had been stopped on the road and rudely treated, the council disregarded the rising, and assumed it would die out. The leaders, however, had gone too far to draw back, and the general excitement was such that old and young flocked together armed with axes and clubs and rusty bows and arrows.

Muster of Insurgents on Blackheath.—Their first rendezvous was Blackheath, and by the way they killed all judges, lawyers, and officers of courts, burned all rolls and records, and compelled the masters of schools to swear that they would abstain from teaching reading and writing. Their first idea was to associate the nobles and gentry with them, and at Rochester they compelled the seneschal of the castle, Sir John Newton, to accompany them as chief captain. They forced all they met, among whom were many pilgrims, to swear that they would be faithful to King Richard and the Commons, that they would never submit to a King John, that they would come on call to join the rising, and that they would consent to no tax in future but the old fifteenth. By the time the insurgents were mustered on Blackheath, they were estimated at 60,000.

Negotiations with the Council.—The Bishop of Rochester was sent to confer with them, and asked them to put forward a leader as spokesman. Wat Tyler at once stepped out. He had been servant of a London merchant, Richard Lyon, in France, and, having gone to live at Dartford, is said to have killed a collector who insulted his daughter. He spoke with great fluency and effect, stating the common grievances, and declaring that the insurgents were all ready to go home if the king would give them promise of redress. The bishop and Sir John Newton, who was deputed to accompany him, reported this answer ; and Sir John assured the king that the people would only be satisfied with a personal interview, but that he need not apprehend any violence. There was a warm discussion in the council, and the archbishop, who was then chancellor, and Robert de Hales, the treasurer, strongly opposed the idea of a conference with these " shoeless ribalds," as the Primate styled them. But other counsels prevailed, and next morning the young king was rowed down in a barge to Rotherhithe. At sight of the wild mob shouting to greet him, " as though all the devils of hell had been among them," the lords in attendance were alarmed, and would not suffer him to land. Neither would the insurgents declare their wishes from the bank, so the king was rowed back to the Tower, and the attempt at negotiation only left the people more exasperated than before.

John Ball's Sermon and Manifestoes.—Down

to this time it is probable that the insurgents generally might have been quieted by promises of redress. But the report of the words used by the Primate, and the distrust shown by the king and council, inclined the people to listen to more violent counsels. At Maidstone they had taken out of the archbishop's prison a certain John Ball, who, if not one of Wycliffe's " poor priests," preached doctrines very similar to theirs; whose dislike of the higher orders had not been softened by a long captivity; and whose self-confidence had not been diminished by the coming true of his prophecy that a great crowd should deliver him. He is said to have preached to the multitude at Blackheath, beginning his sermon with the lines—

> " When Adam delved and Eve span,
> Who was then a gentleman ?"

" What have we deserved," he went on to say, " or why should we thus be kept in servitude ? We are all come from the same parents, Adam and Eve; whereby can they say or show that they are greater lords than we are, except that they cause us to labour and to earn what they spend; they are clothed in sumptuous apparel, and we are habited in poor cloth; they have their wine, spices, and good bread, and we have the chaff and drink water; we are termed their bondsmen, and unless we serve them readily we are beaten. God has now given us the day when we can shake off the yoke of bondage and be free. Wherefore we must play the man, and like good husbandmen clear the land of weeds that are choking its proper increase." It is said he explained this last counsel by a proposal to kill all nobles and gentry, all judges and lawyers, and generally all who might be thought dangerous; and to put all men on the same footing of rank and right before the law. He himself admitted that he had drawn

up letters in rude prose and doggrel rhymes, alluding to
the poem of Piers Plowman, and professing to come
from John Sheep, a priest, who bids Piers Plowman
go to his work and chastise well Hob the robber, and
look only to one head. These letters were sent into the
different counties; they were clearly intended to provoke
a general rising under orders from Wat Tyler; and as the
book quoted had suggested destroying robbers out of the
book of the living, the advice was certainly unsafe or
worse. The popular leaders at this time were said to
have conceived the idea of exterminating the upper
classes, and breaking up England into counties, over each
of which one of themselves should be head. But such a
plan could not be made public. The insurgents generally
desired only a change of government, with John Ball for
primate and chancellor, a general enfranchisement, and
the property in fee of the lands they occupied.

Burning of the Savoy and Temple.—The insurgents now marched upon London. It ought to have
been easy to keep them out of the city, as the only approach to it was by London Bridge, and the mayor and
chief citizens proposed to defend it. But the Londoners
generally, and even three of the aldermen, were well inclined to the rebels, and declared they would not let the
gates be shut against their friends and neighbours, and
would kill the mayor himself if he attempted to do it.
So on the evening of Wednesday, June 13, the insurgents
began to stream in across the bridge, and next morning
marched their whole body across the river, and proceeded
at once to the Savoy, the splendid palace of the Duke of
Lancaster. Proclamation was made that any one found
stealing the smallest article would be beheaded; and the
palace was then wrecked and burned with all the forma-
lities of a solemn act of justice. Gold and silver plate

was shattered with battle-axes and thrown into the Thames; rings and smaller jewels were brayed in mortars; silk and embroidered dresses were trampled under feet and torn up. Then the Temple was burned with all its muniments. The poet Gower was among the lawyers who had to save their lives by flight, and he passed several nights in the woods of Essex, covered with grass and leaves, and living on acorns. Then the great house of the Hospitallers at Clerkenwell was destroyed, taking seven days to burn. The chief motive in this case was the anger against Robert de Hales, the master of the order, who was Lord Treasurer. This completed the work of havoc for the day, and before its close, many of the insurgents were lying drunk about the streets, having been well plied with wine by their London friends, and having also found many cellars left open for them. That evening a council was held in the Tower, and it was proposed to sally out and make a general slaughter of the rebels. There was no lack of soldiers. The garrison of the Tower numbered 600 heavy-armed men and 600 archers; Sir Robert Knolles had 120 men with him guarding his own house; Sir Perdiccas d'Albret, another veteran soldier, was also in London; and altogether it was estimated that 8,000 men could be raised. Walworth, the mayor, recommended this plan. But the Earl of Salisbury opposed it, thinking that it was better to negotiate, as a failure, if arms were tried, would be irreparable. So the council resolved to drift, with the natural result, that the next day had almost ruined the state.

The Tower in the hands of the Mob, who commit many Murders.—For although Wat Tyler, who now commanded, could not keep his men from getting drunk at night, he had them well in hand during the day; and recruits poured in from every quarter now that the

march upon London and its successful occupation began
to be known.   A body of men was detached to Highbury
to burn another house of the Hospitallers.   The rest,
under Tyler, surrounded the Tower, and threatened to
storm it if the king did not come out to speak to them.
The council resolved to risk it, and appointed a rendezvous at Mile-End, whither, accordingly, the body of the
insurgents repaired.   The king and his court, comprising
several earls and barons, went safely among them, quieted
them with a promise of charters of emancipation, and
persuaded a great number to return home.   But during
the interview, Wat Tyler, with Ball and 400 men, had
burst into the Tower to search for the Primate and Sir
Robert de Hales.   So great was the general consternation
that the soldiers dared not raise a hand while these
ruffians searched the different rooms, not sparing even the
king's bedroom, and running spears into the beds, asked
the king's mother to kiss them, and played insolent jokes
on the chief officers.   Unhappily they were not long in
finding the archbishop, who had said mass in the chapel,
and was kneeling at the altar in expectation of their approach.   He was seized and hurried off through a yelling
mob to Tower Hill.   For a moment he tried to speak to
them, and threatened them with the pope's interdict.
There was a shout that they cared neither for pope nor
for interdict.   Then he said a few words of decorous ex-
hortation, declared that he forgave his murderers, and
bowed his neck to the executioner.   A French monk,
accidentally present, and expressing his indignation, was
told by a bystander that before long he should see
more horrible things in France.   Sir Robert de Hales,
John Leg, and the Duke of Lancaster's confessor were
the next to suffer; and the heads of the first and most
conspicuous victims were paraded on pikes through the

streets, and then exposed on London Bridge. Murder now became the order of the day, and foreigners were among the chief victims; thirteen Flemings were dragged out of one church and beheaded, seventeen out of another, and altogether it is said 400 perished. Many private enmities were revenged by the London rabble on this day. Wat Tyler had already put his master, Richard Lyon, to death: his old connection with Latimer and Alice Perrers was probably the excuse for this murder.

Partial Dispersion of the Insurgents.—Next morning (Saturday, June 15) so many of the insurgents had dispersed and gone to their homes, that the streets in the neighbourhood of the Tower seemed fairly clear, and the council resolved that the king had better leave London. He had got so far as St. Bartholomew's, with an escort of about forty knights, when he learned that the men of Kent were encamped in Smithfield under Wat Tyler. Messengers had lately come from the Scotch marches, and had spread a report that the Duke of Lancaster had arranged with the Scotch for an army of 20,000 men, who were to march upon London. In fact, the Scotch had proposed to lend an army, and the Duke had proudly declined the offer, assuring them that the whole power of Scotland could not march as far as York. Under the influence of this rumour, however, the popular leaders, and especially Wat Tyler, for whom there could be no safety, determined to accept no terms, and proposed to protract negotiations till night, and then fire the city, and kill the king and the council. Richard, who showed great decision and ability throughout the proceedings, refused to steal out of the city while there was still any danger of disturbance, and sent to know what the insurgents demanded. Meanwhile, some of his followers reported that the king was in danger, and gathered all the armed men who could be trusted together.　It soon appeared that Tyler had no real wish to negotiate.　He sent back successively three forms of charter which the king offered, and declared them insufficient; though the form the council approved gave all that could be reasonably demanded; a general quittance from all bondage, and a pardon for all offences committed during the riots. His new demands are said to have embraced the abolition of the forest laws throughout England, and he may perhaps have required the removal of restrictions on trade, the preservation of commons, and some security that the serfs now they were freed should retain the lands they lived on at a low rent or for none at all, as we know that these were popular demands of the time.　But that he ever proposed to the king, as one chronicler states, that all lawyers and crown bailiffs should be beheaded, is in the highest degree improbable.

Death of Wat Tyler.—As the negotiation made no progress in the hands of messengers, the king at last sent Sir John Newton to request Tyler to come to a personal conference.　He assented, and came among the king's company, out of sight of his own followers.　He began an angry quarrel with Sir John Newton, whom he accused of treating him disrespectfully, played with a dagger, and threatened to take his life.　On this, Walworth, who had ridden up close to Tyler, asked him if he dared to use such words, and to wear his hat in the king's presence; and then struck him in the throat with a short sword. Sir Ralph Standish followed up the blow with one on the side, and Tyler fell wounded to the ground, and was soon despatched.　For a moment what passed could not be clearly seen, and Tyler's followers believed that the king was knighting him, and cheered in consequence.　When they learned the whole truth, they bent their bows and

raised an angry shout, "Where is our leader?" Richard
seized the moment, and rode out before their ranks, "I will
be your leader, follow me !" and he led them on towards
the field of St. John's, Clerkenwell. Meanwhile, Walworth rode back to quicken the troops that were coming
up ; and by the time the Kentish peasants had deployed
upon the open ground, they found themselves surrounded
by men-at-arms crowding in from every approach, and led
by the first general of the day, Sir Robert Knolles.

Submission of the Insurgents.—The insurgents
lost heart and the soldiers of the king's household urged
him to give the signal that they might ride in and cut
down 100 or 200 at least of the varlets. Richard
himself inclined to a massacre, but Sir Robert Knolles
fortunately was of better mould, and answered promptly,
" No, sire, many of these poor people are here against
their will." He then shouted to them to fall on their
knees, cut the strings of their bows, and leave the city
and its neighbourhood, under pain of death, before night-
fall. This command was instantly obeyed, and so great was
the terror the insurrection had inspired, that they were
allowed to take with them copies of the promised charters.

Insurrections in the Eastern Counties.—Meanwhile the capture of London by the villans had been the
signal for revolts in every part of the country. At St.
Alban's, where the demand of the townsmen chiefly related to rights of commonage and fishing, the abbot was
forced to surrender the Abbey muniments, which were
burned at the town cross, and to make a formal surrender
of the obnoxious privileges. Even when the news of
Tyler's death had arrived, the townsmen and country
people held their ground, and forced the abbot to sign
letters of enfranchisment for the villans on twenty different estates. In this case, though some violence was

threatened to obnoxious officials of the monastery, the leaders of the insurgents seem to have been moderate men, and if they advanced some unfounded claims, it seems certain that they had also real wrongs to complain of; commons enclosed, wages withheld, and obsolete services revived. In Suffolk and Norfolk a worthless priest, one John Wrawe, seems to have been sent by Tyler to rouse the people; and the insurrection broke out on the day of Tyler's death. The chief justiciary, Sir John Cavendish, and the Prior of Bury St. Edmund's, John de Cambridge, were the first and most distinguished victims; but lawyers and church officials everywhere were marked men for the time. The insurgents tried to persuade Sir Robert Salle, who had risen from being a mason's son to be seneschal of Norwich, to put himself at their head, and on his refusal murdered him, one of his own serfs, it is said, giving the fatal blow. This cowed the country gentry, and a number of them swelled the train of John Lyster, a Norwich dyer, who called himself King of the Commons, and affected kingly state, making Sir Stephen Hales his grand carver. Lyster seems to have understood that his best chance was in negotiation, and honestly tried to keep his followers from disorder. Having made the city of Norwich ransom itself, he moved his forces to North Walsham, where there were no temptations to pillage or license, and sent a deputation of two knights and three peasants to the king to offer him the money taken from Norwich, and so purchase a charter of enfranchisement. On its way the deputation met Henry de Spencer, the Bishop of Norwich, who was travelling with a small force of eight men-at-arms and a few archers. He beheaded the peasants, collected the gentry of the neighbouring parts, and then rode at their head with helm, breastplate, and sword, to attack the insurgents.

He found them entrenched behind a moat and palisade, with their waggons in the rear ; and, without pausing a moment, charged so rapidly as to disconcert the aim of their archers He was the first to spur his horse over the ditch, and his charge was so vigorous that after a short sharp fight the serfs broke and tried to fly through the woods. The leaders were all taken, and the bishop himself confessed and absolved John Lyster, and held up his head "as a work of mercy and charity," as he was dragged to the gallows.

This success was the signal for a general reaction. The king sent out a summons for an army, confining it to those of such income that they could serve on horseback, and a number estimated at 40,000 gathered round the royal standard at Blackheath. An unlucky rumour arrived that the Kentish men were again in rebellion ; and the king marched into the country intending to make a bloody example of the rebels, but was stayed from proceeding to the worst extremities by the remonstrances of the local gentry, who did not wish to have their lands ravaged and their labourers massacred. However, a judicial commission went through the chief cities, executing such stern justice that 500 are said to have suffered. The Essex people were naturally alarmed, and rose up in arms, and sent to inquire whether the charters given them would be maintained. The king received the deputation in person, and told them that bondsmen they had been and bondsmen they should remain, in worse bondage than before. An armed force then entered Essex, and scattered the insurgents easily in three engagements. Sir Walter at Lee, who attained a commission to restore order at St. Alban's, told the townsmen that the royal troops had left the country a desert in Essex for a circuit of five miles about the line of march. But the feeling in St. Alban's was so strong that no jury would prosecute or convict offenders; and no surrender of the extorted charters could be obtained till it was known that the king himself was at hand.

The Bloody Assizes.—Richard came with a force of 1,000 archers and men-at-arms; and the justiciary, Sir Robert Tresilian, held a bloody assize (Oct. 15) here, as before in Essex, impannelling three juries, two of which apparently indicted, while the third sentenced. The object was to obtain fuller disclosures, no jury feeling sure how much its neighbours might be doing, or whether it might not itself be taxed with remissness. Fifteen persons were hanged, and nearly 100 were put in prison at St. Alban's alone. Altogether, it was supposed that 1,500 persons suffered judicially; and when at last the Commons petitioned for pardon, it was granted, with 287 exceptions, in eleven counties, of which Somersetshire was one. The eastern and south-eastern counties, from Norfolk to Hampshire, were those chiefly involved. But insurgents from Lincoln, from Stafford, and from Coventry, John Ball's native place, are said to have been present in Lyster's army; and the panic was so great that the Abbot of St. Mary's, Leicester, did not dare receive John of Gaunt's property into the abbey, nor the Earl of Northumberland entertain him as a guest, or give him shelter in Bamborough Castle. In Cambridge, the University was compelled to surrender its privileges, and bind itself to pay the townsmen an indemnity. Part of the timidity shown by the gentry may have arisen from a report, which the rebels carefully spread, that the king favoured them.

Parliament Cancels the Charters.—Parliament met at Westminster in November. Its opening was a stormy one, for the Duke of Lancaster and the Earl of

Northumberland, being now at bitter feud, had each brought up a small army; and Percy had even brought along with him large droves of cattle and sheep, which the Londoners, espousing his cause, took into the city pastures. The king succeeded in patching up an outward reconciliation, Lancaster being so cowed by the sense of the general hatred towards him, that he stooped to court popularity by interceding for the villans; but the insult endured at Bamborough was never forgotten or forgiven. Then the Estates passed to the great question of the day. Hugh Segrave, the new treasurer, explained that the king had granted charters of enfranchisement under constraint with the knowledge that they were illegal, and had cancelled them on the first opportunity. The king now desired to know "the wishes of you Prelates, Lords, and Commons here present, whether you think that in thus repealing them, he has done well or no. For he says, that if you desire to free and discharge the said serfs of your own accord, as he has been told that some of you desire, the king will assent to your prayer." "To which, as well Prelates and Lords temporal, as the knights, citizens, and burgesses, answered with one voice, 'that this repeal was well made;' adding, that this manumission or setting free of the serfs could not be made without the assent of those who have the chief interest in it. Whereto they will never willingly assent, neither otherwise own, were they all to die for it in a day." This, of course, settled the question, and England reverted to its old state. For some time the country was not quiet; there was talk of a new rising in Norfolk, and there was some firing of farm-buildings on the properties of unpopular landlords; then things gradually settled down again, masters were probably a little more cautious, and the serfs were content to wait for gradual enfranchisement. Nevertheless, as late as 1388, it was necessary to pass a new statute of labourers, providing that men should not ask more than the legal rate of wages; that labourers should not go out of their own district without a passport; and that the artisans of towns might be compelled to work in the fields in harvest time. The rate fixed by this tariff varied from six shillings a year and rations for a woman or a swineherd, to ten shillings, also with food, for a carter or a shepherd.

Reaction against Wycliffe's Opinions.— The rising of the serfs had a great effect on the question of church reformation. It would have languished under any circumstances, as the pope recognised in England was no longer a Frenchman; but now John Ball and John Wrawe had done more to destroy Wycliffe's work than the whole church establishment could have effected. Ball— who was scoffingly called the John Baptist of the new Messiah, Wycliffe—was said to have confessed before his execution that he had learned all his doctrine from Wycliffe, and to have added that unless the sect were destroyed, they would undo the whole realm before two years were past. This confession, true or forged, was extensively circulated. Wycliffe and his followers met the coming storm by increased audacity. A day before the Parliament met (May 6, 1382), in which he knew that measures to repress heresy would be discussed, he sent certain propositions to the council, affirming the right of Parliament to provide for all deficiencies in revenue out of church property, and suggesting that no money ought to be sent out of the country to the pope. At the same time, a petition in the English tongue was laid before the king and Estates, praying that members of the religious orders might be allowed to leave them; that the king's right to deal with church property be declared; that people might be authorised to withhold tithes from unworthy clergymen; and that the true doctrine of the eucharist might be taught. In the Commons, Wycliffe's party was still strong enough to ensure a hearing to those opinions, though no action was taken upon them. But the clergy, voting separately, petitioned the king to enforce the laws against heresy by ordering the sheriffs of counties to arrest Wycliffe's " poor preachers," and imprison them till they had been released after trial in the church courts. The petition was assented to, and, though the Commons, six months later (Oct. 1382), procured that it should be cancelled because it had been passed without their consent and infringed their privilege, it had produced considerable effect in the meantime. The new archbishop, Courtenay, was a zealous churchman, and lost no time in formally condemning Wycliffe's doctrines in convocation, and in forcing his chief followers to explain away or recant their opinions. They were not yet prepared for separation from the visible Church; and though the common law of England, which condemned heretics to death, had not often been enforced, there had been several instances that it was no dead letter; one of German heretics, starved to death (1160); one of a renegade deacon, killed with the sword (1223); and one of some Franciscans, burned alive (1330). Wycliffe himself died in peace two years later (1384), having just been saved by his last illness from the necessity of obeying a summons to appear at Rome and answer for his doctrine.

Violence of the Lollards.—It must be borne in mind that the followers of Wycliffe, if they numbered in their ranks many men eminent for learning and piety, numbered not a few, also, who carried out extreme views in a most offensive way. One gentleman of Wiltshire, who had received the sacramental bread from his parish priest, took it home and lunched upon it with wine, oysters, and onions. Two preachers of the sect boasted that they had

cooked vegetables with a saint's image, which they had
broken up.   A great landowner, less violent, contented
himself with stowing away the images of the saints in
cellars, though, in condescension to the wishes of his
household, he allowed one of St Catherine to be kept
in the bakehouse.   A friar, who had turned Lollard, as
Wycliffe's followers were called,[1] had the ingenuity to
purchase a patent as chaplain to the pope, which exempted
him from all jurisdiction except in the pope's own court;
taking advantage of this, he preached in the streets
against the vices of the Mendicant Orders, with such fury
as to excite a riot, in which some friaries would have been
burned if one of the London sheriffs had not come up.
But had the Lollards been all moderate and saintly men,
only recognised, as many were, by their decent lives, and
avoiding of foul language and habitual references to God's
law, they could not have escaped persecution, as long as
they discountenanced pilgrimage; taught that simple
priests might ordain; denied purgatory; objected to idle-
ness on holidays; and maintained that the married state
was holier than life in a monastery.   They soon lost the
patronage of John of Gaunt, who, indeed, as Chancellor of
Oxford, had ordered Wycliffe, in 1381, to abstain from
discussing the Eucharist; and, in 1382, pronounced the
opinions of his followers on that subject to be detestable.
In 1389, the Bishop of Norwich declared he would burn
or behead any one of the sect who dared to preach in his
diocese; and the threat is said to have cleared it of poor
priests.   The Court was supposed to favour the new views
during the lifetime of Queen Anne of Bohemia.   But
Richard II. had what one of his biographers calls two
praiseworthy qualities, that he " loved religion and cher-

---

[1] Probably from a German word, *lollen*, to sing; from their habit of
singing hymns.

ished the clergy, especially the Black Monks." In 1395, he returned from Ireland, at the request of the bishops, to suppress a scheme of church reform, which the Lollards were promulgating, and which had received the countenance of several of the nobility. The king threatened the chief promoters of it with death, and extorted several insincere recantations. The form of recantation imposed at this time in the diocese of York pledged the subscriber to worship images; to obey his ordinary; and to abstain from the study of Lollard books, or the propagating of Lollard doctrines, under pain of forfeiture of goods and punishment by law as a heretic if he relapsed. It does not seem that the penalty of death was ever inflicted during Richard's reign, or, indeed, rendered necessary by the firmness of the persons accused; but torture is said to have been employed in one instance, and in several cases men and women escaped burning only because they preferred to make public and abject recantation of their errors.

CHAPTER XI

RICHARD'S GOVERNMENT.

Character of Richard II.—The insurrection of the serfs had the effect of bringing the young king prominently before the public. Though only fourteen years old, Richard had displayed a courage, presence of mind, and resource in difficulties, that inclined men to augur hopefully of his future. He was at this time a fair, yellow-haired, round-faced boy, with something of his mother's beauty, easily blushing, and speaking with a slight lisp. Events showed that he inherited the sumptuous tastes of his family, and the fierceness of his father; the devotion to friends, and general faithlessness of the second Edward, with a singular power of dissimulation, and great tenacity of purpose. Under better circumstances, Richard might have been a magnificent and glorious king. In Ireland, where he had almost absolute power, he showed himself able to understand the real wants of the country, and to legislate wisely for them. He did not want personal courage, and once challenged the King of France, as it seems, seriously to settle their conflicting pretensions by a duel (Sept. 1383). He was capable of pure affection, though his court was infamous for the profligacy he encouraged; and his relations with his two wives were excellent. But Richard could not bear the restraints of constitutional government. Inheriting a disastrous war and a bankrupt treasury, he required a close economy and the support of all classes in the country. Unhappily, the slightest opposition to his wishes irritated him like an act of treason. While still only fifteen, he took the great seal from the chancellor, who had refused to use it for some unwise grants to favourites, and keeping it for some days in his own hands, gave away with such prodigality, that in the very next year he was compelled to quarter his household in the English monasteries. It added to Richard's difficulties, that England was then very rich in tried statesmen and soldiers, who formed an unrecognised power in the State; that his uncles were ambitious princes, and even, in some slight degree, that he was only the son of a prince, while they were sons of a king. Not unnaturally, perhaps, the king sought the society of young nobles or of officials of low rank; and his hereditary Lord Chamberlain, Robert de Vere, who came of age in 1382, and was henceforth always about the king's person, acquired such ascendency over him "that if he had said, 'Sir, this is white,' though it had been black," says Froissart, "the king would not have contradicted him."

Richard's Marriage.—Several plans for marrying Richard had been proposed and rejected. The Duke of Lancaster had wished to give him his own daughter, but the council objected to the relationship of first cousins as too close. The daughter of Barnabo, Duke of Milan, was offered, and would have brought a large dower, but the alliance would have been unprofitable to England. The council determined to ask the hand of Anne, daughter of the late Emperor Charles the IV., and sister of Wenzel, King of the Romans and King of

Bohemia.   The object no doubt was to detach the House of Luxembourg from the French alliance, and to defeat French diplomacy, which was offering Anne a marriage with the young King of France.   Through the influence of Cardinal Pileus, who represented Urban, the pope recognised in England, Sir Simon Burley, who was sent over for the purpose, succeeded in negotiating the marriage ; though Wenzel took advantage of the eagerness of the English court to stipulate that instead of giving a dower he should be paid £12,000 for his expenses in sending his sister over.   After some weeks' delay at Brussels, for fear of a French fleet that was scouring the Channel to intercept her, Anne, who had already been once captured and ransomed at Richard's expense, obtained passports from the French court, and arrived in England (Dec. 1381). Her marriage did not affect the relations of England with the Continent.   Wenzel was at this time chiefly devoted to hunting and the personal supervision of his dominions, and the conduct of Pope Urban, in filling up some vacant bishoprics without consulting him, gave him such offence that he declined to take any part with England in the crusade against the Anti-Pope and France.

Character of Queen Anne.—Queen Anne's life in England, where she was long remembered as good Queen Anne, seems to have been tranquil and inoffensive. But either she had no influence over her husband, though he was sincerely attached to her, or she used it unwisely. She mixed herself up in one of the worst actions of the king's favourite, Robert de Vere, and she interceded in time of civil dissension for one of the worst offenders against constitutional government.   It is said she was well versed in the Bible, and favoured Lollard opinions.   It is certain that many of her attendants, English and Bohemian, embraced the new faith ; and the most important result of her marriage is perhaps the increased circulation of Wycliffe's books, which passed with other English literature to Prague, and became the starting point of a great schism in the church.

Crusade in Flanders.—The insurrection of the serfs had prevented the Duke of Lancaster from taking an expedition in Portugal, whither the Earl of Cambridge had gone before him ; and the kings of Castile and Portugal had accordingly made peace (1382). Unfortunately, the troubles in Flanders, where Ghent under Philip van Artevelde had for a time subdued the whole country, offered England a new and favourite battle-field, and the crushing defeat of the Flemings, with the death of their leader at the battle of Roosebeke (Nov. 27, 1382), only stimulated the English Council to intervene, while Ghent was still unsubdued. Meanwhile, the warlike Bishop of Norwich had been preaching a crusade against the French anti-pope and his supporters through the length and breadth of England. Favoured by national animosity and religious bigotry, the bishop collected an incredible sum of money in gold and silver, together with jewels, bracelets, rings, dishes, pieces of plates, spoons, and other ornaments, and especially from ladies and women generally. To those who objected that the enterprise was non-Christian, the bishop answered that it was allowable to fight in the cause of God and the pope, and many monks and mendicant friars followed him into the field. Nevertheless, so exhausted was England, that the bishop could only muster 5,000 men-at-arms and archers, of whom 2,000 were Gascons ; and had he not refused to attend a conference with the king, it was thought he would have been countermanded at the last moment. At first the little English army was brilliantly successful. It took Gravelines, defeated 12,000 men near Dunkirk, and besieged Ypres. But it was speedily driven off by an army of 20,000 men commanded by the King of France; and the campaign ended in the surrender of the English conquests, and the return of the expedition (Dec. 1383). Many adventurers had flocked over on the news of the victory to share the plunder of Flanders, and there were loud complaints against the English commanders, who it was said had been cowardly and treacherous. Their defence was that their forces were insufficient to hold the country, and that they thought it better to capitulate on easy terms, taking money from the enemy, than to wait till they were made prisoners. It was not by men of this temper that the English dominion in France had been founded.

There was a nine months' truce with France soon after this (Jan. 26, 1384—Oct. 26, 1384), which gave the two countries a short taste of the blessings of peace and caused a lively trade to spring up, to the great satisfaction of the two peoples, who began to ask themselves if war was a constant necessity.

War between England and Scotland.—But there was still trouble on the Scotch border, and John of Gaunt marched into the Lowlands and employed his men in hewing down and burning the forests which had sheltered the borderers (1384). Next year, when the truce between England and France, which had been prolonged for some months, expired (May 1, 1385), the French sent a compact body of 1,000 men-at-arms, and as many crossbowmen and varlets, under the admiral of France, John de Vienne, into Scotland. There had been many volunteers in France for the honour of sharing in this campaign, and the Scotch mustered 30,000 strong to

do their duty by their allies. As, however, part of the
assistance from France consisted in a hundred suits of
armour it is probable that the Scotch force was indifferently accoutred. Anyhow, the Scotch generals thought
themselves unable to meet the host of England in the field
when it marched in, 16,000 strong in men-at-arms and
archers, besides the light-armed or rascalry, who perhaps
numbered as many more. Even John de Vienne could
not insist on giving battle when Douglas showed him
from a hill the disproportion of the two hosts; and the
Scotch army contented itself with ravaging the north of
England, while the English, retaliating on Scotland, were
soon starved into a retreat. The Scotch inflicted more
damage than they sustained. Their allies wearied of the
inglorious war, and were disgusted to find that they
could not forage safely in the country they came to
defend; they found themselves forced to pay for supplies,
and in default of ready money to give security before
they could quit the country.

Battle known as the Battle of Otterburn.—
Three years later (August 1388), encouraged by the report
of civil war in England, the Scotch again swept over the
border and advanced as far as York; they could not
take the town by assault, and the invasion would probably have been no more than a mere foray, if Douglas
had not captured a pennon of Henry Percy—called Hotspur from his warlike activity. This led to an exchange
of challenges between the two leaders, and while the main
body of the Scotch went westward to Carlisle, Douglas,
having secured his retreat by the capture of Ponteland
Castle, lingered in the neighbourhood of Newcastle, at a
place about six or seven miles on or near the Otterburn
or Jedburgh road. Percy attacked him there at night
with a detachment from Newcastle, and an obstinate

battle, the honour of which was claimed by either side, ended in the death of Douglas and the capture of Percy. As the English were repulsed, and did not dare renew the battle next day when reinforcements had come up, the victory was undoubtedly won by the Scotch, but it had been so obstinately contested, that the conquerors were glad to evacuate the country without further ravage. Froissart has placed this battle at Otterburn twenty miles further north than the real battlefield, and under this name it became much more famous in history than its real importance deserves, and has passed into Border ballads as the battle of Chevy Chase, that is of the " chevauchée," or foray.   The English Parliament next year contributed £3,000 to Henry Percy's ransom, and concluded a three years' truce with Scotland and France, which was prolonged from time to time, and secured peace between England and its two great enemies until the end of the reign.

Irish Difficulty.—There had been good reason for Richard's inactivity against foreign foes in the troubles by which his government was assailed.   After the unsuccessful campaign in Scotland, he held a Parliament (November 1385), in which the affairs of Ireland seem to have been the most important topic of consideration. The last viceroy appointed, Sir Philip Courtenay, though honest and fairly capable, had failed to restore order; and a council of the Irish baronage sent delegates to England to request that Richard would come over in person, or at least would depute one of his greatest nobles.   It was determined to make Ireland a principality for De Vere. But as it was necessary to propitiate the princes of the blood, Richard began by raising his uncles of Cambridge and Buckingham to be Dukes of York and Gloucester, with incomes of £1,000 a year a-piece ; and then proceeded

to make the Earl of Oxford Marquis of Dublin, with
regal power in Ireland, and with a grant of all its revenues, subject to a rent charge of 5,000 marks. Last of
all, the vacant earldom of Suffolk, with £500 a year, was
given to the chancellor, Michel de la Pole. By these
promotions the king hoped farther to balance the power
of the Duke of Lancaster, with whom he had a fresh
quarrel in Scotland. But it seemed safer still to get the
duke out of the country, and the Estates were induced
to vote large sums of money to assist King John of
Castile, as he still styled himself, in an expedition to recover his wife's inheritance. The duke consented to the
arrangement, and left England accordingly. But Richard
was in no position to give pensions. There was an angry
discussion in this very Parliament as to the proportion
clergy and laity were to contribute respectively; and the
county members seem to have proposed a wholesale
scheme of church spoliation, as priests considered it, which
the king would not suffer to remain on record. It was
probably something like a plan, afterwards often pro-
pounded and very popular, for administering the church
lands by the state, paying the clergy fixed and moderate
stipends, and applying their surplus revenues to military
purposes.

Prospect of French Invasion.—Next year the
dread of a French invasion, which was actually planned
on a gigantic scale, kept the whole country on the alert
for several months (August to November), and though the
danger passed away completely, thanks to the autumn
winds, which kept the fleet in harbour at Sluys, the
general feeling in England was almost as much of discontent as of relief.

Parliamentary Inquiry.—Soldiers, with whom the
land swarmed, had blessed the King of France for his

courage, and regretted the plunder of his armament; the villagers for many miles round London murmured at the exactions of their own troops, who had lived at free quarters among them; and Parliament was resolved to find out what had been done with the £300,000 which were said to have been raised by taxation. It was known that the whole management of affairs had been in the hands of the Marquis of Dublin, but it was determined to attack rather the responsible ministers of the crown, the chancellor and treasurer. The treasurer, John Fordam, Bishop of Durham, had not held the office a year, and was only required to resign it. But the chancellor, Michael de la Pole, the new Earl of Suffolk, was impeached on a variety of charges, for abusing his power to his own profit and embezzling the public money. The earl was ably defended by his brother-in-law, Sir Richard Scrope, who pleaded the minister's past services; but he was found guilty of purchasing lands from the king at less than their worth, and of intercepting public money in one particular instance. He was condemned to pay a fine of £12,000, and to remain in prison till it was discharged. Richard's conduct throughout was marked by dissimulation and self-will. At first he took part warmly for his ministers, and it is noteworthy that when he requested to confer with a deputation of the Commons, so general was the belief that he intended to assassinate any who should be sent, that it was thought impossible to designate members for the purpose. Indeed, public feeling ran so high that one member moved that the act of deposition of Edward II. should be sent for and read aloud. The Duke of Gloucester and the Bishop of Ely were at last deputed to urge the king to come in person to Parliament. Richard reluctantly consented; professed to be astonished at the heavy charges proved against his chancellor; and apparently turned against him, observing, " Alas, alas, Michael, see what thou hast done !" Deceived by his manner, the Estates voted him supplies, and allowed him to make De Vere Duke of Ireland, and to give him the ransom of John of Brittany (Charles de Blois' son), the large sum of 30,000 marks, which was soon about to be paid.

Government by Commission.—But they stipulated as a precaution for future good government, that a council of administration should be appointed to sit for a year, to inquire into and redress abuses and to examine thoroughly the state of the public finances. The council was not unfairly constituted, for it contained several such as the Archbishop of York, the Bishop of Winchester, and Sir Richard Scrope, who stood well in the king's favour; and its members were generally recommended by high place or high character. But Richard regarded their appointment as a deliberate insult to himself, and protested at the end of the session in general language against any prejudice to his own power, or to the franchise and prerogatives of the crown. The Estates having separated, Michael de la Pole was at once released from prison and taken into favour again.

Success of the New Administration.—The council was not inclined to let its powers lie idle. It instituted a rigid inquiry into the revenue accounts, and found Sir Simon Burley guilty of peculation to an extent of more than £30,000, which it ordered him to refund. It attempted to ascertain what lands had been alienated from the crown during the reign, and even what had become of the crown jewels left by Edward III. A great victory at sea, which the Earl of Arundel gained (March 24, 1387), over a combined fleet of French, Flemings, and Spaniards, aided the popularity of the new government;

as the Earl of Arundel was in the council, and the Duke of Gloucester was supposed to have contributed very much to the success by his care in seeing the fleet properly manned. The danger of a French invasion was averted by this battle, which gave England the command of the seas. Richard looked on with undisguised displeasure, and occupied himself with a progress in the northern counties. He could still dispense honours and hear complaints; and he courted popularity in York and Coventry by confirming or granting privileges to the citizens. But he found leisure also to promote a scandalous intrigue in his own court.

Conduct of the Duke of Ireland.—The Duke of Ireland, though married to a grand-daughter of Edward III., Philippa de Coucy, had lost his heart to one of Queen Anne's maids of honour, called the Land-gravine; he now proposed to get a divorce from his first wife by interest in the Court of Rome, where the De Coucys were disliked, and the king and queen supported him in the attempt. The Duke of Gloucester was furious at the indignity offered to his niece, and though he could not interfere openly, dropped threats which Robert de Vere resented bitterly.

Conferences with the Judges at Shrewsbury and Nottingham.—As the time drew near when the powers of the council would expire and Parliament meet again, the king prepared for a fresh trial of strength with the popular party; and, marching towards Wales, as if to escort Robert de Vere on his way to Ireland, held a conference with some of the judges at Shrewsbury (1387). Encouraged by their opinions, he arranged to be at Nottingham towards the end of August, and summoned some of the chief citizens of London, the sheriffs of counties, and the judges to meet him there (Aug. 24). The

Londoners seem to have been consulted on the disposition
of the city, and to have answered favourably. The
sheriffs were asked what forces they could raise in case of
a civil war, and how far they could control the elections.
They replied that the Commons generally were in favour
of the council, and would not fight against it or elect re-
presentatives opposed to it. They were, in consequence,
dismissed. Then the judges were called to a conference.
Skipwith, the second justice of the Common Pleas, having
probably been at the council of Shrewsbury, and disliking
the tone of the king's party, professed to be too ill to attend, though he was able to preside in court three weeks
later; Sir John Cary, chief baron of the Exchequer, was
also absent from Nottingham, though he had been present
at Shrewsbury; but Tresilian, the chief justice of the
King's Bench, Bealknap, chief justice of the Common
Pleas, and his three assessors, Fulthorpe, Holt, and Burgh,
were all present, together with Serjeant Lokton, judge-
designate of the King's Bench. A series of questions,
drawn up by two lawyers, John Blake and Thomas Esk,
were now laid before the judges; and under threats of
death, and after some actual violence to Bealknap and
Holt, they consented to subscribe answers in the sense
desired by the king. They declared, amongst other matters, that the late ordinance for reforming the Government
was against the king's prerogative, and that its promoters
had incurred sentence of death; that Parliament had no
right to discuss any other matters than such as the king
laid before it; that the king could dissolve Parliament at
pleasure, and that any one thereafter continuing to act as
if Parliament were sitting was guilty of treason; and that
the Lords and Commons had no right to impeach the
officers of the crown. They were then sworn to secrecy
as members of the king's council, and dismissed.

Richard occupies London.—Richard now intended to raise troops, seize the persons of the Lords Ordainers when their term of office was expired, and try them for the various acts which the judges had declared to be treasonable. But though it was possible to enlist soldiers here and there, where the nature of the service expected was not fully understood, many suspected the king's intentions, and refused to serve. Moreover, Sir Roger Fulthorpe had lost no time in disclosing what had passed at Nottingham to the Earl of Kent, and the Lords Ordainers were thus put upon their guard. The Duke of Gloucester thought it expedient to make public oath before the Bishop of London and a number of the baronage that he had never plotted against the king's person ; though he admitted that he meditated revenge upon the Duke of Ireland. The bishop reported what had occurred to the king, in the hopes of bringing about a reconciliation, but found Richard in the hands of his old favourites, and was ordered angrily back to his diocese. So the barons scattered to prepare for war; and the king made a triumphant entry into London, where a small party of the leading citizens was in his interests (Nov. 10). Next day (Monday) it was rumoured that the Duke of Gloucester and the Earls of Arundel and Warwick had collected large forces, and were preparing to combine and march upon London. The king despatched a small party, under the Earl of Northumberland, to arrest Lord Arundel at his Castle of Reigate ; but the leader dared not, or cared not, to carry out this enterprise ; and a second attempt to intercept the earl on his way to the confederation failed equally.

The Lords Ordainers Invest the City.—On Tuesit was rumoured that the barons had a strong force at Haringay, near London, and in the neighbouring villages.

The king held a hasty council. The Archbishop of York proposed that they should sally out and give battle to the rebels. Others suggested that an envoy should be sent to France to purchase assistance by the surrender of Calais and all the English conquests and claims, except the old dominion of Aquitaine. It was commonly believed that this plan was actually entertained, and only foiled by the decision of the Captain of Calais, William Beauchamp, who arrested the envoy, and sent him back a prisoner to the Duke of Gloucester. But while he craved foreign aid, Richard was well disposed to try the chances of a battle. On inquiry, it appeared that he would have no followers. The Mayor of London, who had answered for 50,000 citizens, had to report that not a man would stir in the quarrel. Even in the king's council the Earl of Northumberland counselled submission, and Ralf Basset declared that he would not have his head broken in the Duke of Ireland's cause. Richard was forced to give way, and to admit the barons to a conference in Westminster Hall (Nov. 17). It is said he laid an ambush for them by the way; it is certain that when they appealed his favourites and counsellors of treason, he broke out into angry railings, and protested he valued the whole faction no more than the meanest varlet in his kitchen. But he was compelled to promise that the impeached persons should answer for their conduct in Parliament six weeks hence (Feb. 3, 1388). Till then, all were to be in the king's peace; a provision which could only be carried out if the treacherous counsellors left the kingdom.

Civil War—Skirmish at Radcot Bridge.—The Earl of Suffolk was wise enough to fly, disguised as a poulterer, and though sent back from Calais, contrived by the king's favour to reach France again, and died in exile. But the Duke of Ireland had the temerity to take the king's commission and attempt to raise an army in Cheshire and North Wales. His success was very slight. His chief partisans were Thomas de Molyneux, a gentleman of Lancashire, Ralph Vernon, and Ralf de Radclyff, not one of whom was a baron or of a baronial family, and though Cheshire was a royal county, many men preferred imprisonment to service against the Duke of Gloucester and the barons. Only 5,000 men in all could be got together ; and when it was known they had taken the field, volunteers flocked from every quarter to join the baronial army. Nevertheless, either because he hoped to be joined by recruits, or that the king would make a diversion, Robert de Vere advanced as far as Radcot Bridge, in Oxfordshire (Dec. 20). He found the bridge partly broken down, and the troops of the Duke of Gloucester coming up to guard it, while the Earl of Derby was advancing along the Oxford bank. The craven's heart failed him, and he leaped his horse into the river, and, favoured by sunset, escaped to the opposite side and rode away ; many of his men trying to follow him were drowned in Carswell Marsh, and Thomas de Molyneux, after some skirmishing, was killed. But there was no slaughter, and the royal troops, having been disarmed and stripped, were sent home. The spoils of the battlefield were rich, and the event decisive.

The " Wonderful Parliament."—It was characteristic of Richard that he now tried to cajole the nobles by fair words and invitations; and significant of the opinion entertained of him, that the chief of the baronage would not enter the Tower till it had been thoroughly searched by their own men. Having put in prison all against whom they intended to proceed, and removed others to whom they objected from the king's person, they separated for the Christmas, to meet again in

Parliament at the beginning of February (February 2, 1388).

Its Impeachments.—When the Estates came together, the Duke of Gloucester knelt before the king and declared his innocence of any plan to depose him ; and then joined by the four Earls of Derby, Arundel, Warwick, and Norfolk, appealed the Archbishop of York, the Duke of Ireland, the Earl of Suffolk, Robert Tresilian, false justice, and Nicholas Brambre, false knight of London, of high treason. They were found guilty on several counts, that they had counselled the king badly, and had made him swear to support them, and had levied war against the king's faithful subjects. Neville, as a churchman could not be touched, but his temporalities were sequestered, and the pope was induced to deprive him of his archbishopric, and translate him to the see of St Andrews, of which the Scotch would not let him take possession. The Duke of Ireland and the Earl of Suffolk having escaped, could only be punished by forfeiture of their lands. Sir Nicholas Brambre, who seems to have been associated with the Peers out of consideration for his former rank as Lord Mayor of London, was specially obnoxious for his intrigues in the city, and was accused of having led the king into immoral courses. His demand to prove his innocence by wager at arms was rejected, and he was beheaded on Tower Hill, the king obtaining as a special favour that he should not be hanged at Tyburn. Tresilian, who might have escaped, was imprudent enough to come to London in disguise, and watch the proceedings of Parliament from the windows of a neighbouring house. He was recognised as he looked out, or betrayed, and within a few hours of detection suffered on the Tyburn gallows. The five judges and Serjeant Lokton were also condemned to death, on the constitutional ground that the king could not have intended them to answer falsely. But as they had certainly been unwilling accomplices in the treasons charged against them, their sentence on intercession of the bishops was commuted to life-long banishment to Ireland, and forfeiture of their property. Blake and Esk, who pleaded the king's orders as sufficient warrant for what they did, were beheaded. The Commons then proceeded to impeach Sir Simon Burley, Sir John Beauchamp, the seneschal of the king's household, Sir James Berners, who had been the king's tutor, and Sir John Salisbury. Burley was found guilty of plotting the death of the Duke of Gloucester's supporters in Parliament; Beauchamp of inciting the king to hate his subjects; and Berners and Salisbury of plotting to give up Calais and other castles in Picardy and Artois to the French. Richard was especially anxious to save Burley, and refused to concur in the sentence passed upon him. The Duke of Gloucester and the Earls of Arundel and Warwick withdrew into a private chamber and tried to convince the young king; at last the duke told him that if he wished to be king it must be done. Queen Anne, it is said, was three hours on her knees pleading for mercy, and was roughly bidden by the Earl of Arundel to pray for herself and her husband. Even the more powerful intercession of the Earl of Derby, though passionately urged, was profitless, and Burley was at last executed without the formality of a royal warrant. But the Bishop of Chichester, who had been equally guilty, escaped with banishment and the forfeiture of his temporalities, as the Estates did not dare to touch a churchman.

Its General Measures.—Before Parliament separated (June 4) it petitioned that all officers of state might in future be nominated in Parliament, or by the Continual

Council with the king's assent; that all forfeited estates might be kept in the king's hands to relieve taxation; and that the Bohemians in the queen's service might be ordered to quit the kingdom. It voted £20,000 to the five lords appellants, probably in compensation of the heavy charges they had been put to. It passed a general act of indemnity for all persons not attainted, except those who had gone beyond sea, and some eighteen who were specified by name; and it enacted that the method of attainder should not be employed in future, nor any points construed as treason which were not treason by statute. This last provision was probably neither a confession of unjust practices, nor an attempt to provide against future retaliation. The Estates must have known that no statute would bind Richard if he recovered power. But they wished not to establish precedents which the ordinary courts of law should misuse, or, on the other hand, to give the impression that Parliament was to interfere in the judicial business of the country. It is difficult at this distance of time to judge how far their leaders were actuated by personal motives of interest or vengeance. But though punishment by death is always to be deplored, the principal victims of the " Wonderful Parliament" deserve little regret. They had used their influence with a young and impressible man to corrupt his morals, encourage his extravagance, and tempt him to breaches of law, civil war, and assassination. They had procured pardons for the worst crimes, interfered with the course of law, embezzled state treasures, and procured large grants of land to themselves. Last of all, they had deliberately tried to subvert the constitution of the country. Either the king or the king's ministers must be held responsible for the proceedings at Nottingham ; and grave as Richard's guilt was, the theory of the constitution demanded that men should hold, in the face of proof, that their sovereign had only acted under ill advice and under constraint.   With the memory of the Black Prince still green, it seemed impossible to deal out hard measures to his son.   It is quite possible that the Duke of Gloucester was an unprincipled and ambitious, as he certainly was a proud and fierce man.   But it is evident that he was so restrained by public opinion, and so fearful of the rumours that taxed him with aiming at the crown, that he could not even take the necessary measures to secure his party a share in the future government of the country.   All that had been done was to purge the court, to make a terrible example of traitors, and to put the finances of the country under upright management for nearly a year.   At the end of that time (May 3, 1389), Richard entered the room where his council was sitting, demanded if he was not of age, and on receiving the only possible answer, declared his intention to govern thenceforward without the counsel of guardians.   He followed this up by removing Gloucester and Warwick from the council, giving the Great Seal to the aged Bishop of Winchester, and appointing four new judges.

Richard Resumes Power.—For some years nothing very noticeable occurred in England; though a general spirit of unrest was abroad, and there were riots in Kent and Cheshire (1390–1393), testifying to local discontents. Richard for a time sought to conciliate public opinion by governing temperately and well, and his ministers, in 1390, demanded and received the approbation of Parliament for their good conduct.   Gradually the king attached himself more and more to the Duke of Lancaster, leaning on his arm in public, wearing his cognisance, and investing him with the principality of Aquitaine (1390).   King and duke agreed on a policy of peace.   Richard knowing that a foreign war would make him dependent upon the Estates, and the duke, sickened of bloodshed, and having nothing to hope from fresh campaigns, as he had made a profitable peace in Spain. It can scarcely be doubted that a renewal of war would have been a great calamity for England and for the world. But, naturally enough, the opposition criticised the king's inglorious policy, and constantly appealed to the old military ardour of the English people. So, although there was apparent reconciliation, and the king endowed the Duke of Gloucester with estates and even with the extended dukedom of Ireland, the relations of the two factions were in reality hostile as before.

Unpopularity of the Government.—The Earl of Arundel, as a young and incautious man, took up the quarrel of his party, and said freely what all thought. In the Parliament of January 27, 1394, he came to open quarrel with the Duke of Lancaster. The duke accused him of having collected an armed force at Holt Castle in Cheshire, to support an insurrection of the country people which John of Gaunt had provoked (Sept. 1393). The earl justified himself on this charge, and retorted with indiscreet accusations against the duke for familiarity with the king, for accepting the duchy of Guienne, and for speaking " such big and sharp words in council and in Parliament, that the earl and others frequently did not dare to say fully what they thought." The king answered the charges himself, and the earl was compelled to apologize before king and peers in a set form of words. " Sire, sith that hit semeth to the king and to the other lords, and eke that yhe ben so mychel (much) greved and displeisid be my wordes, hit forthynketh me (I repent), and byseche yowe of your gode Lordship to remit me your mautalent." It was probably in consequence of this humiliation that

the earl sued for and obtained a writ dispensing him from
attendance on Parliament or from taking any public office.
But he could not avoid giving offence.   In the summer of
this year (June 7, 1394) Queen Anne died, and was buried
with great splendour at Westminster.   The earl came late
to join the funeral procession from St Paul's, and applied
almost instantly for leave to absent himself on private
business.   Richard was so enraged that he struck him
and drew blood before the whole assemblage of mourners.

Troubles in Ireland.—The affairs of Ireland were
beginning to demand instant attention.   In the beginning
of the reign, Art MacMurragh, "in whose might and
puissance all Leinster trembled," and who styled himself
King of Leinster, made a demand on the English Government for a fee of eighty marks.   So impoverished was the
treasury, that it could only muster nine marks, and was
forced to borrow in order to make up the deficiency.
Matters did nòt mend during the next few years, and
became visibly worse when De Vere was made Duke of
Ireland, with power to nominate the great offices of state.
His lieutenant, Sir John Stanley, sacked the house of the
former viceroy, Sir Philip Courtenay, and tried to arrest
him ; for which act Sir Philip afterwards obtained 1000
marks compensation from Parliament.   It was characteristic of Richard that on his recovery of power in 1389
he appointed (Aug. 20) this very Sir John Stanley his
own deputy in Ireland.   Parliament, however, took the
matter up, as complaints of maladministration came over
from Ireland, and Sir John was exiled the kingdom.   It
is probable that the Duke of Gloucester had some share
in this check to the king's policy, as, in 1392, the duke
was commissioned to lead an army into Ireland, and was
stopped when he was just about to set out by counter-
orders from the king   The result of these divisions in

England was fatal to English power, and so many of the settlers returned to England that it was said the English pale was left almost without population. A proclamation was issued, ordering these immigrants to return to their own country ; and they are said to have obeyed with an alacrity which disconcerted the English officials, who had hoped to extort fines for licences to remain. From some notice of their excesses, it is probable that they found English law too severe for the licence learned in the Irish marches.

Richard's First Irish Campaign.—It now became necessary to defend those to whom England refused an asylum ; and Richard, it is said, was the more anxious to pacify the turbulent province, as his ambassadors in Germany, when they canvassed for the imperial crown, were answered with the taunt that their master could not keep France, or govern England, or retrieve Ireland. He made every preparation to ensure success, and landed at Waterford (Oct. 2, 1394) with an army of 4,000 men-at-arms and, as is reported, 30,000 archers, who were embarked at Bristol, Holyhead, and Haverford. His march to Dublin was unopposed ; the English fleet blockaded the coast ; and the Irish chiefs of the more settled parts, who probably had no definite idea of disputing his suzerainty, made submission to the king himself at Drogheda, or to his deputy, the Earl of Nottingham, at Carlow. Their submissions were duly recorded on parchment, and show that they became liegemen in full feudal form for themselves, their land, and their clansmen. In return they received promises of pension, and were, of course, entitled to the protection which every feudal vassal might claim of his seigneur. Richard tried honestly to understand and conciliate his newly-reclaimed subjects. He pointed out, in a letter to his council, that the "rebel Irish" had been provoked by wrongs done to them, and denial of justice; and proposed, with consent of the council, to give them a general pardon (Feb. 1). The council answered, a little grudgingly, that the pardon might be granted, but that heavy fines ought to be imposed for the charges of the war. But during the king's stay in Ireland nothing was done to excite disaffection; and Richard displayed a curious tact in winning the people's favour. He emblazoned the arms of Edward the Confessor, for whom the natives had a great reverence; caused four of the great chiefs to be taught the habits of the English court, knighted them in the English fashion, and made them a present of royal robes. So wild was the state of Ireland still, that there was no distinction of ranks even in the households of the chiefs, and the very kings rode without saddle or stirrups.

Richard Marries a French Princess.—Richard was called back from Ireland by news that the Lollards were assailing the church (May 1395). The reforming movement was easily repressed; and the king now busied himself with hearing the remonstrances of the people of Aquitaine against the grant of their province to the Duke of Lancaster, and with negotiating a marriage for himself with a princess of France. In the end, he determined to resume the government of Aquitaine, and obtained the hand of the young Princess Isabella, a child only seven years old, with a dowry of 800,000 francs. As the war party in England, headed by the Duke of Gloucester, instantly opposed both these measures, it is probable that the court of France preferred to see Aquitaine ruled from London, and did not desire the close neighbourhood of a warlike prince of the blood royal. Richard never seems to have wavered in the policy of maintaining peace between the two kingdoms. He had given back Cherbourg to the King of Navarre (1393); he now proceeded (June 1397) to restore Brest to the Duke of Brittany. It is possible, and even probable, that his chief motives were a sense of his own incapacity as a soldier, and the desire to retrench the cost of foreign garrisons, and apply his money and men to the support of his power at home. But it is certain that the wisest men could only have counselled the same policy, though from different and higher motives; and the government that succeeded Richard's, though constantly challenged to draw the sword, thought it wisest to keep it sheathed. Nevertheless, the truce and alliance with France were viewed with grave displeasure throughout England. The most extravagant stories were circulated against the king; and it was believed that he had spent more than £200,000 on the passage to France and celebration of the marriage, and that he had promised to restore Calais as well as Cherbourg and Brest. There is little doubt that these stories originated with the Duke of Gloucester, who is said to have sold his consent to the marriage for a sum of money and the promise of an earldom to his son, and with whom it may be assumed the king did not keep faith. But Richard's character gave credibility to every charge against him. The king, who had settled £1,000 a year on an exiled king of Armenia, and whose household numbered many hundred persons, might be believed capable of any profusion; and the proposal to give up Calais had already been made at a time when the relations of the French and English courts were less intimate. The nation was right in distrusting its king, and only wrong in trusting one who had no better claim to confidence than an unreasoning opposition to Richard's measures.

CHAPTER XII

RICHARD'S TYRANNY AND FALL.

Intimidation of Parliament. — On Richard's return to England the quarrel between the court and the Duke of Gloucester grew more and more bitter. The king's party were emboldened by the French alliance; the duke felt that he must strike soon if he was to strike successfully. The news of the great battle of Nicopolis (Sept. 1396), in which the flower of French chivalry perished, probably encouraged the duke to renew his attack on the royal administration; and, at his instigation, the principal towns of England held a sort of informal parliament, and sent a deputation to the king at Eltham to complain that the property tax of half a tenth and half a fifteenth, granted in 1392 as a tax of emergency, was still levied, although the country was at peace. The Duke of Lancaster, who was now acting in full concert with the king, told the petitioners to attend at the Parliament which was shortly to meet at Westminster and that they should then have a full answer to their demands. When the Estates came together (Jan. 22, 1397), the Duke of Gloucester and the Earl of Arundel excused themselves on the ground of illness, and the court party succeeded in nominating a dependant of the Earl of Huntingdon's, Sir John Bushey, as Speaker. Nevertheless, the reformers in the Lower House were not

intimidated, and a variety of bills were brought forward
for the redress of abuses. One of these was to restore
the annual appointment of sheriffs, another to provide
for the better defence of the Scotch marches, and a third
to prevent an abuse of men not in a lord's household
wearing his livery, and so defying the law.

Case of Haxey.—Thomas Haxey, Canon of South-
well, in Nottinghamshire, emboldened perhaps by his
privileges as a clergyman, brought forward a bill for the
reform of the king's household, complaining of the bishops
and ladies who thronged it at the public charge, praying
that the prelates might be ordered to reside in their
dioceses, and asking that a tax lately imposed by the pope
might be declared illegal. It is evident that Haxey was
more anxious to reform the church than the state. But
his incautious attack gave Richard the desired opportunity
of punishing a political opponent. The day after Haxey
had brought in his bill (Feb. 2) the Lords were summoned before the king, and the Chancellor was required
to state what matters had lately been discussed in the
conference of the two Houses. Then the king, comment-
ing on the audacious tone of the bills brought in, declared
that Haxey's was against his prerogative, and commissioned the Duke of Lancaster to procure the proposer's
name through the Speaker. Next day the Commons
gave up Haxey's name with abject protestations of
loyalty, which Richard graciously agreed to accept, adding
a promise that he would in future abstain from imposing or
asking for any tenth or fifteenth. Next Monday (Feb. 1)
the Estates, at once intimidated and bribed, voted that if
anyone of whatever state or condition moved or instigated the Commons of Parliament or any other person
to remedy or reform anything that touched the person or
rule or regal rights of the king, he should be accounted a

traitor. On the Wednesday Haxey was brought in before the Council, and condemned to die as a traitor. But the prelates, headed by the Primate, came the same day before the king and interceded for the offender's life, protesting that they only asked it as a matter of grace; and the king, who had probably arranged the scene, granted the petition, and handed Haxey over to be kept in custody by the church. The Parliament now lay at the king's mercy, but as the chief promoters of the opposition could not be seized, Richard contented himself with procuring a confirmation of his right to the customs and the recall of three of the banished judges, Bealknap, Holt, and Burgh, from Ireland. The Duke of Lancaster had sided warmly with his nephew throughout the proceedings, and had lectured the Commons for their inability to understand the reasons of state which might force the king to live beyond his income in time of peace. He was rewarded by a statute legitimating his children by Catharine Swynford, daughter of a Flemish gentleman, Sir Payne Roet, who had been his mistress for years, and whom he had since married, to the great disgust of the higher nobility. The legitimation, however, was not to convey any claim by descent to the crown of England.

Plot Against the Great Nobles.—For some years past the King of England had been negotiating in Germany to obtain the imperial crown, of which the King of the Romans, Wenzel, was generally deemed unworthy. Richard's ephemeral success in Ireland and French marriage had lately increased his prestige, and during the spring of 1397 the English envoys received the homage of Rupert the Elder, Count Palatine and Duke of Bavaria, made a treaty with Rupert the Younger, and were promised the homage of the Archbishop of Cologne. The prospect of new dignity gave the king increased confidence in himself, and the expense which would attend his elevation furnished him with an excuse for borrowing money from his subjects throughout the realm. At the same time, the quarrel with the Duke of Gloucester was unabated. On the return of the English garrison of Brest (June 1397), the duke remonstrated with the king publicly on the small care taken of his soldiers, and his dishonourable policy; and, to show his displeasure more strongly, withdrew from the court. It was customary to refer matters of state to him for his opinion, and to invite him to attend the council; but he seems habitually to have declined on the ground of health, and under no circumstances would attend at London. The Dukes of York and Lancaster withdrew in like manner to their estates, and the seneschal of the royal household, Sir Thomas Percy, anticipating trouble, resigned his appointment. The king was now in the hands of a small clique of violent men, of whom his half-brothers, the Hollands, and William le Scrope were the most dangerous. These men constantly harped on the danger they ran in serving the king, and on the way in which his first advisers had been requited. In July, Thomas de Mowbray, who was then Earl Marshal of England and Captain of Calais, came to Richard with the story of a plot concerted, he said, twelve months before, between the Duke of Gloucester, the Primate, the Earls of Arundel, Warwick, and Derby, and the Abbots of St. Alban's and Westminster, the object of which was to seize the king, and execute summary justice on the lords of the council after the fashion of 1387. The truth of Mowbray's story has often been doubted. He had, by his own account, joined in the conspiracy, and the evidence of a traitor can never be quite trustworthy. He had also a family

feud with the Earl of Warwick about the barony of
Gower.   The story he told, as related by Richard's
French favourites, contains several anachronisms and
discrepancies, and it is at least suspicious that it was
not made part of the indictment against Gloucester and
his fellow-sufferers.   On the other hand, nothing can be
more probable than that some such plans were actually
entertained by the discontented nobility, and Mowbray,
as son-in-law of the Earl of Arundel, was likely to be
taken into their confidence.   That Richard preferred to
punish the old rather than the new offence is in keeping
with his character; but Mowbray's accusation is said to
have been brought forward in Parliament, and the Duke
of Gloucester's language, denying that he had been guilty
of treason since the rising of 1387, seems to prove that a
charge had been made against him.

The Leaders of Opposition Imprisoned.—The
council, in which the king decided on seizing the persons
of the nobles accused of conspiring, was held about the
end of June (June 24).   A fortnight later (July 10) the
Earl of Warwick was in London, staying at the house of
the chancellor, welcomed cordially by the king, and invited to dine with him, when soldiers appeared in the
house, and carried him off to the Tower.   Two days later
(July 12) the Earl of Arundel was seized.   He had been
induced to come to Westminster by his brother, the
Archbishop of Canterbury, on the king's solemn oath
that he should suffer no harm if he came quietly, and
that the only reason for imprisoning him was to show
the German envoys that Richard was supreme in his
dominions.   That same night the city militia was mustered, and the king rode out at their head, and with such
men-at-arms as were in the service of his chief supporters,
to seize the Duke of Gloucester at his country seat of

Plashy, in Essex. The duke was quite unprepared for a siege, and surrendered quietly. There was still dread of a rising among the people; so a proclamation was issued setting forth that there was no intention to revoke the pardons of 1388, and that the nobles arrested had been guilty of new treasons. The clergy were forbidden to offer up prayers for the prisoners. A great council of king and peers was held in the hall of Nottingham Castle (Aug. 1, 1387), and formal indictments of treason were there recited. About seven weeks later (Sept. 17) Parliament met at Westminster to deliberate. The king had collected a number of Cheshire archers, who seemed inclined to revenge Radcot Bridge upon the citizens of London, and his adherents came up escorted by their whole military power. Even, therefore, if Parliament had not been carefully packed with men nominated by the king, it could not have deliberated in freedom. But nobles and knights were alike cowed. The Duke of Lancaster acted throughout as the king's warm partisan. The Duke of York offered no remonstrance. The Earls of Derby and Nottingham applied for a declaration that they had severed themselves from the rebellion of 1387. Among the bishops only the Primate dared say that the king's pardon could not be revoked.

Parliaments of Westminster and Shrewsbury. —Under these circumstances the work of reaction was easy. The Earl of Arundel was condemned to death and executed (September 21). The Earl of Warwick was condemned; but as he implored his life abjectly and with prayers, which moved even Richard to tears, and with a confession of guilt which the king said was dearer to him than the forfeitures of Gloucester and Arundel, the sentence was commuted to life-long imprisonment (Sept. 28). The Duke of Gloucester was cited to appear, but his gaoler, the Earl Marshal, answered for him that he had died in prison at Calais (Sept. 24). As afterwards appeared, Sir William Brickhill, one of the banished judges, had been sent over to question him on the articles of indictment (Sept. 7), and the duke's answers being thought unsatisfactory he had been suffocated with a feather bed. Next to Gloucester and Arundel the king hated the Archbishop of Canterbury, and Parliament readily sentenced him to banishment. It was afterwards said that he did not appear to answer, under a promise that nothing should be done. But it was not safe to enforce the law against a prelate, and Richard had to content himself with persuading the Primate to leave England, by a promise that he should be soon recalled, and with trying to murder him on his way to Rome. A liberal distribution of honours followed. Five earls were made dukes, and one a marquis, and four barons were raised to the rank of earls. Before Parliament adjourned (Sept. 29), its members swore before the shrine of St Edward to maintain without deceit all the statutes and judgments they had consented to.

Richard becomes Despotic.—Four months later the Estates met again at Shrewsbury (Jan. 27, 1398). The king's revenge was not yet satiated, and Sir John Cobham and Sir John Cheyny were condemned to death, and the punishment commuted to imprisonment for life. Then the judges and sergeants-at-law were desired to give their opinion on the answers returned by their predecessors at Nottingham in 1387. They unanimously replied that the answers were good and loyal, and that they should themselves have answered in like manner. Accordingly the king and Estates declared that the acts of the Wonderful Parliament should be annulled and utterly set aside. As if to show more distinctly the king's purpose to destroy all precedents against royal authority, the Act of 1327, by which the De Spensers had been declared traitors, was reversed; and even Alice de Windsor, better known as Alice Perrers, got a promise that her case should be reviewed by the king. It was impossible, as the judges told Richard, that this Parliament could bind its successors, but the members all swore to maintain the ordinances established in it; and Richard announced his intention of communicating with the pope, that church censures might be denounced against any who violated the compact. Then the Commons prayed the king to name a committee of lords and others, to whom the powers of Parliament might be delegated, to examine, answer, and despatch divers petitions, and other matters which the Estates had not time to consider. A precedent for this had been established in the last sitting, when Thomas Percy had been named proctor for the clergy, with power to give assent in their name. Richard willingly assented, and of course formed the committee of his own creatures. Before separating, the Estates granted the king a tax of 20 per cent. upon personalty, and the duties on wool for life, as if with the view of making him for ever independent of Parliament. It was necessary to acknowledge their generosity by some act of grace, and the king issued a general pardon, clogged, however, with three conditions, that the rebels of 1387 must make composition separately; that in case Parliament should hereafter dispute the grant of the wool-tax, the pardon should be revoked; and that all who had compassed the king's life should be excepted. Richard intimated that he had a list, which he would not at present divulge, of fifty persons who had offended in this way. Even his most trusted counsellors professed themselves ignorant of the names thus registered. Practically, therefore, power was reserved to except any man who might offend the king hereafter from the Shrewsbury Act of Grace.

Quarrel of Norfolk and Hereford.—It was afterwards charged against Richard, and seems probable, that he falsified the rolls of Parliament so as to give the committee sanctioned by the Estates a general and lasting power, instead of the mere right to terminate certain arrears of Parliamentary business. It seems certain that he intended to dispense thenceforward with Parliament, at least till it should be necessary to levy extraordinary taxes, and that he meant to pass laws and judge tenants-in-chief by the authority of himself and of the committee. A case of great importance occupied the attention of the committee in the first days of its sitting. There is reason to believe that John of Gaunt had expressed strong displeasure on learning of the Duke of Gloucester's death; and his son, Henry Earl of Derby, and now Duke of Hereford, had been implicated in the insurrection of 1387, and had nothing to trust to but the king's assurance of favour. While Hereford was riding from Brentford to London in the month of December, Mowbray Duke of Norfolk, came up with him, and, as Hereford said, entered into discourse about the danger they were both in, saying that the king had never forgiven the affairs of 1387; and that there was a party about him who wished to reverse the attainder of Earl Thomas of Lancaster, so as to dispossess those among whom his estates had been distributed. Hereford urged the king's pardon and promises, and Mowbray rejoined that neither could be trusted, and that ten years hence he might be plotting their deaths. It is uncertain whether Richard was informed by a spy of the nature of this conversation and forced Hereford to disclose it, or whether Hereford himself volunteered the discovery, or whether John of Gaunt disclosed it, or even

whether Mowbray himself was not the first to charge
Hereford with treason. But the second supposition is,
perhaps, the more probable. Hereford might naturally
distrust a double-dyed traitor like Mowbray, who had
accused his own father-in-law, and who was perhaps employed by the king to elicit fatal confidences. Moreover,
under any circumstances, to denounce the king's projects
beforehand was to force the king to disown them, and so
purchase a reprieve of some years. In fact, Hereford
profited by his disclosures to demand and obtain a fresh
general pardon under the great seal, and by afterwards
appealing to the king in Parliament, forced Richard to
confirm his grace in a set speech before the Estates of the
realm.

Banishment of Norfolk and Hereford.—By the
Parliamentary Commissioners the quarrel of the two
noblemen was referred to the Court of. Chivalry. As
either nobleman flatly denied the words imputed to him
by the other, it was impossible in the absence of witnesses to decide which was speaking the truth, and the
court accordingly decided that they should void the
quarrel by single combat. Some months' delay was
granted that they might prepare themselves, and the
best armourers of Milan and Germany were put in request
to equip them. Richard's first thought was to let the
combat take place. It would rid him of one man at
least whom he regarded as an enemy, perhaps of both ;
and the estates of the vanquished nobleman could be
forfeited. But he had not counted on the strength of
public opinion. Even in France it was considered mon-
strous, that two princes, allied to royalty, should be
suffered to fight in the public lists ; and a special French
envoy was charged to make representations to Richard on
the subject. In England, Hereford, who had served

with some distinction as a crusader, and who was a man
of scholarly acquirement, and with genial and popular
manners, was well liked by all classes, especially in
London; and the belief that he would in some way be
sacrificed to the Duke of Norfolk, who appeared con-
fident of royal support, produced a ferment of indignation.　Richard was warned that the Londoners would
interfere forcibly if their favourite seemed to be getting
the worst, and that even at Coventry, the place fixed
for the duel, Hereford's partisans would preponderate.
Accordingly on the very day of the combat, when the
two dukes had already entered the lists, the king, to the
great disappointment of all present, forbade the duel.
Presently Sir John Bushey appeared, and read out the
king's sentence.　It stated that inasmuch as the Duke
of Hereford had communicated with the Duke of Norfolk
and with the banished Primate, after being forbidden to
do so, he was banished the realm for ten years.　The
Duke of Norfolk having hung back from prosecuting the
appeal of the traitors of 1387, having spoken against the
king's government, and embezzled money allowed for
the good governance of Calais, so that the walls were out
of repair, was condemned to banishment for life with
sequestration of his estates, except a yearly pension of a
£1,000.　The two exiles were to sail from different
ports, and not to come into one another's company.
Among the people there was great murmuring at a
sentence which seemed to bear so heavily on Hereford,
against whom nothing worse was charged than suspicious
communications with men of his own rank.　But the
nobles, understanding that Richard was willing to reduce
Hereford's term of banishment from ten years to six, and
that he would receive letters patent securing to him the
right of inheriting property during his exile, regarded

the sentence with approval, and said that the duke, who was a young man, might well spend a few years in seeing the world, and winning credit in some crusade against the infidel. For Mowbray, whose best friends could only say of him that he had been half-hearted in his treachery, the sole feeling was of execration, and his death in Venice a year later, only called out the comment that it was "the just judgment of God."

Richard was now absolute, and though the violence of his late acts had offended the moral sense of the nation, they were so far excused by the provocation he had received, that a little wisdom and moderation would have made him popular among all classes. Unhappily, he had learned nothing during the long years of dissimulation. The case with which he had beaten down opposition, and the dazzling prospect of an imperial crown, blinded him to the insecure tenure of his power; and some wretched prophecies, which a certain John of Bridlington had composed at the time of our French victories, were interpreted by the king's flatterers to promise him the greatest sovereignty in the world. Richard made progresses about the country, surrounded by his guard of Cheshire archers, forcing nobles and gentry to swear fidelity to the ordinances of the Parliament at Shrewsbury, imposing fines on seventeen counties, forcing many towns to subscribe blank covenants, which he might fill up as he chose, and exacting confiscations from many private persons. A hermit who ventured to intercede for the disinherited earls and their families was straightway sent to the Tower. Even the clergy shared the general discontent, when the king forced a new Primate upon them, left them to sustain the battle against papal provisions single-handed; and out of deference to French policy, desired them to remain

neutral in the church schism that was then raging.
Yet it is probable that all these grievances would have
been endured in silent discontent, if the king had not
ventured on the one breach of public faith that gave the
opposition against him a warlike and popular chief.
John of Gaunt died, it was said of grief for private and
public troubles, early in 1399 (Feb. 3). The Duke of
Hereford lost no time in applying by attorney to have
seisin of his lands. No covenant could be more solemn
than that by which Richard had promised that his cousin
should not be defrauded of his inheritance. But he now
declared that the letters patent had been issued inad-
vertently, and were opposed to the judgment given at
Coventry; and he ordered that the clerk who had procured
them should be drawn, hanged, and quartered as a traitor.
The Duke of Albemarle, Henry's cousin, afterwards protested that he had done his utmost to dissuade Richard
from these proceedings; and Henry's half-brother, the
Marquis of Dorset, declared that he had only given his
consent in fear for his life.

Richard's Second Visit to Ireland.—Richard
himself was beginning to feel uneasy. It is said the
discovery of a new prophecy that might be interpreted
against himself discouraged him. It is probable he per-
ceived at last that he had not a single trustworthy
partisan, except among those whose lives would be forfeited if he were dethroned. Yet with what has since
appeared desperate rashness, he resolved to leave England
at this most critical time, and make a campaign in Ireland.
There was some reason for his presence in that country,
for Mac Murchad, furious that a barony promised him
had been granted away to the Duke of Surrey, was again
harrying the English pale; and the Earl of March,
Richard's cousin and viceroy, had been dragged from his

horse, and torn limb from limb in a battle with the
natives. Having determined upon the expedition,
Richard omitted no precaution that could make it safe.
He reduced the following of the baronage, so that his
own troops might be a match for any revolt in the camp,
and he took with him hostages from every great family
in England; and among them the Duke of Hereford's
eldest son, afterwards Henry V. He carried over the
crown jewels and a large treasure; leaving, however,
more than enough to defray the cost of government at
the disposition of the Council of Regency. These precautions only increased the general disquiet. It was said
the king intended to hold a Parliament in Ireland, and
make a fresh proscription of his most eminent subjects;
after which he would fix his residence in Wales or
Ireland, and govern England from thence as a conquered
province. It was said that William le Scrope, the king's
most obnoxious favourite, had farmed the escheats for
the next three years, and was preparing a series of
indictments to make his contract profitable. It was
noticed that a race of villainous informers was springing
into existence. Men prayed everywhere that the king
might never return. Even a sumptuous tournament which
he celebrated before his departure attracted scarcely any
guests. Men were too sullen to rejoice, or too fearful of
being murdered to attend.

**Henry of Lancaster Invades and Overruns
England.**—The king's campaign in Ireland (June to
Aug.) was only partially successful. Some loss was inflicted upon Art Mac Murragh, and the gallant savage
amused the enemy, whom he was too weak to meet in the
field, with negotiations which were only meant to consume
time and exhaust their provisions. The king was forced
to march hastily upon Dublin, where the Constable of

England, the Duke of Albemarle, arrived with fresh supplies and a fleet of 100 sail. Preparations were made for a new march into the interior. Meanwhile England was lost. Henry of Lancaster had other injuries to avenge beside the loss of his inheritance; for an English ambassador had been sent to break off his engagement to a French princess. He was in communication with the Primate, who came over from Utrecht to be near him, and was joined by the English exiles, who held council in his house. The French court could not openly support Henry against the king's brother-in-law. But the feeling of the French nobles was so strongly in favour of the exiled duke that he was offered any number of French soldiers if he liked to recover his inheritance by force. Henry wisely declined the aid of foreigners, except that he borrowed three ships from his cousin, the Duke of Brittany. With these he coasted from Vannes to Boulogne, where the rest of his followers joined him, when the whole force amounted to less than 100 persons, of whom fifteen only were men-at-arms, in ten or twelve ships. It seems to have sailed first along the southern coast of England, spreading the news of the duke's return, and then made directly for the north, went up the Humber, and put in at the ruined port of Ravenspur some time in July (? July 4). Henry first marched north upon Pickering, one of his own castles, which was surrendered to him, and then, with equally good results, upon two of his other castles, Knaresborough and Pontefract. He was soon joined by the Earls of Northumberland and Westmoreland, who carried with them the whole power of the north. Only a few years before, the Percys had been at deadly feud with the House of Lancaster, and throughout the reign they had taken part with Richard. But the king, probably thinking them only half-hearted in his cause, had

withdrawn his favour from them of late ; and the Duke of
Exeter had advanced a claim to the earl's homage for one
of the oldest manors the Percys held. Some imprudent
language used by the earl and his son, Hotspur, was reported at court, and Richard summoned them to attend
nim on his passage to Ireland with the intention of punishing them ; they were warned, and refused to, obey the
summons, pleading that their presence was needed on the
Scotch marches, and that Richard had men enough without them. The king accordingly banished them, and they
so far obeyed the sentence as to retire into Scotland, where
their old enemies gave them a hearty welcome. Ralf
Neville, Earl of Westmoreland, was in favour at court,
and connected by his son's marriage with the Hollands.
But he was still more closely connected with the Duke of
Lancaster, whose sister he had married ; and he probably
feared that Northumberland's fate might one day be his
own.

From the day the northern earls joined him, Henry's
victory was assured. He proceeded at first with great
caution, dismissing the few foreigners who were with him,
professing to have no thought except to claim his inheritance, and at the same time circulating manifestoes, in
which he accused Richard of intending to massacre his
chief opponents, and to increase the burdens laid upon
the villans, and to sell all his possessions in France to the
French king. In the Council of Regency, the Duke of
York was at best half-hearted to the king, and the Marquis
of Dorset was planning how to desert ; Scrope and the
counsellors of inferior rank were paralysed with alarm ;
and only the Bishop of Norwich had the wish and the
capacity to make head against the insurrection. Even he
soon found that he was powerless. Thousands of men
assembled at the royal summons, and took the liberal pay

offered ; but the language of all was that they would do
nothing to hurt the Duke of Lancaster.   Unable to stay
in London or to muster at St Albans, where the country
people remembered the massacres of 1382, the Council
shifted their place of rendezvous to Oxford, and resolved
to march hastily across country, secure Bristol, and wait
at some Welsh port with such forces as they could command.   The plan was good, and perhaps the only one
feasible, but it could not be carried out, for Henry
marched across country to intercept them, and though he
reached Bristol later than the king's army, the mere sight
of his banner was sufficient to disarm resistance.   York
and Dorset made terms (July 27), and Sir Peter Courtenay,
by York's orders, surrendered Bristol Castle with the persons of Scrope, Bushey and Green, who were beheaded
next morning.   Henry of Lancaster was now at the head of
an army estimated at 100,000 men.   He at once marched
upon Cheshire and North Wales, the one part in which
Richard was popular, and where his adherents were collecting forces.   Hearing nothing from the king, and dis-
mayed by Henry's summary execution of Sir Piers Legh,
the justice of the principality, the royalists dispersed to
their own homes.

Richard's Army Disperses.—While Henry of
Lancaster had been carrying out his invasion of England,
contrary winds had suspended all communication with
Ireland.   The first messenger who brought news of what
had happened had been sent at a time when the danger
seemed small, and the king accordingly contented himself
with securing the persons of his two chief hostages, and
with making arrangements for the government of the province.   The next messenger reported the progress of the
rebellion, and the march of the royal army toward Milford
Haven.   More time was now lost in transferring the

troops to Waterford as the best port of embarkation, and
when the king at last landed in Wales (Aug. 5), instead
of finding an army of loyal subjects ready to support him,
he was greeted with the news of the surrender of Bristol,
and the defection of the whole kingdom to his cousin.
Next morning the troops he brought over, 32,000 in all,
were reduced by desertions to some 6,000, and even of
these many were foreign mercenaries. The King's Council
debated what should be done. The Earl of Salisbury and
the Bishop of Carlisle advised that the king should take
refuge in Bordeaux; but the Duke of Exeter urged that
to fly the kingdom would be to renounce the crown, and
that Conway Castle on the sea would be perfectly safe,
would allow of escape to France, and that from it Richard
might arrange a compromise or prepare to raise his standard again. This opinion prevailed, and Richard left the
camp secretly that night. Next morning the army dispersed in dismay. The king's steward, Sir Thomas Percy,
announced with tears to the royal household that the king
thanked them for their good service, and exhorted them
to care for themselves as they best might. He then broke
his wand of office, and set out himself with the Duke of
Albemarle to make their peace with Henry of Lancaster.

Richard is made Prisoner.—Thus far the success
of the insurrection had been miraculous. But its leaders
knew that their position was insecure. They could not
keep a large army in the field, and if Richard escaped to
France, or was able to hold out in Conway, popular feeling was not unlikely to declare itself, after a time, in favour
of a compromise. Accordingly, when the Duke of Exeter
arrived at Henry's headquarters with a commission to
negotiate, he was detained in camp and the Earl of Northumberland sent to Conway in his place. What then happened cannot be exactly known. Richard's partisans say

that Northumberland produced a forged letter from the Duke of Exeter, telling the king to trust the earl implicitly, and that Northumberland represented Henry of Lancaster as desiring nothing but restoration to his lands and dignities, and confirmed the assertion with an oath on the Eucharist. On the other hand, Henry's official narrative, entered on the Rolls of Parliament, declares that the Primate was present at the interview with Northumberland, and that the king declared to both that he was willing to renounce the crown, and only delayed the formal act of cession till he had met the Duke in a private interview. It is admitted by the royalist writer that Richard expressed his determination of breaking faith if he ever recovered power; and it may be assumed that Northumberland promised and even swore to something which he knew would not be granted. Richard probably expected to be subjected to another Council of Regency like that of 1387, and did not understand how completely his own bad faith had made compromise or reconciliation impossible. He seems to have been first disenchanted when he found himself at Flint Castle in the midst of a large army, and was told by his cousin that there was no chance of saving him from the wrath of the Londoners, unless he consented to be taken along with the army as a prisoner. At the same time, the Primate overwhelmed him with savage reproaches, till even the Duke of Lancaster was moved to pity and bade the speaker be silent. Richard's powers of dissimulation did not forsake him. He professed himself satisfied; and seeing a favourite greyhound of his own fawn upon the duke, told him to accept it as an omen that he was to be king. He also consented to issue writs for a Parliament, and letters ordering the great abbots to send up the chronicles of the country and persons skilled in them; but when he found himself with none but his own friends about him, he gave way to passionate wailings, lamenting that he had ever spared his cousin's life, vowing that he had never transgressed in anything against the kingdom of England, and hoping that his French and German kinsmen would avenge him. The one redeeming circumstance in his grief was the genuine love and anxiety he displayed for his young queen (Aug. 19).

The Estates Depose Richard and Elect Henry of Lancaster.—There was some delay in making provision for Richard's progress across country, apparently from a fear lest the Welsh royalists should rescue him, and there was time in consequence for the Londoners to send a deputation, which met the army at Coventry, and requested the Duke to put his captive to death summarily. This Henry of course declined to do without authority of Parliament. The Estates met on Michaelmas day at Westminster. On the first day a deputation of peers and judges waited upon Richard in the Tower, and reminded him, by the Lancastrian account, of the promise to abdicate which he had given at Conway. The king desired to speak in private with his cousin of Lancaster, and having done this, received the deputation again with a cheerful countenance, and insisted on reading over the act of abdication himself. It was chiefly a formal release to his subjects of their allegiance, but it contained a clause in which he was made to say that he confessed himself to be altogether useless and insufficient, and worthy to be deposed for his manifest demerits. At the end he said that, if it depended upon himself, he should like the Duke of Lancaster to be his successor; and in sign of this he placed his own signet ring on the duke's finger. But as the power to fill the throne rested with the Estates of the realm, he constituted the Archbishop of York and the Bishop of Hereford proctors to

announce his abdication.   Next day Parliament met in
the great hall at Westminster; the empty throne was
covered with cloth of gold, and the royal proctors
appeared, and read out the king's act of abdication in
Latin and English.   There was a general feeling that the
surrender ought to be accompanied with a statement of
the various acts by which the king had alienated his
people.   Accordingly, a formal act of indictment, which
had already been prepared, was read aloud.   It began by
rehearsing those clauses of the coronation oath in which
the king swore to protect the church, to govern in justice
and mercy, and to maintain thé laws and customs of the
realm, and it proceeded to enumerate thirty-three instances in which the king had violated his oath.   The
most important of these were, of course, the questions put
to the judges in 1387, and the *coup d'état* of 1397,
with the murder of the Duke of Gloucester, and the surrender of power procured from the Parliament of Shrewsbury.   The injustice done to the Duke of Lancaster
figured prominently.   It was also urged that the king
had taxed his people in time of peace more heavily
than had been customary in time of war; that he had
borrowed and not repaid; that he had alienated the crown
lands; that he had raised money by forcing individuals,
and even whole counties, to fine for offences more or less
imaginary; that he had caused men to be imprisoned
arbitrarily; and that he had tried to subvert the Constitution by procuring letters of dispensation from the pope,
and by often saying that the laws of the realm were as he
chose to declare or think, and that the life and property
of his subjects were held in his good pleasure.   An extract from his will showed that he had bound over his
successor to maintain the ordinances of Shrewsbury under
penalty of forfeiting the royal treasure.   It was charged

against him that his faithlessness was notorious throughout Europe; and an instance of even grotesque swindling was alleged, in which the king had induced the Primate, by protestations of affection and the sending a private token, to transport his treasure to the royal palace for safe keeping when he was driven into exile, an act of confidence which the king had requited by breaking open the boxes and spending the treasure. The truth of most of these charges was matter of notoriety. The Estates agreed unanimously to depose the king, and appointed commissioners to renounce their homage to him in behalf of the whole people of England; thus not so much accepting the king's abdication, as using it to justify the act of their own sovereign power. The throne was now considered vacant; and the Duke of Lancaster, rising up and crossing himself, said, "In the name of Father, Son, and Holy Ghost, I, Henry of Lancaster, challenge this realm of England and the crown, with all the members and the appurtenances, as that I am descended by right line of the blood arising from the good lord King Henry the Third, and through that right that God of his grace hath sent me, with help of my kin and of my friends, to recover it, the which realm was in point to be undone for default of governance and undoing of the good laws." The Estates were questioned one by one what they thought of the claim, and replied unanimously that the duke should be their king. So the Primate led Henry to the vacant throne, and preached a short sermon from the text, "A man shall rule over the people," with well understood references to the mischievous rule of Richard, who had been crowned as a child, and with oblique reflections on the proper heir, the young Earl of March. Then the king-elect thanked the Estates in a short speech, promising to disturb no man in his right, and pointing out that he had come to save the country in urgent public necessity. "And I maintain that when a king sets his kingdom in a blaze, or destroys town or village by fire, as King Richard has done, that he has forfeited his crown."

Richard Abdicates.—Next day the Estates met again; and as the deputation charged to announce his deposition to King Richard had not yet executed their mission, Merks, Bishop of Carlisle, rose up and protested against the course of proceedings. He pointed out that the worst malefactor ought not to be condemned unheard, much less a sovereign who had ruled them more than twenty years, and argued that Henry of Lancaster had violated the laws by his return to England. He wound up by demanding that Richard should be brought before the Estates, and questioned if he were willing to resign his crown. It is probable that this desperate proposition was suggested by the king himself, who hoped to recover the old allegiance of his subjects by a personal appeal. Henry, of course, could not permit such an interview; and Merks, who was in high discredit, having been the king's boon companion, was taken into custody for disputing the late settlement. Then the proctors of Parliament waited upon Richard, and the justiciary, Sir William Thirning, a judge of Richard's appointment, and who had vindicated the Nottingham consultation in the Shrewsbury Parliament, read out the renunciation of homage based on the king's confession of inability to govern. The deposed king answered to the last words, giving up obeisance and faith, that he looked not thereafter, but hoped that his cousin would be good lord to him. Some explanatory remarks from the justiciary provoked a declaration from Richard that he did not and could not renounce the religious character of kingship given him by his anointing, and the justiciary's rejoinder that he had confessed himself unworthy, was met by the answer that he had only admitted that his government was not pleasing to the people. Even in this supreme moment of powerlessness the king was evidently devising subterfuges, by which at some happier time he might cancel every oath he had taken. Sir William pointed out that the abdication had been complete and unconditional, and the king instantly acquiesced with a pleasant countenance, and only expressed a hope that he might receive an honourable sustenance.

Rebellion in Favour of Richard.—In what manner he should be maintained was the next question with which Parliament busied itself; and sentence was given that John of Bordeaux, styled Richard, King of England, should be put in a royal prison, and fed with the best food that could be had for money, and that if there should be any trouble of people in arms to deliver him, he should be the first to die for it. In all likelihood this was only regarded as a provisional arrangement, for three weeks later the first Parliament summoned by Henry IV. requested that the captive king might be brought to public trial. Public feeling at the time was very warm from the angry discussions which had taken place between Richard's old partisans and the aggrieved nobility, the deposed king's favourites constantly protesting that in all they did they had acted under fear of death. The new king, however, was honourably anxious to avoid proceeding to extremities, and perhaps a little influenced by a French embassy which had come to intercede. He postponed proceedings for a few days, on pretence that all the bishops were not present, and it was finally determined (Oct. 24) in a conference of the peers, where all were sworn to secresy, that Richard should be

put in sure custody in a place where there was no resort
of people, that none of his friends should be allowed
access to him, and that he should not be suffered to
write or receive letters. There is reason to believe that
the general feeling of Lords and Commons was in favour
of putting him to death, and that only the king's positive
determination not to shed his blood saved him. Henry's
clemency was ill requited by the royalists. Within
three months an army was in the field, headed by the
Earls of Kent, Huntingdon, and Salisbury, who carried
with them a priest named Maudeleyn, who strongly resembled King Richard, and gave out that the king had
escaped from prison. Betrayed, surprised, and almost
taken, Henry was saved by the enthusiasm of the people,
who mustered to support him in such numbers that the
insurgents were compelled to fall back hastily from
Windsor and Oxford upon the western counties. There
the people of Cirencester rose in arms, and captured and
killed the Earls of Kent and Salisbury, while the men of
Bristol did equally stern justice on the Lords Lumley
and Despenser, and the men of Essex on the Earl of
Huntingdon, who had remained near London.

Richard's Death.—There can be no doubt that the
lenity which the king had shown was generally distaste-
ful, and that men generally were resolved not to leave any
more noble traitors to the doubtful justice of their peers in
Parliament. Richard learned in his prison at Pontefract
of the utter ruin of his cause, and sunk under the blow
(Feb. 14, 1400), refusing it is said to eat till it was too
late to take food, when he was better counselled and
repented. His body with the face exposed for general
recognition was brought by easy stages to Langley, and
there buried without pomp. But there were not wanting
men who declared that he had been starved to death by

his gaolers, or others, who pointed suspiciously to the bands in which his forehead was swathed, and declared that he had been brained with an axe by Sir Piers Exton, after a desperate hand fight against seven assailants. The first can only be refuted by our trust in Henry's character; the second has been so far disproved that the skull has been examined and displays no trace of a wound. Later on another romance found belief: it was said that the dead body exposed had been that of Maudeleyn, the king's chaplain, who had been beheaded at Tyburn (Feb. 4), and that Richard himself had escaped into Scotland. It is certain that some one pretending to be Richard, and acknowledged for Richard by the Scotch court, was maintained at the charge of the Scotch kings till he died in 1419, and there is strong evidence that during the whole of this time some persons at least in England believed their old monarch to be alive. That he took no steps to recover his throne may be explained by the statement that his intellect was disordered. But the arguments against this story are strong. It would seem that Creton, a Frenchman, who knew Richard personally and believed him to be alive was sent into Scotland in 1405 on a diplomatic mission by the French court. Soon after his return, Isabella of France, Richard's second queen, was married to the Duke of Orleans. The inference seems irresistible that Creton was sent to ascertain the truth of the story, and reported against it. Why the Scotch Government should have entertained and pensioned an impostor is easily accounted for. For purposes of hostility against England a false Richard was preferable to a true one. But it is suspicious that he was never seriously put forward by the enemies of England, or dreaded by the English Government.

Henry IV.'s Mercy.—Few things are more remarkable, or more creditable to Henry IV., than the blood-lessness of the first period of the revolution. Except that Scrope, Bushey, and Green were sacrificed to popular indignation at Bristol, and that one Hall was put to death as the murderer of the Duke of Gloucester, not a single Englishman suffered on the scaffold. This lenity could not of course be maintained after the insurrection of the three earls ; and, besides the leaders, twenty-six persons suffered at Oxford, and four in London. It is said that in the case of the prisoners tried in London, the judges declared that they could not be found guilty on any capital charge, and that the Earl of Arundel ordered them to death on his own authority, to please the populace. But the story comes from a foreigner, and seems unworthy of full credit, as two at least of the number, Shelley and Maudeleyn, had actually been in arms against the king recognised by Parliament.. It is not unlikely, however, that here as elsewhere Henry IV.'s partisans were more zealous than himself. Three church-men, who from their eminent rank escaped the penalty of the law on this occasion, were soon liberated without worse punishment than a short imprisonment, and two of them afterwards obtained promotion from the crown.

Reversal of Richard's Acts.—All Richard's violent changes were cancelled in the first Parliament which the new king called. The Speaker, Sir William Durward, presented a petition from the Commons, praying that the king's lieges might be as free as in time past; that the acts of the Parliament of Shrewsbury might be annulled, and the acts of the Wonderful Parliament confirmed; and that all the disinherited lords might be restored to their inheritances. The king, with advice of the Peers, at once assented to the petition. By a series of subsequent acts the new titles of Richard's creation were cancelled.

But the Duke of Brittany's services did not procure him
the restoration of the earldom of Richmond, which
Richard had given to the Earl of Westmoreland; and the
only forfeitures of property, till the rebellion of the three
earls, were of those who had suffered at Bristol. History
does not record a more orderly revolution. The union of
all classes made Henry of Lancaster irresistible; and his
own moderation and decision enabled him to put aside
the violent counsels which were freely rendered, and
which the nation at large approved. There is a story
that he once thought of challenging the crown as his by
right of conquest, and was dissuaded by the justiciary,
Sir William Thirning, who showed him that such a claim
would invalidate every title deed in England. He accordingly was careful to disclaim the right of conquest in his
first speech in Parliament. The expression that he was
of "the right line of blood," may, and probably does,
mean only that he wished to limit the Parliamentary
right of election to a prince of the blood. But it served
in later times as the pretext for an extravagant fable,
probably fathered during the Wars of the Roses, that
Henry's great-great-grandfather, Edmund Hunchback, Earl
of Lancaster, was really the elder brother of Edward I.,
and had been unjustly set aside from the succession on
account of his deformity.

Character of Richard II.—Another more ancient
fable, that Richard II. was a bastard, originated no doubt
in the disposition to account for his degeneracy from the
Black Prince, and has no shadow of probability except
from his mother's light fame. To us who look across
time, it is evident that never man was more justified in
his child, than Prince Edward in Richard of Bordeaux.
Both the redeeming and the worse traits of either character were for the most part the same; the uxoriousness, the

affection for friends, the sumptuousness of taste, the liberality, the devotion, the ready insight, and the fearless presence of mind, no less than the unscrupulousness, the ferocity, the drift toward low profligacy, and the inability to listen to wise counsel. But the father was trained a soldier, and fell upon times when to be a brilliant general was to be the saviour and darling of the English people; while the son, probably with less aptitude, certainly with less taste for war, was partly unable to attempt costly campaigns, and partly reluctant to renounce the struggle against constitutional liberty. Very different from Edward II., whom he seems superficially to resemble, Richard II. in later years at least was never governed by his favourites, but pursued a policy of his own, with which they were not trusted, and which kept them in constant terror by its breadth, its thoroughness, and its secrecy. Could he have held his hands from his cousin's heritage, at least till that cousin was in his power, Richard would probably have succeeded in transforming the English monarchy after the French model. But he misunderstood the nature of his own success. He had triumphed for a time, because in a small and thinly scattered population, even a small force could easily overawe resistance for a time, and because his opponents had committed many mistakes. But the mere presence of a hostile leader, the mere raising of a rival flag, were sufficient in a country where half the able-bodied men were soldiers, to transfer the crown to one who a few days before had been a beggared exile. The deposition of an unworthy king was repeated for the second time in a century, and Magna Charta never needed to be confirmed again.

State of the People during Richard II.'s Reign. —To his people Richard's misgovernment was less costly, and even less dangerous, than the splendid successes of the third Edward and of his son had been.　Men demoralised by war murmured at peace; men accustomed to plunder in foreign countries sate down sullenly to till the fields and pay taxes.　But population increased again; trade found new channels in the German and Baltic Seas, and agriculture revived.　Langley gave the highest expression to the old forms of English poetry in the vision of Piers Plowman; and Gower and Chaucer founded a new school.　Wycliffe and his followers stirred religious thought and feeling to their depths.　Questions of constitutional change, questions of personal freedom, questions of reform in church and law, all were in the air and in men's minds and on their lips.　Could the country have consented to forego its miserable ambition, and the dreams of foreign dominion, it might have retrieved all that the policy of a single warlike king had given to wreck.　But the curse of blood wantonly shed, which had overtaken the heir of the victorious princes, was yet to work itself out upon the nation which had escaped their policy.　Exhausted, held back from war, or occupied with other and better impulses as England might seem to be, it had no stronger wish than to renew the struggle which had been the heroic episode of the 14th century.

INDEX

HISTORICAL HANDBOOKS

EDITED BY

OSCAR BROWNING, M.A.,
FELLOW OF KING'S COLLEGE, CAMBRIDGE.

Crown 8vo.

ENGLISH HISTORY IN THE XIVth CENTURY.

By CHARLES H. PEARSON, M.A., *Principal of the Presbyterian Ladies' College, Melbourne, late Fellow of Oriel College, Oxford, and Professor of History in the University of Melbourne ; sometime Professor of Modern History in King's College, London.* 3s. 6d.

CONTENTS.

Introduction—State of Scotland in the Thirteenth Century—Misgovernment of Edward II.—Death of Edward II.—First years of Edward III.—The war with France—Subjugation of France—The Loss of the French Conquests—The results of Foreign Aggression—The minority of Richard II.—Richard's Government—Richard's Tyranny and Fall.

THE REIGN OF LEWIS XI.

By P. F. WILLERT, M.A., *Fellow of Exeter College, Oxford. With Map and Genealogical Table.* 3s. 6d.

EXTRACT FROM PREFACE.

"The consolidation of the French kingdom by the most able of the Valois, and the struggle between France and Burgundy has been fully traced by many distinguished authors, among others by M. de Barante in his most interesting "History of the Dukes of Burgundy," by Sismondi, and Michelet, and Henry Martin in the course of their great works, and by Mr Kirk in his "Life of Charles the Bold." But these books may not happen to be easily within reach of the schoolboy or even of the undergraduate. This little book, accordingly, attempts to give a connected, a clear, and a tolerably full account of the events and the nature of a reign which left France a consolidated and powerful nation, fully prepared for the part she was destined to play in the great struggle of the next century."

THE ROMAN EMPIRE. A.D. 395–800.

By A. M. CURTEIS, M.A., *Assistant-Master at Sherborne School, late Fellow of Trinity College, Oxford. With Maps.* 3s. 6d.

CONTENTS.

Administrative and Legal Unity—The Christian Church in the First Four Centuries—The Barbarians on the Frontier—Century IV.—Church and State in Constantinople, Eutropius and Chrysostom—Chrysostom and the Empress Eudoxia—Alaric and the Visigoths, 396-419—Genseric and the Vandals, 423-533—Attila and the Huns, 435-453—The "Change of Government," commonly called the Fall of the Western Empire, 475-526—The Emperor Justinian, 527-563—The Empire in relation to the Barbarians of the East, 450-650—Mohammed and Mohammedanism, 622-711—The Popes and the Lombards in Italy, 540-740—The Franks and the Papacy, 500-800—Synopsis of Historical Events.

MAPS :—Central Europe, about A.D. 400—The Roman Empire at the beginning of the sixth Century.—Italy, 600-750.—Europe in the time of Charles the Great.

RIVINGTONS : Waterloo Place, London ; Oxford ; and Cambridge.

[B—504]

HISTORY OF THE ENGLISH INSTITUTIONS.

By PHILIP V. SMITH, M.A., *Barrister-at-Law; Fellow of King's College, Cambridge.* 3s. 6d.

CONTENTS.

Social and Local Development of the Constitution.

Origin of the English Institutions—The People—Local Government.

Constituents of the Central Authority.

The King—Parliament—The King's Council.

Central Government.

Legislation—Judicature—The Executive—Taxation—Chronological Table—Index and Glossary.

[*Used as a Text-Book for the Cambridge University Lectures in Populous Towns.*]

HISTORY OF MODERN ENGLISH LAW.

By Sir ROLAND KNYVET WILSON, Bart., M.A., *Barrister-at-Law; late Fellow of King's College, Cambridge.* 3s. 6d.

CONTENTS.

The English Law in the Time of Blackstone.

The form in which it was Enunciated—Property, Contract, and Absolute Duties—Wrongs and Remedies, Civil and Criminal—Procedure—Laws relating to Special Classes of Persons.

Life and Work of Bentham.

Biography—The Writings of Bentham—Early Attempts at Law Reform.

Legal Changes since 1825.

Changes as to the Form in which the Law is Enunciated—Changes in the Law of Property, Contract, and Absolute Duties—Changes in the Laws as to Wrongs and Remedies—Changes in the Laws relating to Procedure and Evidence—Changes in the Laws relating to Special Classes of Persons—Chronological Table of Cases and Statutes.

HISTORY OF FRENCH LITERATURE.

Adapted from the French of M. DEMOGEOT. *By* CHRISTIANA BRIDGE. 3s. 6d.

CONTENTS.

Introduction.

THE MIDDLE AGES:—Epic Poetry—Lyric Poetry—Clerical Society in the Middle Ages—History in the Middle Ages—The Drama—The Fifteenth Century—an Age of Transition.

THE RENAISSANCE:—Roman Jurisprudence—Moral and Political Philosophy—Oratory—Pamphlets—Memoirs—History—Poetry and Reform of Literature.

THE SEVENTEENTH CENTURY:—Foreign Influence—Novelists—The Drama—The Age of Richelieu—Philosophy and Eloquence—Louis XIV. and his Court—Age of Louis XIV.—The Drama and Poetry—Philosophy and Oratory.

THE EIGHTEENTH CENTURY:—Voltaire—Strife of Doctrines—The Encyclopædists and the Religious Party—Jean Jacques Rousseau—End of the Eighteenth Century.

THE NINETEENTH CENTURY:—The First Empire—The Restoration—History and Criticism—Conclusion.

IN PREPARATION.

THE GREAT REBELLION.

By the EDITOR.

HISTORY OF THE FRENCH REVOLUTION.

By the Rev. J. FRANK BRIGHT, M.A., *Fellow of University College, and Historical Lecturer in Balliol, New, and University Colleges, Oxford; late Master of the Modern School at Marlborough College, author of " An English History for the use of Public Schools."*

THE AGE OF CHATHAM.

By Sir W. R. ANSON, Bart., M.A., *Fellow of All Souls' College, and Vinerian Reader of Law, Oxford.*

THE AGE OF PITT.

By the Same.

THE SUPREMACY OF ATHENS.

By R. C. JEBB, M.A., *Professor of Greek in the University of Glasgow, and Public Orator of the University of Cambridge.*

THE ROMAN REVOLUTION. From B.C. 133 to the Battle of Actium.

By H. F. PELHAM, M.A., *Fellow and Lecturer of Exeter College, Oxford.*

HISTORY OF THE UNITED STATES.

By Sir GEORGE YOUNG, Bart., M.A., *late Fellow of Trinity College, Cambridge.*

HISTORY OF ROMAN POLITICAL INSTITUTIONS.

By J. S. REID, M.L., *Christ's College, Cambridge.*

OPINIONS OF THE PRESS.

WILSON'S MODERN ENGLISH LAW.

"We have in Blackstone's *Commentaries*, in so far as they are to be trusted, a comprehensive view of the state of the law at the time at which he wrote, and there are also abundant means of ascertaining what the law is at the present moment. It is of great importance, however, to observe the nature of the changes which have taken place during the intervening period, and the student has hitherto been at a loss for any systematic information on this subject. It has been Sir R. Wilson's object to supply this deficiency, and he has succeeded in doing so to a certain extent in a very clear and interesting manner."—*Saturday Review.*

"The style and method of the book are so clear and orderly that an ordinary reader is never puzzled by a sentence, and a copious index renders it both valuable and available as a book of reference."—*Morning Post.*

SMITH'S ENGLISH INSTITUTIONS.

[*Used as a Text Book for the Cambridge University Lectures in Populous Towns.*]

"It contains in a short compass an amount of information not otherwise accessible to students without considerable research. The chapter on Local Government in particular is well executed. It would be hard to name any other book in which the history of our local institutions, from the Gemots of the first Teutonic settlers down to the County Court, the Local Government Board, and the School Board of our own day, is to be found."—*Athenæum.*

"It is an admirable guide, and worthy of our warmest commendation."—*Standard.*

"It is emphatically one which ought to find its way into all schools, as an introduction to the more important works of Hallam, May, and Blackstone, and a companion to the histories of England."—*Educational Times.*

CURTEIS' ROMAN EMPIRE, A.D. 395–800.

"We have very carefully examined the chapters on the 'Barbarians,' the Visigoths, the Vandals, and the Huns, and can pronounce them the best condensed account that we have read of the westerly migrations."—*Athenæum.*

"An admirable specimen of careful condensation and good arrangement, and as a school book it will assuredly possess a high value."—*Scotsman.*

BRIDGE'S FRENCH LITERATURE.

"An excellent manual."—*Athenæum.*

"A clever adaptation."—*London Quarterly Review.*

"It is clear, idiomatic, and flowing, possessing all the characteristics of good English composition. Its perusal will furnish abundant evidence of the richness and variety of French Literature, of which it is a good and sufficient handbook."—*British Quarterly Review.*

"We cannot too highly commend this careful analysis of the characteristics of the great French writers."—*Standard.*

3, WATERLOO PLACE, PALL MALL.
November, 1876.

𝔅ooks for 𝔖chools and ℭolleges

PUBLISHED BY

MESSRS. RIVINGTON

HISTORY

An English History for the Use of Public Schools.

By the Rev. J. FRANCK BRIGHT, M.A., *Fellow of University College, and Historical Lecturer in Balliol, New, and University Colleges, Oxford; late Master of the Modern School at Marlborough College.*

With numerous Maps and Plans.   Crown 8vo.

This work is divided into three Periods of convenient and handy size, especially adapted for use in Schools, as well as for Students reading special portions of History for local and other Examinations. It will also be issued in one complete Volume.

Period I.—MEDIÆVAL MONARCHY: The departure of the Romans, to Richard III.   From A.D. 449 to A.D. 1485.   4*s.* 6*d.*

Period II.—PERSONAL MONARCHY: Henry VII. to James II.   From A.D. 1485 to A.D. 1688.   5*s.*

Period III.—CONSTITUTIONAL MONARCHY: William and Mary, to the present time.   From A.D. 1688 to A.D. 1837.   [*Now Ready.*

"Amid the numerous crude and hastily compiled historical manuals that the press is now pouring forth, it is a relief to meet with a piece of sterling, careful work like this first instalment of Mr. Bright's English History. . . . A careful examination of its pages can hardly fail to suggest that it has cost the compiler a great deal of trouble, and is likely, in consequence, to save both teacher and learner a proportionate amount.   For the use for which it is especially designed—that of a text-book in our public schools—it is excellently adapted."—*Academy.*

"An air of good common sense pervades it; the style is entirely free from affectation or inflation, and is at the same time tolerably clear and easy to follow."
Athenæum.

"We do not know a book more suitable for school use, or one more likely to stimulate in boys an intelligent interest in constitutional and social history.   We confess to having read the greater part of it with a very real pleasure."—*Educational Times.*

"It is written in a clear, straightforward, sensible way, and contains as much instruction as possible, put in a way that can be easily understood."—*Examiner.*

"It is a critical and thoughtful examination of the growth of this great nation; and while the facts are given always with clearness and force, the student is led to understand and to reflect not merely upon the events themselves, but upon a number of interesting and important considerations arising out of these events."
School Board Chronicle.

"A model of what a clear, attractive, well-arranged, and trustworthy manual of historical information ought to be."
Glasgow Herald.

"We can speak with entire satisfaction of the style in which the work is done, Mr. Bright's is a lucid, steady, vigorous style, which leaves nothing in doubt, and is comprehensive and thoroughly practical."
Liverpool Albion.

"Admirably adapted for the purpose intended, and should rank high as a text-book in all educational establishments."
Civil Service Gazette.

"Mr. Bright has done his work, as it seems to us, in a very careful manner."
Scotsman.

"The narrative is clear and concise, and illustrated by useful plans and maps."
Notes and Queries.

(*See Specimen Page, No.* 1.)

LONDON, OXFORD AND CAMBRIDGE.

HISTORICAL HANDBOOKS

Edited by

OSCAR BROWNING, M.A.,

FELLOW OF KING'S COLLEGE, CAMBRIDGE.

Crown 8vo.

(*See Specimen Pages, Nos.* 3 *and* 4.)

HISTORY OF THE ENGLISH INSTITUTIONS.

By PHILIP V. SMITH, M.A.; *Barrister-at-Law; Fellow of King's College, Cambridge.* 3s. 6d.

CONTENTS.

Social and Local Development of the Constitution.

Origin of the English Institutions—The People—Local Government.

Constituents of the Central Authority.

The King—Parliament—The King's Council.

Central Government.

Legislation—Judicature—The Executive—Taxation—Chronological Table.
Index and Glossary.

ENGLISH HISTORY IN THE XIVth CENTURY.

By CHARLES H. PEARSON, M.A., *Head Master of the Presbyterian Ladies' College, Melbourne, late Fellow of Oriel College, Oxford.*
3s. 6d.

CONTENTS.

Introduction—State of Scotland in the Thirteenth Century—Misgovernment of Edward II.—Death of Edward II.—First Years of Edward III.—The War with France—Subjugation of France—The Loss of the French Conquests—The Results of Foreign Aggression—The Minority of Richard II.—Richard's Government—Richard's Tyranny and Fall.

THE REIGN OF LEWIS XI.

By P. F. WILLERT, M.A., *Fellow of Exeter College, Oxford.*
With Map. 3s. 6d.

LONDON, OXFORD, AND CAMBRIDGE.

HISTORICAL HANDBOOKS—continued.

THE ROMAN EMPIRE. A.D. 395–800.

By A. M. CURTEIS, M.A., *Assistant-Master at Sherborne School, late Fellow of Trinity College, Oxford.*

With Maps. 3*s.* 6*d.*

CONTENTS.

Administrative and Legal Unity—The Christian Church in the First Four Centuries—The Barbarians on the Frontier—Century IV.—Church and State in Constantinople, Eutropius and Chrysostom—Chrysostom and the Empress Eudoxia—Alaric and the Visigoths, 396–419—Genseric and the Vandals, 423–533—Attila and the Huns, 435–453—The "Change of Government," commonly called the Fall of the Western Empire, 475–526—The Emperor Justinian, 527–565—The Empire in relation to the Barbarians of the East, 450–650—Mohammed and Mohammedanism, 622–711—The Popes and the Lombards in Italy, 540–740—The Franks and the Papacy, 500–800—Synopsis of Historical Events—Index.

MAPS.

Central Europe, about A.D. 400—The Roman Empire at the beginning of the sixth Century.—Italy, 600–750.—Europe in the time of Charles the Great.

"We have very carefully examined the chapters on the 'Barbarians,' the Visigoths, the Vandals, and the Huns, and can pronounce them the best condensed account that we have read of the westerly migrations."—*Athenæum.*

"An admirable specimen of careful condensation and good arrangement, and as a school book it will assuredly possess a high value."—*Scotsman.*

"The period with which it deals is neglected in schools for want of text-books, but is full of most important historical teaching. Mr. Curteis' little book is admirably written for teaching purposes; it is clear, definite, well-arranged, and interesting."—*Academy.*

"Appears to be a good school book for the higher forms."—*Westminster Review.*

"Will prove of great service to students, and we commend it to the notice of those who intend competing in the Civil Service Examinations. Mr. Curteis has executed his task with great care and judgment."

Civil Service Gazette

HISTORY OF MODERN ENGLISH LAW.

By Sir ROLAND KNYVET WILSON, Bart., M.A., *Barrister-at-Law; late Fellow of King's College, Cambridge.*

3*s.* 6*d.*

CONTENTS.

The English Law in the Time of Blackstone.

The Form in which it was Enunciated—Property, Contract, and Absolute Duties—Wrongs and Remedies, Civil and Criminal—Procedure—Laws relating to Special Classes of Persons.

Life and Work of Bentham.

Biography—The Writings of Bentham—Early Attempts at Law Reform.

Legal Changes since 1825.

Changes as to the Form in which the Law is Enunciated—Changes in the Law of Property, Contract, and Absolute Duties—Changes in the Laws as to Wrongs and Remedies—Changes in the Laws relating to Procedure and Evidence—Changes in the Laws relating to Special Classes of Persons—Chronological Table of Cases and Statutes—Index.

[*HISTORICAL HANDBOOKS*—*Continued.*

LONDON, OXFORD, AND CAMBRIDGE.

HISTORICAL HANDBOOKS—continued.

HISTORY OF FRENCH LITERATURE.

Adapted from the French of M. DEMOGEOT, *by* C. BRIDGE.
3*s.* 6*d.*

"An excellent manual."—*Athenæum.*
"A clever adaptation."—*London Quarterly Review.*
"It is clear, idiomatic, and flowing, possessing all the characteristics of good English composition. Its perusal will furnish abundant evidence of the richness and variety of French literature, of which it is a good and sufficient handbook."—*British Quarterly Review.*
"We cannot too highly commend this careful analysis of the characteristics of the great French writer."—*Standard.*
"Unlike most manuals, it is readable as well as accurate."—*Echo.*

THE GREAT REBELLION.

By the EDITOR.

HISTORY OF THE FRENCH REVOLUTION.

By the Rev. J. FRANCK BRIGHT, M.A., *Fellow of University College, and Historical Lecturer in Balliol, New, and University Colleges, Oxford; late Master of the Modern School at Marlborough College.*

THE AGE OF CHATHAM.

By Sir W. R. ANSON, Bart., M.A., *Fellow of All Souls' College, and Vinerian Reader of Law, Oxford.*

THE AGE OF PITT.

By the Same.

THE SUPREMACY OF ATHENS.

By R. C. JEBB, M.A. *Cambridge, Professor of Greek in the University of Glasgow.*

THE ROMAN REVOLUTION. From B.C. 133 to the

Battle of Actium.

By H. F. PELHAM, M.A., *Fellow and Lecturer of Exeter College, Oxford.*

HISTORY OF THE UNITED STATES.

By SIR GEORGE YOUNG, BART., M.A., *late Fellow of Trinity College, Cambridge.*

HISTORY OF ROMAN POLITICAL INSTITUTIONS.

By J. S. REID, M.L., *Christ's College, Cambridge.*

LONDON, OXFORD AND CAMBRIDGE

HISTORICAL BIOGRAPHIES

Edited by

THE REV. M. CREIGHTON, M.A.,

LATE FELLOW AND TUTOR OF MERTON COLLEGE, OXFORD.

With Maps and Plans.   Small 8vo.

The most important and the most difficult point in Historical Teaching is to awaken a real interest in the minds of Beginners.   For this purpose concise handbooks are seldom useful.   General sketches, however accurate in their outlines of political or constitutional development, and however well adapted to dispel false ideas, still do not make history a living thing to the *young*.   They are most valuable as maps on which to trace the route beforehand and show its direction, but they will seldom allure any one to take a walk.

The object of this series of Historical Biographies is to try and select from English History a few men whose lives were lived in stirring times.   The intention is to treat their lives and times in some little detail, and to group round them the most distinctive features of the periods before and after those in which they lived.

It is hoped that in this way interest may be awakened without any sacrifice of accuracy, and that personal sympathies may be kindled without forgetfulness of the principles involved.

It may be added that round the lives of individuals it will be possible to bring together facts of social life in a clearer way, and to reproduce a more vivid picture of particular times than is possible in a historical handbook.

By reading short Biographies a few clear ideas may be formed in the pupil's mind, which may stimulate to further reading.   A vivid impression of one period, however short, will carry the pupil onward and give more general histories an interest in their turn.   Something, at least, will be gained if the pupil realises that men in past times lived and moved in the same sort of way as they do at present.

The following Biographies:—

Now ready, 2s. 6d. each.

1. SIMON DE MONTFORT.   2.   THE BLACK PRINCE.

In preparation.

3. SIR WALTER RALEIGH.   4.   OLIVER CROMWELL.
5. THE DUKE OF MARLBOROUGH.   6.   THE DUKE OF WELLINGTON.

History of the Church under the Roman Empire, A.D. 30-476.

By the Rev. A. D. CRAKE, B.A., *Chaplain of All Saints' School, Bloxham.*

Crown 8vo.   7s. 6d.

A History of England for Children.

By GEORGE DAVYS, D.D., *formerly Bishop of Peterborough.*
New Edition.   18mo.   1s. 6d.
With twelve Coloured Illustrations.   Square cr. 8vo.   3s. 6d.

LONDON, OXFORD, AND CAMBRIDGE.

ENGLISH

ENGLISH SCHOOL-CLASSICS

With Introductions, and Notes at the end of each Book.

Edited by FRANCIS STORR, B.A.,

CHIEF MASTER OF MODERN SUBJECTS IN MERCHANT TAYLORS' SCHOOL, LATE SCHOLAR
OF TRINITY COLLEGE, CAMBRIDGE, AND BELL UNIVERSITY SCHOLAR.

Small 8vo.

THOMSON'S SEASONS: Winter.
With Introduction to the Series, by the Rev. J. FRANCK BRIGHT, M.A., Fellow of
University College, and Historical Lecturer in Balliol, New, and University Colleges,
Oxford; late Master of the Modern School at Marlborough College. 1s.

COWPER'S TASK.
By FRANCIS STORR, B.A., Chief Master of Modern Subjects in Merchant Taylors'
School. 2s.
 Part I. (Book I.—The Sofa; Book II.—The Timepiece) 9d. Part II. (Book III.
—The Garden; Book IV.—The Winter Evening) 9d. Part III. (Book V.—The
Winter Morning Walk; Book VI.—The Winter Walk at Noon) 9d.

SCOTT'S LAY OF THE LAST MINSTREL.
By J. SURTEES PHILLPOTTS, M.A., Head Master of Bedford School, formerly
Fellow of New College, Oxford. 2s. 6d.
 Part I. (Canto I., with Introduction, &c.) 9d. Part II. (Cantos II. and III.) 9d.
Part III. (Cantos IV. and V.) 9d. Part IV. (Canto VI.) 9d.

SCOTT'S LADY OF THE LAKE.
By R. W. TAYLOR, M.A., Assistant-Master at Rugby School. 2s.
 Part I. (Cantos I. and II.) 9d. Part II. (Cantos III. and IV.) 9d. Part III.
(Cantos V. and VI.) 9d.

NOTES TO SCOTT'S WAVERLEY.
By H. W. EVE, M.A., Head-Master of University College School, London. 1s., or
with the Text, 2s. 6d.

TWENTY OF BACON'S ESSAYS.
By FRANCIS STORR, B.A., Chief Master of Modern Subjects in Merchant Taylors'
School. 1s.

SIMPLE POEMS.
Edited by W. E. MULLINS, M.A. Assistant-Master at Marlborough College. 8d.

SELECTIONS FROM WORDSWORTH'S POEMS.
By H. H. TURNER, B.A., late Scholar of Trinity College, Cambridge. 1s.

WORDSWORTH'S EXCURSION: The Wanderer.
By H. H. TURNER, B.A., late Scholar of Trinity College, Cambridge. 1s.

MILTON'S PARADISE LOST.
By FRANCIS STORR, B.A., Chief Master of Modern Subjects in Merchant Taylors'
School.
 Book I. 9d. Book II. 9d.

ENGLISH SCHOOL-CLASSICS—continued.

SELECTIONS FROM THE SPECTATOR.
By OSMUND AIRY, M.A., Assistant-Master at Wellington College. 1s.

BROWNE'S RELIGIO MEDICI.
By W. P. SMITH, M.A., Assistant-Master at Winchester College. 1s.

GOLDSMITH'S TRAVELLER AND DESERTED VILLAGE.
By C. SANKEY, M.A., Assistant-Master at Marlborough College. 1s.

EXTRACTS FROM GOLDSMITH'S VICAR OF WAKEFIELD.
By C. SANKEY, M.A., Assistant-Master at Marlborough College. 1s.

POEMS SELECTED FROM THE WORKS OF ROBERT BURNS.
By A. M. BELL, M.A., Balliol College, Oxford. 2s.

MACAULAY'S ESSAYS.
MOORE'S LIFE OF BYRON. By FRANCIS STORR, B.A. 9d.
BOSWELL'S LIFE OF JOHNSON. By FRANCIS STORR, B.A. 9d.
HALLAM'S CONSTITUTIONAL HISTORY. By H. F. BOYD, late Scholar of Brasenose College, Oxford. 1s.

SOUTHEY'S LIFE OF NELSON.
By W. E. MULLINS, M.A., Assistant-Master at Marlborough College.

*** The General Introduction to the Series will be found in* Thomson's WINTER.

(See Specimen Pages, Nos. 5 *and* 6.)

OPINIONS OF TUTORS AND SCHOOLMASTERS.

"Nothing can be better than the idea and the execution of the English School-Classics, edited by Mr. Storr. Their cheapness and excellence encourage us to the hope that the study of our own language, too long neglected in our schools, may take its proper place in our curriculum, and may be the means of inspiring that taste for literature which it is one of the chief objects of education to give, and which is apt to be lost sight of in the modern style of teaching Greek and Latin Classics with a view to success in examinations."—*Oscar Browning, M.A., Fellow of King's College, Cambridge.*

"I think the plan of them is excellent; and those volumes which I have used I have found carefully and judiciously edited, neither passing over difficulties, nor preventing thought and work on the pupil's part by excessive annotation."—*Rev. C. B. Hutchinson, M.A., Assistant-Master in Rugby School.*

"I think that these books are likely to prove most valuable. There is great variety in the choice of authors. The notes seem sensible, as far as I have been able to examine them, and give just enough help, and not too much; and the size of each volume is so small, that in most cases it need not form more than one term's work.

Something of the kind was greatly wanted."—*E. E. Bowen, M.A., Master of the Modern Side, Harrow School.*

"I have used some of the volumes of your English School-Classics for several months in my ordinary form work, and I have recommended others to be set as subjects for different examinations for which the boys have to prepare themselves. I shall certainly continue to use them, as I have found them to be very well suited to the wants of my form."—*C. M. Bull, M.A., Master of the Modern School in Marlborough College.*

"I have no hesitation in saying that the volumes of your Series which I have examined appear to me far better adapted for school use than any others which have come under my notice. The notes are sufficiently full to supply all the information which a boy needs to understand the text without superseding the necessity of his thinking. The occasional questions call the learner's attention to points which he can decide from his own resources. The general plan, and the execution of the volumes which have come before me, leave little to be desired in a School Edition of the English Classics."—*The Rev. Chas. Grant Chittenden, M.A., The Grange, Hoddesdon, Herts.*

SELECT PLAYS OF SHAKSPERE

RUGBY EDITION.

With Introduction and Notes to each Play.

Small 8vo.

AS YOU LIKE IT. *2s.* HAMLET. *2s. 6d.*

MACBETH. *2s.* KING LEAR. *2s. 6d.*

Edited by the Rev. CHARLES E. MOBERLY, M.A., *Assistant-Master at Rugby School, and formerly Scholar of Balliol College, Oxford.*

CORIOLANUS. *2s. 6d.*

Edited by ROBERT WHITELAW, M.A., *Assistant-Master at Rugby School, formerly Fellow of Trinity College, Cambridge.*

THE TEMPEST.

Edited by J. SURTEES PHILLPOTTS, M.A., *Head-Master of Bedford Grammar School, formerly Fellow of New College, Oxford.*

With Notes at the end of the Volume. *2s.*

THE MERCHANT OF VENICE.

Edited by R. W. TAYLOR, M.A., *Assistant-Master at Rugby School.*

With Notes at the end of the Volume.

[*In preparation.*

Dictionary of the English Language.

By R. G. LATHAM, M.A., M.D., *late Fellow of King's College, Cambridge.*

Abridged from Dr. Latham's Edition of Johnson's English Dictionary. In 1 vol. medium 8vo. *24s.*

The Rudiments of English Grammar and Composition.

By J. HAMBLIN SMITH, M.A., *of Gonville and Caius College, Cambridge; late Lecturer of St. Peter's College, Cambridge.*

Crown 8vo. *2s. 6d.*

LONDON, OXFORD, AND CAMBRIDGE.

MATHEMATICS
RIVINGTONS' MATHEMATICAL SERIES

The following Schools, amongst many others, use this Series :—Eton : Harrow : Rugby : Winchester : Charterhouse : Marlborough : Shrewsbury : Cheltenham : Clifton : City of London School : Haileybury : Tonbridge : Durham : Fettes College, Edinburgh : H.M.'s Dockyard Schools, Sheerness and Devonport : Hurstpierpoint : King William's College, Isle of Man : St. Peter's, Clifton, York : Birmingham : Bedford : Felsted : Christ's College, Finchley : Liverpool College : Windermere College : Eastbourne College : Competitive College, Bath : Brentwood : Perse School, Cambridge : Queen's College, Cork. Also in use in the Royal Naval College, Greenwich : H.M. Training Ships : the Owen's College, Manchester : Harvard College, U.S. : the Grammar and High Schools of Canada : Melbourne University, Australia : the other Colonies : and some of the Government Schools in India.

OPINIONS OF TUTORS AND SCHOOLMASTERS.

"A person who carefully studies these books will have a thorough and accurate knowledge of the subjects on which they treat."—*H. A. Morgan, M.A., Tutor of Jesus College, Cambridge.*

"We have for some time used your Mathematical books in our Lecture Room, and find them well arranged, and well calculated to clear up the difficulties of the subjects. The examples also are numerous and well-selected."—*N. M. Ferrers, M.A., Fellow and Tutor of Gonville and Caius College, Cambridge.*

"I have used in my Lecture Room Mr. Hamblin Smith's text-books with very great advantage."—*James Porter, M.A., Fellow and Tutor of St. Peter's College, Cambridge.*

"For beginners there could be no better books, as I have found when examining different schools."—*A. W. W. Steel, M.A., Fellow and Assistant-Tutor of Gonville and Caius College, Cambridge.*

"I consider Mr. Hamblin Smith's Mathematical Works to be a very valuable series for beginners. His Algebra in particular I think is the best book of its kind for schools and for the ordinary course at Cambridge."—*F. Patrick, M.A., Fellow and Tutor of Magdalen College, Cambridge.*

"The series is a model of clearness and insight into possible difficulties."—*Rev. J. F. Blake, St. Peter's College, Clifton, York.*

"I can say with pleasure that I have used your books extensively in my work at Haileybury, and have found them on the whole well adapted for boys."—*Thomas Pitts, M.A., Assistant Mathematical Master at Haileybury College.*

"I can strongly recommend them all."—*W. Henry, M.A., Sub-Warden, Trinity College, Glenalmond.*

"I consider Mr. Smith has supplied a great want, and cannot but think that his works must command extensive use in good schools."—*J. Henry, B.A., Head-Master, H.M. Dockyard School, Sheerness, and Instructor of Engineers, R.N.*

"We have used your Algebra and Trigonometry extensively at this School from the time they were first published, and I thoroughly agree with every mathematical teacher I have met, that, as school text-books, they have no equals. We are introducing your Euclid gradually into the School."—*Rev. B. Edwardes, sen., Mathematical Master at the College, Hurstpierpoint, Sussex.*

"I consider them to be the best books of their kind on the subject which I have yet seen."—*Joshua Jones, D.C.L., Head-Master, King William's College, Isle of Man.*

"I have very great pleasure in expressing an opinion as to the value of these books. I have used them under very different circumstances, and have always been satisfied with the results obtained."—*C. H. W. Biggs, Editor of the 'Educational Times,' and the 'Monthly Journal of Education.'*

RIVINGTONS' MATHEMATICAL SERIES—continued.

ELEMENTARY ALGEBRA.

By J. HAMBLIN SMITH, M.A., *of Gonville and Caius College, and late Lecturer at St. Peter's College, Cambridge.*

12mo. 3*s*. Without Answers, 2*s*. 6*d*.

A KEY TO ELEMENTARY ALGEBRA.

Crown 8vo. 9*s*.

EXERCISES ON ALGEBRA.

By J. HAMBLIN SMITH, M.A.

Small 8vo. 2*s*. 6*d*.

(Copies may be had without the Answers.)

ALGEBRA. Part II.

By E. J. GROSS, M.A., *Fellow of Gonville and Caius College, Cambridge, and Secretary to the Oxford and Cambridge Schools Examination Board.*

Crown 8vo. 8*s*. 6*d*.

"We have to congratulate Mr. Gross on his excellent treatment of the more difficult chapters in Elementary Algebra. His work satisfies not only in every respect the requirements of a first-rate text-book on the subject, but is not open to the standing reproach of most English mathematical treatises for students, a minimum of teaching and a maximum of problems. The hard work and considerable thought which Mr. Gross has devoted to the book will be seen on every page by the experienced teacher; there is not a word too much, nor is the student left without genuine assistance where it is needful. The language is precise, clear, and to the point. The problems are not too numerous, and selected with much tact and judgment. The range of the book has been very rightly somewhat extended beyond that assigned to simpler treatises, and it includes the elementary principles of Determinants. This chapter especially will be read with satisfaction by earnest students, and the mode of exposition will certainly have the approval of teachers. Altogether we think that this *Algebra* will soon become a general text-book, and will remain so for a long time to come." — *Westminster Review.*

KINEMATICS AND KINETICS.

By E. J. GROSS, M.A.

Crown 8vo. 5*s*. 6*d*.

A TREATISE ON ARITHMETIC.

By J. HAMBLIN SMITH, M.A.

Small 8vo. 3*s*. 6*d*.

(*See Specimen Page, No.* 7.)

A KEY TO ARITHMETIC.

Crown 8vo. 9*s*.

RIVINGTONS' MATHEMATICAL SERIES—continued.

ELEMENTS OF GEOMETRY. Small 8vo. 3*s.* 6*d.*

By J. HAMBLIN SMITH, M.A.

Containing Books 1 to 6, and portions of Books 11 and 12, of EUCLID, with Exercises and Notes, arranged with the Abbreviations admitted in the Cambridge Examinations.

Part I., containing Books 1 and 2 of Euclid, limp cloth, 1*s.* 6*d.*, may be had separately.

(*See Specimen Page, No.* 8.)

GEOMETRICAL CONIC SECTIONS. Crown 8vo. 4*s.* 6*d.*

By G. RICHARDSON, M.A., *Assistant-Master at Winchester College, and late Fellow of St. John's College, Cambridge.*

TRIGONOMETRY. Small 8vo. 4*s.* 6*d.*   A Key, *in the Press.*

By J. HAMBLIN SMITH, M.A.

ELEMENTARY STATICS. Small 8vo. 3*s.*

By J. HAMBLIN SMITH, M.A.

ELEMENTARY HYDROSTATICS. Small 8vo. 3*s.*

By J. HAMBLIN SMITH, M.A.

BOOK OF ENUNCIATIONS FOR HAMBLIN SMITH'S

GEOMETRY, ALGEBRA, TRIGONOMETRY, STATICS, AND HYDROSTATICS. Small 8vo. 1*s.*

The Principles of Dynamics.

An Elementary Text-book for Science Students.

By R. WORMELL, D.Sc., M.A., *Head-Master of the City of London Middle-Class School.*

Crown 8vo. 6*s.*

Arithmetic, Theoretical and Practical.

By W. H. GIRDLESTONE, M.A., *of Christ's College, Cambridge, Principal of the Theological College, Gloucester.*

New Edition. Crown 8vo. 6*s.* 6*d.*

Also a School Edition. Small 8vo. 3*s.* 6*d.*

LONDON, OXFORD, AND CAMBRIDGE.

SCIENCE

Preparing for Publication,

SCIENCE CLASS-BOOKS

Edited by

The Rev. ARTHUR RIGG, M.A.,

LATE PRINCIPAL OF THE COLLEGE, CHESTER.

These Volumes are designed expressly for School use, and by their especial reference to the requirements of a School Class-Book, aim at making Science-teaching a subject for regular and methodical study in Public and Private Schools.

AN ELEMENTARY CLASS-BOOK ON SOUND.

By GEORGE CAREY FOSTER, B.A., F.R.S., *Fellow of, and Professor of Physics in, University College, London.*

AN ELEMENTARY CLASS-BOOK ON ELECTRICITY.

By GEORGE CAREY FOSTER, B.A., F.R.S., *Fellow of, and Professor of Physics in, University College, London.*

BOTANY FOR CLASS-TEACHING.

With Exercises for Private Work.

By F. E. KITCHENER, M.A., F.L.S., *Assistant-Master at Rugby School, and late Fellow of Trinity College, Cambridge.*

ASTRONOMY FOR CLASS-TEACHING.

With Exercises for Private Work.

By WALLIS HAY LAVERTY, M.A., *late Fellow of Queen's College, Oxford.*

The knowledge of Mathematics assumed will be Euclid, Books I.–VI., and Quadratic Equations.

Other Works are in preparation.

LONDON, OXFORD, AND CAMBRIDGE.

A Year's Botany.

Adapted to Home and School Use.
By FRANCES ANNA KITCHENER.
Illustrated by the Author.   Crown 8vo.   5*s.*
(*See Specimen Page, No.* 2.)

CONTENTS.

General Description of Flowers—Flowers with Simple Pistils—Flowers with Compound Pistils — Flowers with Apocarpous Fruits — Flowers with Syncarpous Fruits—Stamens and Morphology of Branches—Fertilisation—Seeds—Early Growth and Food of Plants—Wood, Stems, and Roots—Leaves—Classification—Umbellates, Composites, Spurges, and Pines—Some Monocotyledonous Families—Orchids—Appendix of Technical Terms—Index.

"One and only one English book do I know that might almost make a stupid man teach one science well; and that is Mrs. Kitchener's 'A Year's Botany' (Rivingtons). That happily does not teach facts only; but is the expression of the method of a first-rate teacher in such a form as to enable any one to follow it."—*J. M. Wilson, M.A., in 'Nature' of April* 13, 1876.

An Easy Introduction to Chemistry.

For the use of Schools.
Edited by the Rev. ARTHUR RIGG, M.A., *late Principal of The College, Chester, and* WALTER T. GOOLDEN, B.A., *late Science Scholar of Merton College, Oxford; and Lecturer in Natural Science at Tonbridge School.*
New Edition, revised.   With Illustrations.   Crown 8vo.   2*s.* 6*d.*
(*See Specimen Page, No.* 9.)

Notes on Building Construction.

Arranged to meet the requirements of the syllabus of the Science and Art Department of the Committee of Council on Education, South Kensington Museum.   Medium 8vo.

PART I.—FIRST STAGE, OR ELEMENTARY COURSE.
With 325 woodcuts, 10*s.* 6*d.*

PART II.—COMMENCEMENT OF SECOND STAGE, OR ADVANCED COURSE.   With 277 woodcuts, 10*s.* 6*d.*

PART III.—ADVANCED COURSE.   [*In the Press.*

REPORT ON THE EXAMINATION IN BUILDING CONSTRUCTION, HELD BY THE SCIENCE AND ART DEPARTMENT, SOUTH KENSINGTON, IN MAY, 1875.—"The want of a text-book in this subject, arranged in accordance with the published syllabus, and therefore limiting the students and teachers to the prescribed course, has lately been well met by a work published by Messrs. Rivingtons, entitled '*Notes on Building Construction,* arranged to meet the requirements of the Syllabus of the Science and Art Department of the Committee of Council on Education, South Kensington.'
June 18, 1875.   (Signed)   H. C. SEDDON, Major, R.E."

"Something of the sort was very much needed. The whole series when published will be a great boon to young students."
Builder.
"The text is prepared in an extremely simple and consecutive manner, advancing from rudimental and general statements to those which are comparatively advanced; it is a thoroughly coherent, self-sustained account."—*Athenæum.*

LATIN

Easy Latin Stories for Beginners.

With Vocabulary and Notes. Forming a First Latin Reading Book for Junior Forms in Schools.

By G. L. BENNETT, M.A., *Assistant-Master at Rugby School; formerly Fellow of St. John's College, Cambridge.*

Crown 8vo.   [*Now Ready.*

Elementary Rules of Latin Pronunciation.

By ARTHUR HOLMES, M.A., *late Senior Fellow and Dean of Clare College, Cambridge.*

Crown 8vo.   On a card, 9*d*.

Outlines of Latin Sentence Construction.

By E. D. MANSFIELD, B.A., *Assistant-Master at Clifton College.*

Demy 8vo.   On a card, 1*s*.

Easy Exercises in Latin Prose.

By CHARLES BIGG, M.A., *Principal of Brighton College.*

Small 8vo.   1*s*. 4*d*.; sewed, 9*d*.

Latin Prose Exercises.

For Beginners, and Junior Forms of Schools.

By R. PROWDE SMITH, B.A., *Assist.-Master at Cheltenham College.*

New Edition.   Crown 8vo.   2*s*. 6*d*.

An Elementary Latin Grammar.

By J. HAMBLIN SMITH, M.A., *of Gonville and Caius College, Cambridge; late Lecturer of S. Peter's College, Cambridge.*

Small 8vo.   3*s*. 6*d*.

Henry's First Latin Book.

By THOMAS KERCHEVER ARNOLD, M.A.

Twenty-third Edition. 12mo. 3s. Tutor's Key, 1s.

Recommended in the *Guide to the Choice of Classical Books* by J. B. Mayor, M.A., Professor of Classical Literature at King's College, late Fellow and Tutor of St. John's College, Cambridge.

A Practical Introduction to Latin Prose Composition.

By THOMAS KERCHEVER ARNOLD, M.A.

Seventeenth Edition. 8vo. 6s. 6d. Tutor's Key, 1s. 6d.

Cornelius Nepos.

With Critical Questions and Answers, and an Imitative Exercise on each Chapter.

By THOMAS KERCHEVER ARNOLD, M.A.

Fifth Edition. 12mo. 4s.

A First Verse Book.

Being an Easy Introduction to the Mechanism of the Latin Hexameter and Pentameter.

By THOMAS KERCHEVER ARNOLD, M.A.

Eleventh Edition. 12mo. 2s. Tutor's Key, 1s.

Progressive Exercises in Latin Elegiac Verse.

By C. G. GEPP, B.A., *late Junior Student of Christ Church, Oxford; Head-Master of the College, Stratford-on-Avon.*

Third Edition, Revised. Crown 8vo. 3s. 6d. Tutor's Key, 5s.

Recommended in the *Guide to the Choice of Classical Books* by J. B. Mayor, M.A., Professor of Classical Literature at King's College, late Fellow and Tutor of St. John's College, Cambridge.

Selections from Livy, Books VIII. and IX.

With Notes and Map.

By E. CALVERT, LL.D., *St. John's College, Cambridge; and* R. SAWARD, M.A., *Fellow of St. John's College, Cambridge; Assistant-Master in Shrewsbury School.*

Small 8vo. 2s.

LONDON, OXFORD, AND CAMBRIDGE.

New Edition, re-arranged, with fresh Pieces and additional References.

Materials and Models for Latin Prose Composition.

Selected and arranged by J. Y. SARGENT, M.A., *Fellow and Tutor of Magdalen College, Oxford; and* T. F. DALLIN, M.A., *Tutor, late Fellow, of Queen's College, Oxford.*

Crown 8vo. 6s. 6d.

(*See Specimen Page, No.* 10.)

Latin Version of (60) Selected Pieces from Materials and Models.

By J. Y. SARGENT, M.A.

Crown 8vo. 5s.

May be had by Tutors only, on direct application to the Publishers.

Stories from Ovid in Elegiac Verse.

With Notes for School Use and Marginal References to the PUBLIC SCHOOL LATIN PRIMER.

By R. W. TAYLOR, M.A., *Assistant-Master at Rugby School, late Fellow of St. John's College, Cambridge.*

Crown 8vo. 3s. 6d.

(*See Specimen Pages, Nos.* 11 *and* 12.)

The Æneid of Vergil.

Edited, with Notes at the end, by FRANCIS STORR, B.A., *Chief Master of Modern Subjects in Merchant Taylors' School.*

BOOKS XI and XII.

Crown 8vo. 2s. 6d.

(*See Specimen Pages, Nos.* 13 *and* 14.)

Classical Examination Papers.

Edited, with Notes and References, by P. J. F. GANTILLON, M.A., *Classical Master in Cheltenham College.*

Crown 8vo. 7s. 6d.

Or interleaved with writing-paper, half-bound, 10s. 6d.

Eclogæ Ovidianæ.

From the Elegiac Poems. With English Notes.

By THOMAS KERCHEVER ARNOLD, M.A.

Thirteenth Edition. 12mo. 2s. 6d.

Terenti Comoediae.

Edited by T. L. PAPILLON, M.A., *Fellow of New College, and late Fellow of Merton, Oxford.*
ANDRIA ET EUNUCHUS. 4s. 6d.
ANDRIA. New Edition, with Introduction on Prosody. 3s. 6d.
Crown 8vo.
Forming a Part of the " Catena Classicorum."

Juvenalis Satirae.

Edited by G. A. SIMCOX, M.A., *Fellow of Queen's College, Oxford.*
THIRTEEN SATIRES.
Second Edition, enlarged and revised. Crown 8vo. 5s.
Forming a Part of the " Catena Classicorum."

Persii Satirae.

Edited by A. PRETOR, M.A., *of Trinity College, Cambridge, Classical Lecturer of Trinity Hall, Composition Lecturer of the Perse Grammar School, Cambridge.*
Crown 8vo. 3s. 6d.
Forming a Part of the " Catena Classicorum."

Horati Opera.

By J. M. MARSHALL, M.A., *Under-Master in Dulwich College.*
VOL. I.—THE ODES, CARMEN SECULARE, AND EPODES.
Crown 8vo. 7s. 6d.
Forming a Part of the " Catena Classicorum."

Taciti Historiae. BOOKS I. and II.

Edited by W. H. SIMCOX, M.A., *Fellow of Queen's College, Oxford.*
Crown 8vo. 6s.
Forming a Part of the " Catena Classicorum."

Taciti Historiae. BOOKS III. IV. and V.

Edited by W. H. SIMCOX, M.A., *Fellow of Queen's College, Oxford.*
Crown 8vo. 6s.
Forming a Part of the " Catena Classicorum."

LONDON, OXFORD, AND CAMBRIDGE.

GREEK

An Elementary Greek Grammar for the Use of Beginners.

By EVELYN ABBOTT, M.A., *Lecturer in Balliol College, Oxford, and late Assistant-Master in Clifton College.*

Crown 8vo.   [*In the Press.*

Elements of Greek Accidence.

By EVELYN ABBOTT, M.A., *Lecturer in Balliol College, Oxford, and late Assistant-Master in Clifton College.*

Crown 8vo.   4s. 6d.

"This is an excellent book. The compilers of elementary Greek Grammars have not before, so far as we are aware, made full use of the results obtained by the labours of philologists during the last twenty-five years. Mr. Abbott's great merit is that he has; and a comparison between his book and the *Rudimenta* of the late Dr. Donaldson—a most excellent volume for the time at which it was published—will show how considerable the advance has been; while a comparison with the works in ordinary use, which have never attained anything like the standard reached by Dr. Donaldson, will really surprise the teacher."—*Athenæum.*

An Introduction to Greek Prose Composition, with Exercises.

By ARTHUR SIDGWICK, M.A., *Assistant-Master at Rugby School, and formerly Fellow of Trinity College, Cambridge.*

Crown 8vo.   5s.   A Key, *in preparation.*

Zeugma; or, Greek Steps from Primer to Author.

By *the* Rev. LANCELOT SANDERSON, M.A., *Principal of Elstree School, late Scholar of Clare College, Cambridge; and the* Rev. F. B. FIRMAN, M.A., *Assistant-Master at Elstree School, late Scholar of Jesus College, Cambridge.*

Small 8vo.   1s. 6d.

A Table of Irregular Greek Verbs.

Classified according to the arrangement of Curtius's Greek Grammar.

By FRANCIS STORR, B.A., *Chief-Master of Modern Subjects in Merchant Taylors' School, late Scholar of Trinity College, Cambridge, and Bell University Scholar.*

On a Card.   1s.

LONDON, OXFORD, AND CAMBRIDGE.

Selections from Lucian.

With English Notes.

By EVELYN ABBOTT, M.A., *Lecturer in Balliol College, Oxford, and late Assistant-Master in Clifton College.*

Small 8vo. 3*s.* 6*d.*

Alexander the Great in the Punjaub.

Adapted from Arrian, Book V.

An easy Greek Reading Book, with Notes at the end and a Map.

By the Rev. CHARLES E. MOBERLY, M.A., *Assistant-Master in Rugby School, and formerly Scholar of Balliol College, Oxford.*

Small 8vo. 2*s.*

Stories from Herodotus.

The Tales of Rhampsinitus and Polycrates, and the Battle of Marathon and the Alcmæonidae. *In Attic Greek.*

Adapted for use in Schools, by J. SURTEES PHILLPOTTS, M.A., *Head Master of Bedford School; formerly Fellow of New College, Oxford.*

Crown 8vo. 1*s.* 6*d.*

Iophon: an Introduction to the Art of Writing Greek Iambic Verses.

By the WRITER *of* " *Nuces* " *and* " *Lucretilis.*"

Crown 8vo. 2*s.*

The First Greek Book.

On the plan of *Henry's First Latin Book.*

By THOMAS KERCHEVER ARNOLD, M.A.

Sixth Edition. 12mo. 5*s.* Tutor's Key, 1*s.* 6*d.*

A Practical Introduction to Greek Accidence.

By THOMAS KERCHEVER ARNOLD, M.A.

Ninth Edition. 8vo. 5*s.* 6*d.*

A Practical Introduction to Greek Prose Composition.

By THOMAS KERCHEVER ARNOLD, M.A.

Twelfth Edition. 8vo. 5*s.* 6*d.* Tutor's Key, 1*s.* 6*d.*

LONDON, OXFORD, AND CAMBRIDGE.

SCENES FROM GREEK PLAYS

RUGBY EDITION

Abridged and adapted for the use of Schools, by

ARTHUR SIDGWICK, M.A.,

ASSISTANT-MASTER AT RUGBY SCHOOL, AND FORMERLY FELLOW OF
TRINITY COLLEGE, CAMBRIDGE.

Small 8vo. 1*s.* 6*d.* each.

Aristophanes.

THE CLOUDS. THE FROGS. THE KNIGHTS. PLUTUS.

Euripides.

IPHIGENIA IN TAURIS. THE CYCLOPS. ION.
ELECTRA. ALCESTIS. BACCHÆ. HECUBA.

Recommended in the *Guide to the Choice of Classical Books*, by J. B.
Mayor, M.A., Professor of Classical Literature at King's College, late
Fellow and Tutor of St. John's College, Cambridge.

Homer without a Lexicon, for Beginners.

ILIAD, Book VI.

*Edited, with Notes giving the meanings of all the less common words,
by* J. SURTEES PHILLPOTTS, M.A., *Head Master of Bedford Grammar
School, formerly Fellow of New College, Oxford.*

Small 8vo, 2*s.*

Xenophon's Memorabilia.

Book I. With an Introduction, and Notes at the end of the
volume.

By the Rev. C. E. MOBERLY, *Assistant-Master in Rugby School.*

Small 8vo. 2*s.*

LONDON, OXFORD, AND CAMBRIDGE.

Homer's Iliad.

Edited, with Notes at the end for the Use of Junior Students, by ARTHUR SIDGWICK, M.A., *Assistant-Master at Rugby School, and formerly Fellow of Trinity College, Cambridge.*

Books I. and II. forming one Volume, Books III. and IV. forming a second Volume. Crown 8vo. [*In preparation.*

Homer for Beginners.

ILIAD, Books I.—III. With English Notes.
By THOMAS KERCHEVER ARNOLD, M.A.
Fourth Edition. 12mo. 3s. 6d.

The Iliad of Homer.

From the Text of Dindorf. With Preface and Notes.
By S. H. REYNOLDS, M.A., *Fellow and Tutor of Brasenose College, Oxford.*

Books I.—XII. Crown 8vo. 6s.
Forming a Part of the " Catena Classicorum."

The Iliad of Homer.

With English Notes and Grammatical References.
By THOMAS KERCHEVER ARNOLD, M.A.
Fifth Edition. 12mo. Half-bound, 12s.

A Complete Greek and English Lexicon for the Poems of Homer and the Homeridæ.

By G. CH. CRUSIUS. *Translated from the German. Edited by* T. K. ARNOLD, M.A.
New Edition. 12mo. 9s.

In the Press, New Edition, re-arranged, with fresh Pieces and additional References.

Materials and Models for Greek Prose Composition.

Selected and arranged by J. Y. SARGENT, M.A., *Fellow and Tutor of Magdalen College, Oxford; and* T. F. DALLIN, M.A., *Tutor, late Fellow of Queen's College, Oxford.*
Crown 8vo.

LONDON, OXFORD, AND CAMBRIDGE.

Classical Examination Papers.

Edited, with Notes and References, by P. J. F. GANTILLON, M.A., *sometime Scholar of St. John's College, Cambridge; Classical Master at Cheltenham College.*

Crown 8vo.   7*s.* 6*d.*

Or interleaved with writing-paper, half-bound, 10*s.* 6*d.*

Recommended in the *Guide to the Choice of Classical Books*, by J. B. Mayor, M.A., Professor of Classical Literature at King's College, late Fellow and Tutor of St. John's College, Cambridge.

Demosthenes.

Edited, with English Notes and Grammatical References, by THOMAS KERCHEVER ARNOLD, M.A.

12mo.

OLYNTHIAC ORATIONS.   Third Edition.   3*s.*
PHILIPPIC ORATIONS.   Third Edition.   4*s.*
ORATION ON THE CROWN.   Second Edition.   4*s.* 6*d.*

Demosthenis Orationes Privatae.

Edited by ARTHUR HOLMES, M.A., *late Senior Fellow and Dean of Clare College, Cambridge, and Preacher at the Chapel Royal, Whitehall.*

Crown 8vo.

DE CORONA.   5*s.*

Forming a Part of the "Catena Classicorum."

Demosthenis Orationes Publicae.

Edited by G. H. HESLOP, M.A., *late Fellow and Assistant-Tutor of Queen's College, Oxford; Head-Master of St. Bees.*

Crown 8vo.

OLYNTHIACS, 2*s.* 6*d.* } or, in One Volume, 4*s.* 6*d.*
PHILIPPICS, 3*s.*
DE FALSA LEGATIONE, 6*s.*

Forming Parts of the "Catena Classicorum."

Isocratis Orationes.

Edited by JOHN EDWIN SANDYS, M.A., *Fellow and Tutor of St. John's College, Cambridge.*

Crown 8vo.

AD DEMONICUM ET PANEGYRICUS.   4*s.* 6*d.*

Forming a Part of the "Catena Classicorum."

LONDON, OXFORD, AND CAMBRIDGE.

The Greek Testament.

With a Critically Revised Text ; a Digest of Various Readings ;
Marginal References to Verbal and Idiomatic Usage ; Prolegomena ;
and a Critical and Exegetical Commentary. For the use of Theological Students and Ministers.

By HENRY ALFORD, D.D., *late Dean of Canterbury.*

New Edition. 4 vols. 8vo. 102*s.*

The Volumes are sold separately, as follows :

Vol. I.—The FOUR GOSPELS. 28*s.*
Vol. II.—ACTS to 2 CORINTHIANS. 24*s.*
Vol. III.—GALATIANS to PHILEMON. 18*s.*
Vol. IV.—HEBREWS to REVELATION. 32*s.*

The Greek Testament.

With Notes, Introductions, and Index.
By CHR. WORDSWORTH, D.D., *Bishop of Lincoln.*

New Edition. 2 vols. Impl. 8vo. 60*s.*

The Parts may be had separately, as follows :—

The GOSPELS. 16*s.*
The ACTS. 8*s.*
St. Paul's EPISTLES. 23*s.*
GENERAL EPISTLES, REVELATION, and INDEX. 16*s.*

Notes on the Greek Testament.

By the Rev. ARTHUR CARR, M.A., *Assistant-Master at Wellington
College, late Fellow of Oriel College, Oxford.*
THE GOSPEL ACCORDING TO S. LUKE.
Crown 8vo. 6*s.*
(*See Specimen Page No.* 15.)

Madvig's Syntax of the Greek Lan-guage, especially of the Attic Dialect.

For the use of Schools.
Edited by THOMAS KERCHEVER ARNOLD, M.A.
Second Edition. Imperial 16mo. 8*s.* 6*d.*
Recommended by the Cambridge Board of Classical Studies for the
Classical Tripos.

LONDON, OXFORD, AND CAMBRIDGE.

Sophocles.

With English Notes from SCHNEIDEWIN.

Edited by T. K. ARNOLD, M.A., ARCHDEACON PAUL, *and* HENRY BROWNE, M.A.

12mo.

AJAX. 3*s.* PHILOCTETES. 3*s.* ŒDIPUS TYRANNUS. 4*s.* ŒDIPUS COLONEUS. 4*s.*

Sophoclis Tragoediae.

Edited by R. C. JEBB, M.A., *Professor of Greek in the University of Glasgow, late Fellow and Assistant-Tutor of Trinity College, Cambridge, and Public Orator of the University.*

Crown 8vo.

ELECTRA.   Second Edition, revised.   3*s.* 6*d.*
AJAX.   3*s.* 6*d.*

Forming Parts of the "Catena Classicorum."

Aristophanis Comoediae.

Edited by W. C. GREEN, M.A., *late Fellow of King's College, Cambridge; Assistant-Master at Rugby School.*

Crown 8vo.

THE ACHARNIANS and THE KNIGHTS.   4*s.*
THE CLOUDS.   3*s.* 6*d.*
THE WASPS.   3*s.* 6*d.*

An Edition of "THE ACHARNIANS and THE KNIGHTS," revised and especially prepared for Schools.   4*s.*

Forming Parts of the "Catena Classicorum."

Herodoti Historia.

Edited by H. G. WOODS, M.A., *Fellow and Tutor of Trinity College, Oxford.*

Crown 8vo.

BOOK I.   6*s.*   BOOK II.   5*s.*
Forming Parts of the "Catena Classicorum."

A Copious Phraseological English-Greek Lexicon.

Founded on a work prepared by J. W. FRÄDERSDORFF, Ph.D., *late Professor of Modern Languages, Queen's College, Belfast.*

Revised, Enlarged, and Improved by the late THOMAS KERCHEVER ARNOLD, M.A., *and* HENRY BROWNE, M.A.

Fifth Edition. 8vo. **21s.**

Thucydidis Historia. Books I. and II.

Edited by CHARLES BIGG, M.A., *late Senior Student and Tutor of Christ Church, Oxford ; Principal of Brighton College.*

Crown 8vo. 6s.

Forming a Part of the "Catena Classicorum.

Thucydidis Historia. Books III. and IV.

Edited by G. A. SIMCOX, M.A., *Fellow of Queen's College, Oxford.*

Crown 8vo. 6s.

Forming a Part of the "Catena Classicorum."

An Introduction to Aristotle's Ethics.

Books I.—IV. (Book X., c. vi.—ix. in an Appendix). With a Continuous Analysis and Notes. Intended for the use of Beginners and Junior Students.

By the Rev. EDWARD MOORE, B.D., *Principal of S. Edmund Hall, and late Fellow and Tutor of Queen's College, Oxford.*

Crown 8vo. 10s. 6d.

Aristotelis Ethica Nicomachea.

Edidit, emendavit, crebrisque locis parallelis e libro ipso, aliisque ejusdem Auctoris scriptis, illustravit JACOBUS E. T. ROGERS, A.M. Small 8vo. 4s. 6d. Interleaved with writing-paper, half-bound. 6s.

Selections from Aristotle's Organon.

Edited by JOHN R. MAGRATH, M.A., *Fellow and Tutor of Queen's College, Oxford.*

Second Edition. Crown 8vo. *[In the Press.*

LONDON, OXFORD, AND CAMBRIDGE.

CATENA CLASSICORUM

Crown 8vo.

Sophoclis Tragoediae.   By R. C. JEBB, M.A.
  THE ELECTRA. 3s. 6d.   THE AJAX. 3s. 6d.

Juvenalis Satirae.   By G. A. SIMCOX, M.A. 5s.

Thucydidis Historia.—Books I. & II.
  By CHARLES BIGG, M.A. 6s.

Thucydidis Historia.—Books III. & IV.
  By G. A. SIMCOX, M.A. 6s.

Demosthenis Orationes Publicae.   By G. H. HESLOP, M.A.
  THE OLYNTHIACS. 2s. 6d. } or, in One Volume, 4s. 6d.
  THE PHILIPPICS. 3s.
  DE FALSA LEGATIONE. 6s.

Demosthenis Orationes Privatae.
  By ARTHUR HOLMES, M.A.
  DE CORONA. 5s.

Aristophanis Comoediae.   By W. C. GREEN, M.A.
  THE ACHARNIANS AND THE KNIGHTS. 4s.
  THE WASPS. 3s. 6d.   THE CLOUDS. 3s. 6d.
    An Edition of THE ACHARNIANS AND THE KNIGHTS, revised and especially adapted
  for use in Schools. 4s.

Isocratis Orationes.   By JOHN EDWIN SANDYS, M.A.
  AD DEMONICUM ET PANEGYRICUS. 4s. 6d.

Persii Satirae.   By A. PRETOR, M.A.   3s. 6d.

Homeri Ilias.   By S. H. REYNOLDS, M.A.
      BOOKS I. TO XII. 6s.

Terenti Comoediae.   By T. L. PAPILLON, M.A.
  ANDRIA AND EUNUCHUS. 4s. 6d.
  ANDRIA. New Edition, with Introduction on Prosody. 3s. 6d.

Herodoti Historia.   By H. G. WOODS, M.A.
      BOOK I., 6s.   BOOK II., 5s.

Horati Opera.   By J. M. MARSHALL, M.A.
VOL. I.—THE ODES, CARMEN SECULARE, AND EPODES. 7s. 6d.

Taciti Historiae.   By W. H. SIMCOX, M.A.
  BOOKS I. AND II. 6s. BOOKS III., IV., and V. 6s.

LONDON, OXFORD, AND CAMBRIDGE.

DIVINITY

MANUALS OF RELIGIOUS INSTRUCTION

Edited by

JOHN PILKINGTON NORRIS, B.D.,

CANON OF BRISTOL, AND EXAMINING CHAPLAIN TO THE BISHOP OF MANCHESTER.

Three Volumes. Small 8vo. 3*s.* 6*d.* each.

Or each Book in Five Parts. 1*s.* each Part.

"Contain the maximum of requisite information within a surprising minimum of space. They are the best and fullest and simplest compilation we have hitherto examined on the subject treated."
Standard.

"Carefully prepared, and admirably suited for their purpose, they supply an acknowledged want in Primary Schools, and will doubtless be in great demand by the teachers for whom they are intended."
Educational Times.

THE OLD TESTAMENT.

By the Rev. E. I. GREGORY, M.A., *Vicar of Halberton.*

PART I. The Creation to the Exodus. PART II. Joshua to the Death of Solomon. PART III. The Kingdoms of Judah and Israel. PART IV. Hebrew Poetry—The Psalms. PART V. The Prophets of the Captivity and of the Return—The Maccabees—Messianic Teaching of the Old Testament.

THE NEW TESTAMENT.

By C. T. WINTER.

PART I. St. Matthew's Gospel. PART II. St. Mark's Gospel. PART III. St. Luke's Gospel. PART IV. St. John's Gospel. PART V. The Acts of the Apostles.

THE PRAYER BOOK.

By JOHN PILKINGTON NORRIS, B.D., *Canon of Bristol, &c.*

PART I. The Catechism to the end of the Lord's Prayer—The Order for Morning and Evening Prayer. PART II. The Catechism, concluding portion — The Office of Holy Baptism — The Order of Confirmation. PART III. The Theology of the Catechism—The Litany—The Office of Holy Communion. PART IV. The Collects, Epistles, and Gospels, to be used throughout the year. PART V. The Thirty-Nine Articles.

LONDON, OXFORD, AND CAMBRIDGE.

Rudiments of Theology.

A First Book for Students.

By John Pilkington Norris, B.D., *Canon of Bristol, and Examining Chaplain to the Bishop of Manchester.*

Crown 8vo. 7s. 6d.

"We can recommend this book to theological students as a useful and compendious manual. It is clear and well arranged. . . . We venture to believe that, on the whole, he is a very fair exponent of the teaching of the English Church, and that his book may be profitably used by those for whom it is chiefly intended—that is, candidates for ordination."—*Spectator.*

"This is a work of real help to candidates for ordination, and to the general student of theology."—*Standard.*

A Manual of Devotion, chiefly for the use of School-boys.

By the Rev. William Baker, D.D., *Head Master of Merchant Taylors' School.*

With Preface by J. R. Woodford, D.D., *Lord Bishop of Ely.*

Crown 16mo. 2s. 6d.

A Companion to the Old Testament.

Being a plain Commentary on Scripture History down to the Birth of our Lord.

Small 8vo. 3s. 6d.

Also in Two Parts:

Part I.—The Creation of the World to the Reign of Saul.
Part II.—The Reign of Saul to the Birth of Our Lord.

Small 8vo. 2s. each.

A Companion to the New Testament.

Small 8vo. [*In the Press.*

The Young Churchman's Companion to the Prayer Book.

By the Rev. J. W. Gedge, M.A., *Diocesan Inspector of Schools for the Archdeaconry of Surrey.*

Part I.—Morning and Evening Prayer and Litany.
Part II.—Baptismal and Confirmation Services.

18mo. 1s. each, or in Paper Cover, 6d.

Recommended by the late and present Lord Bishops of Winchester.

A Manual of Confirmation.

With a Pastoral Letter instructing Catechumens how to prepare themselves for their First Communion.

By EDWARD MEYRICK GOULBURN, D.D., *Dean of Norwich.*
Ninth Edition. Small 8vo. 1*s.* 6*d.*

The Way of Life.

A Book of Prayers and Instruction for the Young at School. With
a Preparation for Holy Communion.

Compiled by a Priest.   Edited by the Rev. T. T. CARTER, M.A.,
Rector of Clewer, Berks.
Imperial 32mo, 1*s.* 6*d.*

Household Theology.

A Handbook of Religious Information respecting the Holy Bible, the
Prayer Book, the Church, the Ministry, Divine Worship, the Creeds,
&c., &c.

By the Rev. JOHN HENRY BLUNT, M.A.
New Edition. Small 8vo. 3*s.* 6*d.*

Keys to Christian Knowledge.

Small 8vo. 2*s.* 6*d.* each.

" Of cheap and reliable text-books of this nature there has hitherto been a great want. We are often asked to recommend books for use in Church Sunday schools, and we therefore take this opportunity of saying that we know of none more likely to be of service both to teachers and scholars than these *Keys.*" — *Churchman's Shilling Magazine.*

" Will be very useful for the higher classes in Sunday schools, or rather for the fuller instruction of the Sunday-school teachers themselves, where the parish Priest is wise enough to devote a certain time regularly to their preparation for their voluntary task."—*Union Review.*

By J. H. BLUNT, M.A., Editor of the *Annotated Book of Common Prayer.*

THE HOLY BIBLE.

THE BOOK OF COMMON PRAYER.

THE CHURCH CATECHISM.

CHURCH HISTORY, ANCIENT.

CHURCH HISTORY, MODERN.

By JOHN PILKINGTON NORRIS, B.D., *Canon of Bristol.*

THE FOUR GOSPELS.

THE ACTS OF THE APOSTLES.

MISCELLANEOUS

A German Accidence for the Use of Schools.

By J. W. J. VECQUERAY, *Assistant-Master at Rugby School.*
New Edition, revised. 4to. 3*s.* 6*d.*

Selections from La Fontaine's Fables.

Edited, with English Notes at the end, for use in Schools, by
P. BOWDEN-SMITH, M.A., *Assistant-Master at Rugby School.*

[*In preparation.*

Le Maréchal de Villars, from Sainte-Beuve's "Causeries du Lundi."

Edited, with English Notes at the end, for use in Schools, by H. W.
EVE, M.A., *Head-Master of University College School, London.*

[*In preparation.*

The Campaigns of Napoleon.

The Text (in French) from M. THIERS' *"Histoire de la Révolution
Française," and "Histoire du Consulat et de l'Empire." Edited, with
English Notes, for the use of Schools, by* EDWARD E. BOWEN, M.A.,
Master of the Modern Side, Harrow School.

With Maps. Crown 8vo.

ARCOLA. 4*s.* 6*d.*   MARENGO. 4*s.* 6*d.*
JENA. 3*s.* 6*d.*   WATERLOO. 6*s.*

Selections from Modern French Authors.

Edited, with English Notes and Introductory Notice, by HENRI VAN LAUN, *Translator of Taine's* HISTORY OF ENGLISH LITERATURE.

Crown 8vo.   3*s.* 6*d.* each.

HONORÉ DE BALZAC.   H. A. TAINE.

The First French Book.

By T. K. ARNOLD, M.A.

Sixth Edition.   12mo.   5*s.* 6*d.*   Key, 2*s.* 6*d.*

The First German Book.

By T. K. ARNOLD, M.A., *and* J. W. FRÄDERSDORFF, Ph.D.

Seventh Edition.   12mo.   5*s.* 6*d.*   Key, 2*s.* 6*d.*

The First Hebrew Book.

By T. K. ARNOLD, M.A.

Fifth Edition.   12mo.   7*s.* 6*d.*   Key, 3*s.* 6*d.*

The Chorister's Guide.

By W. A. BARRETT, Mus. Bac., Oxon., *of St. Paul's Cathedral, Author of "Flowers and Festivals," &c.*

Second Edition.   Crown 8vo.   2*s.* 6*d.*

Form and Instrumentation.

By W. A. BARRETT, Mus. Bac., Oxon., *Author of "The Chorister's Guide," &c.*

[*In preparation.*

these too far apart, and the intercourse of the defenders with an army
of relief under the Count of Clermont at Blois was not broken off.
Early in the following year, this army hoped to raise the siege by
falling on a large body of provisions coming to the besiegers from
Battle of the   Paris under Sir John Fastolf. The attack was made at
Herrings.   Rouvray, but Fastolf had made careful preparations.
The waggons were arranged in a square, and, with the stakes of the
archers, formed a fortification on which the disorderly attack of the
French made but little impression. Broken in the assault, they fell
an easy prey to the English, as they advanced beyond their lines.
The skirmish is known by the name of the Battle of the Herrings.
This victory, which deprived the besieged of hope of external succour,
seemed to render the capture of the city certain.

Already at the French King's court at Chinon there was talk of a
Danger of   hasty withdrawal to Dauphiné, Spain, or even Scotland;
Orleans.   when suddenly there arose one of those strange effects
of enthusiasm which sometimes set all calculation at defiance.

In Domrémi, a village belonging to the duchy of Bar, the inhabitants of which, though in the midst of Lorraine, a province under
Burgundian influence, were of patriotic views, lived a village maiden
called Joan of Arc. The period was one of great mental excitement ;
as in other times of wide prevailing misery, prophecies and mystical
preachings were current. Joan of Arc's mind was particularly
Joan of Arc.   susceptible to such influences, and from the time she
was thirteen years old, she had fancied that she heard
voices, and had even seen forms, sometimes of the Archangel Michael,
sometimes of St. Catherine and St. Margaret, who called her to
the assistance of the Dauphin. She persuaded herself that she was destined to fulfil an old prophecy which said that the kingdom, destroyed
by a woman—meaning, as she thought, Queen Isabella,—should be
saved by a maiden of Lorraine. The burning of Domrémi in the
summer of 1428 by a troop of Burgundians at length gave a practical
form to her imaginations, and early in the following year she succeeded in persuading Robert of Baudricourt to send her, armed and
accompanied by a herald, to Chinon. She there, as it is said by the
wonderful knowledge she displayed, convinced the court of the truth
of her mission. At all events, it was thought wise to take advantage
of the infectious enthusiasm she displayed, and in April she was
intrusted with an army of 6000 or 7000 men, which was to march up
the river from Blois to the relief of Orleans. When she appeared
upon the scene of war, she supplied exactly that element of success

of all of them open by two slits turned towards the centre of the flower. Their stalks have expanded and joined together, so as to form a thin sheath round the central column (fig. 12). The dust-

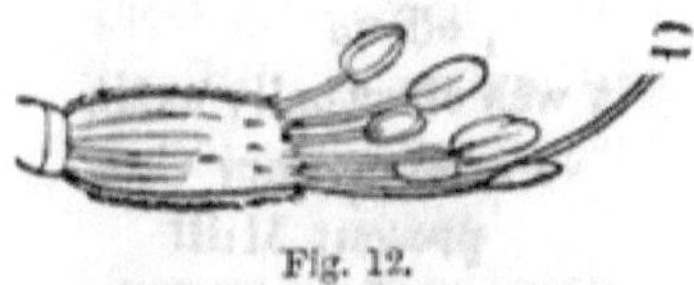
Fig. 12.
Dust-spikes of gorse (*enlarged*).

spikes are so variable in length in this flower, that it may not be possible to see that one short one comes between two long ones, though this ought to be the case.

The *seed-organ* is in the form of a longish rounded pod, with a curved neck, stretching out beyond the dust-spikes. The top of it is sticky, and if you look at a bush of gorse, you will see it projecting beyond the keel in most of the fully-blown flowers, because the neck has become more curved than in fig. 12. Cut open the pod; it contains only one cavity (not, as that of the wall-flower, two separated by a thin partition), and the grains are suspended by short cords from the top (fig. 13). These grains may be plainly seen in the seed-organ of even a young flower. It is evident that they are the most important part of the plant, as upon them depends its diffu-

Fig. 13.
Split seed-pod of gorse.

sion and multiplication. We have already seen how carefully their well-being is considered in the matter of their perfection, how even insects are pressed into their service for this purpose! Now let us glance again at our flower, and see how wonderfully contrivance is heaped upon contrivance for their protection!

First (see fig. 10, p. 14), we have the outer covering, so covered with hairs, that it is as good for keeping out rain as a waterproof cloak; in the buttercup, when you pressed the bud, it separated into five leaves; here there are five leaves, just the same, but they are so tightly joined that you may press till the whole bud is bent without making them separate at all, and when the bud is older, they only separate into two, and continue to enfold the flower to a certain extent till it fades. When the flower pushes back its waterproof cloak, it has the additional shelter of the big struction, and at last, after nearly twenty years of alternate hopes and fears, of tedious negotiations, official evasions, and sterile Parliamentary debates, it was effectually extinguished by the adverse report of a Parliamentary Committee, followed by the erection of the present Millbank Penitentiary at a vastly greater expense and on a totally different system.

Transportation.—In the meantime the common gaols were relieved in a makeshift fashion by working gangs of prisoners in hulks at the seaports; but the resource mainly relied on for getting rid of more dangerous criminals was the old one of transportation, Botany Bay having succeeded to America. As at first employed, there was no mistake as to the reality of the punishment; the misfortune was that the worst elements in the real were not so made known as to form any part of the apparent punishment. If the judge, in sentencing the convict, had thought fit to explain, for the warning of would-be offenders, exactly what was going to be done with their associate, the sentence would have been something of this sort: "You shall first be kept, for days or months as it may happen, in a common gaol, or in the hulks, in company with other criminals better or worse than yourself, with nothing to do, and every facility for mutual instruction in wickedness. You shall then be taken on board ship with similar associates of both sexes, crammed down between decks, under such circumstances that about one in ten of you will probably die in the course of the six months' voyage. If you survive the voyage you will either be employed as a slave in some public works, or let out as a slave to some of the few free settlers whom we have induced to go out there. In either case you will be under very little regular inspection, and will have every opportunity of indulging those natural wealth into the treasury. Churches remained open day and night, and frequent addresses kept up the enthusiasm to a high pitch. It was (for the moment) a genuine "revival" or reawakening of the whole Roman world. The occasion, too, appeared favourable. Italy was quiet, and the Exarchate at peace with its neighbours. Clotaire the Frank was no enemy to Heraclius, and in common with his clergy (being orthodox and not Arian) might be expected to sympathise in so holy a cause.

Treachery of the Avars—A.D. 616.—In one quarter only was there room for fear. The Avars were on the Danube, and the turbulence of the Avars was only equalled by their perfidy. Already, in A.D. 610, they had fallen suddenly on North Italy, and pillaged and harassed those same Lombards whom they had before helped to destroy the Gepidæ. Previous to an absence, therefore, of years from his capital, it was essential for the Emperor to sound their intentions, and, if possible, to secure their neutrality. His ambassadors were welcomed with apparent cordiality, and an interview was arranged between the Chagan and Heraclius. The place was to be Heraclea. At the appointed time the Emperor set out from Selymbria to meet the Khan, decked with Imperial crown and mantle to honour the occasion. The escort was a handful of soldiers; but there was an immense cortége of high officials and of the fashionable world of Constantinople, and the whole country side was there to see. Presently some terrified peasants were seen making their way hurriedly towards Heraclius. They urged him to flee for his life; for armed Avars had been seen in small bodies, and might even now be between him and the capital. Heraclius knew too much to hesitate. He threw off his robes and fled, and but just in time. The Chagan had laid a deep plot. A large mass of men had been told off in small detachments

I say the pulpit (in the sober use
Of its legitimate peculiar pow'rs)
Must stand acknowledg'd, while the world shall stand,
The most important and effectual guard,
Support and ornament of virtue's cause.
There stands the messenger of truth: there stands
The legate of the skies; his theme divine,
His office sacred, his credentials clear.
By him, the violated law speaks out   340
Its thunders, and by him, in strains as sweet
As angels use, the Gospel whispers peace.
He stablishes the strong, restores the weak,
Reclaims the wand'rer, binds the broken heart,
And, arm'd himself in panoply complete
Of heav'nly temper, furnishes with arms
Bright as his own, and trains, by ev'ry rule
Of holy discipline, to glorious war,
The sacramental host of God's elect.
Are all such teachers? would to heav'n all were!   350
But hark—the Doctor's voice—fast wedged between
Two empirics he stands, and with swoln cheeks
Inspires the news, his trumpet.   Keener far
Than all invective is his bold harangue,
While through that public organ of report
He hails the clergy; and, defying shame,
Announces to the world his own and theirs.
He teaches those to read, whom schools dismiss'd,
And colleges, untaught; sells accent, tone,
And emphasis in score, and gives to pray'r   360
Th' *adagio* and *andante* it demands.
He grinds divinity of other days
Down into modern use; transforms old print
To zigzag manuscript, and cheats the eyes
Of gall'ry critics by a thousand arts.—
Are there who purchase of the Doctor's ware?
Oh name it not in Gath!—it cannot be,
That grave and learned Clerks should need such aid.
He doubtless is in sport, and does but droll,
Assuming thus a rank unknown before,   370
Grand caterer and dry-nurse of the church.

    I venerate the man whose heart is warm,
Whose hands are pure, whose doctrine and whose life.

[COWPER'S TASK—*See Page* 6.]

gether as with a close seal. . . . . The flakes of his flesh are joined together : they are firm in themselves ; they cannot be moved."

Hobbes, in his famous book to which he gave the title *Levia-than*, symbolised thereby the force of civil society, which he made the foundation of all right.

315–325 Cowper's limitation of the province of satire—that it is fitted to laugh at foibles, not to subdue vices—is on the whole well-founded.   But we cannot forget Juvenal's famous "facit indignatio versum," or Pope's no less famous—

> "Yes, I am proud : I must be proud to see
> Men not afraid of God, afraid of me :
> Safe from the bar, the pulpit, and the throne,
> Yet touched and shamed by ridicule alone."

326–372 *The pulpit, not satire, is the proper corrector of sin. A description of the true preacher and his office, followed by one of the false preacher, "the reverend advertiser of engraved sermons."*
330 *Strutting and vapouring.* Cf. *Macbeth*, v. 5.

> "Life's but a walking shadow, a poor player,
> That struts and frets his hour upon the stage,
> And then is heard no more ; it is a tale
> Told by an idiot, full of sound and fury,
> Signifying nothing."

> "And what in real value's wanting,
> Supply with vapouring and ranting."—HUDIBRAS.

331 *Proselyte.* προσήλυτος, a new comer, a convert to Judaism.
338 *His theme divine.* Nominative absolute.
343 *Stablishes.* Notice the complete revolution the word has made—stabilire, établir, establish, stablish ; cf. state, &c.
346 *Of heavenly temper.* Cf. *Par. Lost*, i. 284, "his ponderous shield etherial temper."   See note on *Winter Morning Walk*, l. 664.
349 *Sacramental.* Used in the Latin sense. Sacramentum was the oath of allegiance of a Roman soldier.   The word in its Christian sense was first applied to baptism—the vow to serve faithfully under the banner of the cross. See *Browne on the Thirty-nine Articles*, p. 576.
350 *Would to heaven.* A confusion between "would God" and "I pray to heaven."
351 A picture from the life of a certain Dr Trusler, who seems to have combined the trades of preacher, teacher of elocution, writer of sermons, and literary hack.
352 *Empirics.* ἐμπειρικός, one who trusts solely to experience or practice instead of rule, hence a quack.   The accent is the same as in Milton (an exception to the rule. See note on *Sofa*, l. 52).

thus : if the articles had cost £1 each, the total cost would have been £2478 ;

∴ as they cost ⅙ of £1 each. the cost will be £$\frac{2478}{6}$, or £413.

The process may be written thus :

3s. 4d. is ⅙ of £1 | £2478 = cost of the articles at £1 each.

£413 = cost .... at 3s. 4d. ...

Ex. (2). Find the cost of 2897 articles at £2. 12s. 9d. each.

£2 is 2 × £1	2897 . 0 . 0 = cost at £1 each.
10s. is ½ of £1	5794 . 0 . 0 = ... £2 ....
2s. is ⅕ of 10s.	1448 . 10 · 0 = ... 10s.....
8d. is ⅓ of 2s.	289 · 14 · 0 = ... 2s. ....
1d. is ⅛ of 8d.	96 . 11 . 4 = ... 8d. ....
	12 . 1 . 5 = ... 1d. ....
	£7640 . 16 . 9 = ... £2. 12s. 9d. each.

NOTE.—A shorter method would be to take the parts thus :

10s. = ½ of £1 ; 2s. 6d. = ¼ of 10s. ; 3d. = $\frac{1}{10}$ of 2s. 6d.

Ex. (3). Find the cost of 425 articles at £2. 18s. 4d. each.

Since £2. 18s. 4d. is the difference between £3 and 1s. 8d. (which is $\frac{1}{12}$ of £1), the shortest course is to find the cost at £3 each, and to *subtract from it* the cost at 1s. 8d. each, thus :

	£ s. d.
£3 is 3 × £1	425 . 0 . 0 = cost at £1 each.
1s. 8d. is $\frac{1}{12}$ of £1	1275 . 0 . 0 = ... £3 ....
	35 . 8 . 4 = ... 1s. 8d. each.
	£1239 . 11 . 8 = ... £2. 18s. 4d. each.

[J. HAMBLIN SMITH'S ARITHMETIC—*See Page* 10.]

Proposition XLI. Theorem.

If a parallelogram and a triangle be upon the same base, and between the same parallels, the parallelogram is double of the triangle.

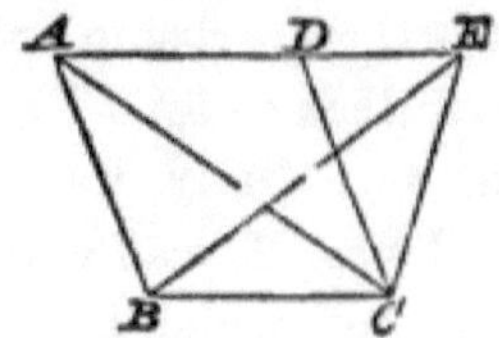

Let the ▱ *ABCD* and the △ *EBC* be on the same base *BC* and between the same ‖s *AE, BC*.

Then must ▱ ABCD be double of △ EBC.

Join *AC*.

Then △ *ABC* = △ *EBC*, ∵ they are on the same base and between the same ‖s ;   I. 37.

and ▱ *ABCD* is double of △ *ABC*, ∵ *AC* is a diagonal of *ABCD* ;   I. 34.

∴ ▱ *ABCD* is double of △ *EBC*.

Q. E. D.

Ex. 1. If from a point, without a parallelogram, there be drawn two straight lines to the extremities of the two opposite sides, between which, when produced, the point does not lie, the difference of the triangles thus formed is equal to half the parallelogram.

Ex. 2. The two triangles, formed by drawing straight lines from any point within a parallelogram to the extremities of its opposite sides, are together half of the parallelogram.

Sometimes carbonic anhydride is produced in wells, and, being so much heavier than air, it remains at the bottom. If a man goes down into such a well, he will have no difficulty at first, because the air is good; but when he is near the bottom, where the gas has accumulated, he will gasp for breath and fall; and if anyone, not understanding the cause of his trouble, goes down to assist him, he too will fall senseless, and both will quickly die. The way to ascertain whether carbonic anhydride has accumulated at the bottom of a well is to let a light down into it. If it goes out, or even burns very dimly, there is enough of the gas to make the descent perilous. A man going down a well should always take a candle with him, which he should hold a considerable distance below his mouth. If the light burns dimly, he should at once stop, before his mouth gets any lower and he takes some of the gas into his lungs.

When this gas is in a well or pit, of course it must be expelled before a man can descend. There are several expedients for doing this. One is to let a bucket down frequently, turning it upside down, away from the mouth of the well, every time it is brought up, a plan which will remind you of the experiment represented in Fig. 24.

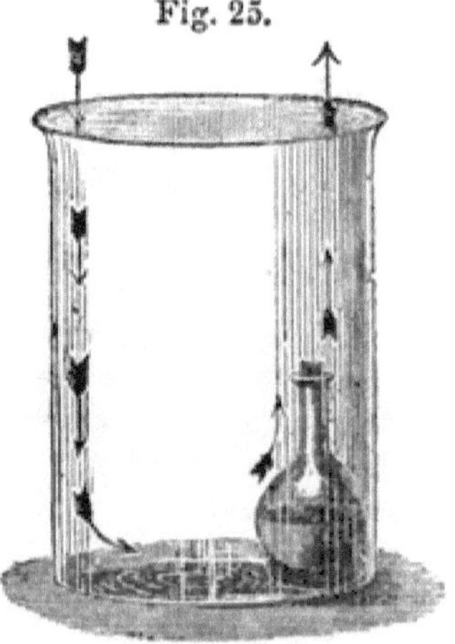

Fig. 25.

But a better way is to let down a bundle of burning straw or shavings, so as to heat the gas. Now heated bodies expand, gases very much more than solids or liquids, and, in expanding, the weight of a certain volume, say of a gallon, becomes lessened. So that if we can heat the carbonic anhydride enough to make a gallon of it weigh less than a gallon of air, it will rise out of the well just as hydrogen gas would do. Fig. 25 shows how you may perform this experiment upon a small scale.

DISASTROUS RETREAT OF THE ENGLISH FROM CABUL.

IT took two days of disorder, suffering, and death to carry the army, now an army no more, to the jaws of the fatal pass. Akbar Khan, who appeared like the Greeks' dread marshal from the spirit-land at intervals upon the route, here demanded four fresh hostages. The demand was acquiesced in. Madly along the narrow defile crowded the undistinguishable host, whose diminished numbers were still too numerous for speed : on every side rang the war-cry of the barbarians : on every side plundered and butchered the mountaineers : on every side, palsied with fatigue, terror, and cold, the soldiers dropped down to rise no more. The next day, in spite of all remonstrance, the general halted his army, expecting in vain provisions from Akbar Khan. That day the ladies, the children, and the married officers were given up. The march was resumed. By the following night not more than one-fourth of the original number survived. Even the haste which might once have saved now added nothing to the chances of life. In the middle of the pass a barrier was prepared. There twelve officers died sword in hand. A handful of the bravest or the strongest only reached the further side alive : as men hurry for life, they hurried on their way, but were surrounded and cut to pieces, all save a few that had yet escaped. Six officers better mounted or more fortunate than the rest, reached a spot within sixteen miles of the goal ; but into the town itself rode painfully on a jaded steed, with the stump of a broken sword in his hand, but one.

LIVY, xxi. c. 25, § 7-10. xxxv. c. 30. xxiii. c. 24.
CÆSAR, *Bell. Gall.* v. c. 35-37.

DEFEAT OF CHARLES THE BOLD AND MASSACRE OF HIS TROOPS AT MORAT.

IN such a predicament braver soldiers might well have ceased to struggle. The poor wretches, Italians and Savoyards, six thousand or more in number, threw away their arms and made

II.

ARIADNE'S LAMENT.

Madam, 'twas Ariadne passioning
For Theseus' perjury and unjust flight.
Two Gentlemen of Verona, IV. 4, 172.

ARGUMENT.

ARIADNE *tells the story of her first waking, to find herself abandoned by Theseus and left on an unknown island, exposed to a host of dangers.*—(HEROIDES, x.)

The story is beautifully told by Catullus, in the "Epithalamium Pelei et Thetidos:" it also forms one of the episodes in Chaucer's "Legende of Goode Women."

I woke before it was day to find myself alone, no trace of my companions to be seen. In vain I felt and called for Theseus ; the echoes alone gave me answer.

QUAE legis, ex illo, Theseu, tibi litore mitto,
    Unde tuam sine me vela tulere ratem :
In quo me somnusque meus male prodidit et tu,
    Per facinus somnis insidiate meis.   107
Tempus erat, vitrea quo primum terra pruina   112
    Spargitur et tectae fronde queruntur aves :
Incertum vigilans, a somno languida, movi   97
    Thesea prensuras semisupina manus :
Nullus erat, referoque manus, iterumque retempto,
10   Perque torum moveo brachia : nullus erat.
Excussere metus somnum : conterrita surgo,
    Membraque sunt viduo praecipitata toro.   123
Protinus adductis sonuerunt pectora palmis,   111
    Utque erat e somno turbida, rapta coma est.
Luna fuit : specto, siquid nisi litora cernam ;
    Quod videant, oculi nil nisi litus habent.   150
Nunc huc, nunc illuc. et utroque sine ordine curro ;
    Alta puellares tardat arena pedes.
Interea toto clamanti litore "Theseu !"   121
20   Reddebant nomen concava saxa tuum,
Et quoties ego te, toties locus ipse vocabat :
    Ipse locus miserae ferre volebat opem.   106 3

STORIES FROM OVID.

174. **Punica poma,** pomegranates.
178. **Taenarum,** at the southern extremity of Peloponnesus, was one of the numerous descents to Tartarus. Cf. Virgil, Georg. IV. 467:

>Taenarias etiam fauces, alta ostia Ditis.

179. **Factura fuit.** This periphrasis for *fecisset* is to be noted; it is the one from which the oblique forms are all constructed, *e.g., facturam fuisse,* or *factura fuisset.*
183. **Cessatis,** one of a goodly number of intransitive verbs of the first conjugation which have a passive participle. Cf. **erratas,** above, 139, **clamata,** 35. So Horace, regnata Phalanto rura (Odes, II. 6, 12); triumphatae gentes (Virgil).

II.—IV.

ARIADNE.

THIS and the two following extracts, though taken from different works, form a definite sequence. Ariadne, daughter of Minos, king of Crete, has helped Theseus to conquer the Minotaur, by giving him a clew to the maze in which the monster was hid, and, being in love with him, has fled in his company. They put in for the night to the island of Dia, and Theseus on the next morning treacherously sails away, leaving the poor girl alone. The first extract is part of an epistle which she is supposed to write on the day when she discovers his perfidy.

The name Dia, which belonged properly to a small island off the north coast of Crete, was also a poetical name for Naxos, one of the largest of the Cyclades. It may have been this fact which led to the further legend which is recounted in the next extract, how Ariadne, lorn of Theseus, becomes the bride of Bacchus; for Naxos was the home of the Bacchic worship. As the completion of the legend she is raised to share in Bacchus' divine honours, and as the Cretan Crown becomes one of the signs of the heavens.

II.

ARIADNE'S LAMENT.

1. **Illo,** sc. *Diae.*
4. **Per facinus,** criminally.
5. Describing apparently the early dawn, or the hour that precedes it, when the night is at its coldest, and the birds, half-awake, begin to stir in their nests. **Pruina** hints that it is autumn.
7. A beautifully descriptive line—But half-awake, with all the languor of sleep still on me.
   A somno = after, as the *result* of.
8. **Semisupina,** on my side, lit., half on my back, describes the motion of a person thus groping about on waking. Cf. Chaucer:

>Ryght in the dawenynge awaketh shee,
>And gropeth in the bed, and fonde ryghte noghte.

[TAYLOR'S OVID—*See Page* 16.]

55 haec mea magna fides? at non, Euandre, pudendis
      volneribus pulsum aspicies, nec sospite dirum
      optabis nato funus pater. ei mihi, quantum
      praesidium Ausonia, et quantum tu perdis, Iule!
            Haec ubi deflevit, tolli miserabile corpus
60 imperat, et toto lectos ex agmine mittit
      mille viros, qui supremum comitentur honorem,
      intersintque patris lacrimis, solacia luctus
      exigua ingentis, misero set debita patri.
      haut segnes alii crates et molle feretrum
65 arbuteis texunt virgis et vimine querno,
      extructosque toros obtentu frondis inumbrant.
      hic iuvenem agresti sublimem stramine ponunt;
      qualem virgineo demessum pollice florem
      seu mollis violae, seu languentis hyacinthi,
70 cui neque fulgor adhuc, nec dum sua forma recessit;
      non iam mater alit tellus, viresque ministrat.
      tunc geminas vestes auroque ostroque rigentis
      extulit Aeneas, quas illi laeta laborum
      ipsa suis quondam manibus Sidonia Dido
75 fecerat, et tenui telas discreverat auro.
      harum unam iuveni supremum maestus honorem
      induit, arsurasque comas obnubit amictu;
      multaque praeterea Laurentis praemia pugnae
      aggerat, et longo praedam iubet ordine duci.
80 addit equos et tela, quibus spoliaverat hostem.
      vinxerat et post terga manus, quos mitteret umbris
      inferias, caeso sparsuros sanguine flammam;
      indutosque iubet truncos hostilibus armis
      ipsos ferre duces, inimicaque nomina figi.
85 ducitur infelix aevo confectus Acoetes,
      pectora nunc foedans pugnis, nunc unguibus ora;
      sternitur et toto proiectus corpore terrae.

Comp. *Geor.* ii. 80, *Nec longum tempus et . . . exiit . . . arbos,* C. But as these are the only two instances of the construction adduced it is perhaps safer to take *et* = even.

51 **nil iam,** etc.] The father is making vows to heaven in his son's behalf, but the son is gone where vows are neither made nor paid.

55 **haec mea magna fides**] 'Is this the end of all my promises?' *Magna* may be taken as 'solemn,' or 'boastful.'

pudendis volneribus] All his wounds are on his breast.

56 **dirum optabis funus** = *morti devovebis.* Compare the meaning of *dirae,* xii. 845.

59-99] A description of the funeral rites. Aeneas bids his last farewell.

59 **Haec ubi deflevit**] 'His moan thus made.' *De* in composition has two opposite meanings : (1) cessation from or removal of the fundamental ideas, as in *decresco, dedoceo,* etc.; (2) (as here) in intensifying, as *debello, demiror, desaevio.*

61 **honorem**] *Honos* is used by V. for (1) a sacrifice, iii. 118; (2) a hymn, *Geor.* ii. 393; (3) beauty, *Aen.* x. 24; (4) the 'leafy honours' of trees, *Geor.* ii. 404; (5) funeral rites, vi. 333, and here. See below, *l.* 76.

63 **solatia**] In apposition to the whole sentence ; whether it is nom. or acc. depends on how we resolve the principal sentence ; here, though *solatia* applies to the whole sentence, its construction probably depends on the last clause, which we may paraphrase, *ut praesentes* (τὸ μετεῖναι) *sint solatia ;* therefore it is nom.

64 **crates et molle feretrum**] The bier of pliant osier : cf. *l.* 22.

66] Cf. Statius, *Theb.* vi. 55, *torus* et puerile feretrum.

obtentu frondis] 'A leafy canopy.' C. understands 'a layer of leaves.

67 **agresti stramine**] 'The rude litter.'

68] Cf. ix. 435 ; *Il.* viii. 306,

> μήκων δ' ὡς ἑτέρωσε κάρη βάλεν, ἥτ' ἐνὶ κήπῳ
> καρπῷ βριθομένη νοτίῃσί τε εἰαρινῇσιν·
> ὡς ἑτέρωσ' ἤμυσε κάρη πήληκι βαρυνθέν.

> 'Even as a flower,
> Poppy or hyacinth, on its broken stem
> Languidly raises its encumbered head.'—MILMAN.

69 **languentis hyacinthi**] The rhythm is Greek. The 'drooping hyacinth' is probably the Lilium Martagon or Turk's-cap lily, 'the sanguine flower inscribed with woe.'

70] 'That hath not yet lost its gloss nor all its native loveliness.' *Recessit* must apply to both clauses. 'If we suppose the two parts of the line to contain a contrast, the following line will lose much of its force,' C. Compare the well-known lines from the *Giaour,* 'He who hath bent him o'er the dead,' etc.

71] Contrast the force of *neque adhuc, nec dum,* and *non iam :* 'the brightness not all gone,' 'the lines where beauty lingers,' and 'the support and nurture of mother earth cut off once and for all.'

36. ἵνα φάγῃ] In modern Greek, which properly speaking has no infinitive, the sense of the infinitive is expressed by νά (ἵνα) with subjunctive (as in this passage), *e.g.* ἐπιθυμῶ νὰ γράφῃ, 'I wish him to write;' see Corfe's *Modern Greek Grammar*, p. 78. This extension of the force of ἵνα to oblique petition, and even to consecutive clauses, may be partly due to the influence of the Latin *ut;* cf. ch. xvi. 27, ἐρωτῶ οὖν, πάτερ, ἵνα πέμψῃς : see note on ch. iv. 3.

The following incident is recorded by St. Luke alone. Simon the Pharisee is not to be identified with Simon the leper, Matt. xxvi., Mark xiv. 3.

ἀνεκλίθη] The Jews had adopted the Roman, or rather Greek, fashion of reclining at meals—a sign of advancing luxury and of Hellenism, in which however even the Pharisee acquiesces.

37. γυνή] There is no proof that this woman was Mary Magdalene. But mediæval art has identified the two, and great pictures have almost disarmed argument in this as in other incidents of the gospel narrative.

38. ἀλάβαστρον] The neuter sing. is Hellenistic. The classical form is ἀλάβαστρος with a heteroclite plural ἀλάβαστρα, hence probably the late sing. ἀλάβαστρον. The grammarian stage of a language loves uniformity, Herod. iii. 20 ; Theocr. xv. 114 :

Συρίω δὲ μύρω χρύσει' ἀλάβαστρα.

στᾶσα παρὰ τοὺς πόδας αὐτοῦ] This would be possible from the arrangement of the triclinium.

39. ἐγίνωσκεν ἄν] 'Would (all the while) have been recognising.'

40. χρεωφειλέται] A late word; the form varies between χρεωφειλέται and χρεοφειλέται.

41. δηνάρια] The denarius was a silver coin originally containing ten ases (deni), afterwards, when the weight of the as was reduced, sixteen ases. Its equivalent modern value is reckoned at 7½d. But such calculations are misleading ; it is more to the point to regard the denarius as an average day's pay for a labourer.

42. μὴ ἐχόντων] Because *he saw that* they had not.

INDEX